Behind the pure surging power of our finest orchestral music, behind the flawless attunement of America's most magnificent orchestras, are men in whose souls lie the living forces that create splendid symphonic music from instrumentalists and written notes.

These are our orchestral conductors, whom David Ewen affectionately terms *Dictators of the Baton*.

To know these men is to have a richer appreciation of fine music. And, through David Ewen's deep-searching analyses of thirty of the leading conductors in America's contemporary orchestral scene—in biographical, critical, and personal portraits—*Dictators of the Baton* compels you to know them intimately.

Artists all, from the paragon, Toscanini, to such rising young leaders as Izler Solomon, Dean Dixon, and Sylvan Levin, these conductors are revealed as vital forces molding and elevating the musical tastes of our people. Fused with these biographies are the histories of our nation's leading orchestras, a score of which are discussed in this important new addition to musical literature.

Thanks to David Ewen, readers can now find fuller enjoyment from the better recordings, concerts, and musical radio programs. Now they can have a behind-the-scenes visit with great music in the making. For *Dictators of the Baton* plumbs the superficial and wrenches the heartbreak and triumphs, the institutions and the men behind our greatest symphonic music from their seclusion.

Books by Mr. Ewen

———

THE UNFINISHED SYMPHONY

FROM BACH TO STRAVINSKY

WINE, WOMEN AND WALTZ

THE MAN WITH THE BATON

COMPOSERS OF TODAY

HEBREW MUSIC

COMPOSERS OF YESTERDAY

TWENTIETH CENTURY COMPOSERS

MUSICAL VIENNA
(in collaboration with Dr. Frederic Ewen)

MEN AND WOMEN WHO MAKE MUSIC

PIONEERS IN MUSIC

LIVING MUSICIANS

MUSIC COMES TO AMERICA

THE BOOK OF MODERN COMPOSERS

ARTURO TOSCANINI

Dictators
of the Baton

BY DAVID EWEN

CHICAGO · NEW YORK

THIRD PRINTING · OCTOBER, 1943

For
ROBERT

Preface

Several years ago, I published a book about conductors and conducting* which was handsomely received by the critics, and generously acclaimed by the book-buying public. The present book is not intended to supplant its predecessor but to supplement it. *The Man With the Baton* placed emphasis on the past: thus the greatest portion of that book was devoted to a history of conducting and of world-famous orchestras and to the careers of the distinguished baton personalities of yesterday. Only incidentally—and briefly—did it concern itself with present-day conductors.

Dictators of the Baton is devoted exclusively to the contemporary orchestral scene in America. In a sense, therefore, it continues from where *The Man With the Baton* ended—except, of course, for certain essential (but minor) duplications. Feeling as strongly as I do that America is the musical center of the world (a position, I am sure, it will retain long after a sick and ravaged world is restored to a semblance of normalcy) and sensing the ever-increasing fascination of American music-lovers for symphonic music in general and the orchestral conductor in particular, I decided to produce a new work surveying the ground exhaustively.

This book presents thirty of the leading conductors now functioning in this country. It presents these men in biographical, critical, and personal portraits. Through these men, it is

---

* *The Man With the Baton,* Thos Y. Crowell Co., 1936.

hoped, the reader will gain an insight not only into the art of conducting, but also into the state of orchestral music in this country, for a part of this work is devoted to brief histories of about twenty of our major symphony orchestras.

[As the book was going to press, Frederick Stock, for nearly forty years conductor of the Chicago Symphony Orchestra, died suddenly—October 20, 1942—at his home in Chicago, less than a month before his seventieth birthday. Although the author speaks of "leading conductors now functioning in this country," Dr. Stock's influence on "the contemporary orchestral scene in America" must surely continue to be felt, and it has therefore been thought desirable to make no present alteration in the chapter dealing with Frederick Stock.—*Editor*]

Contents

Table of Illustrations

Introduction

The Conductor

There was a time when the artistic function of the conductor mystified many untrained music lovers. After all, they argued, were not the men of the orchestra expertly trained musicians? And did they not have the printed music in front of them to guide them? Of what possible use, then, was the man with the baton? Some of those who questioned the conductor's usefulness went so far as to describe him as a "frustrated instrumentalist" (in much the same way that critics are supposed to be frustrated novelists and playwrights)—unable to create great art themselves, they enter a field in which others create it for them.

Then the pendulum of public opinion swung to the other extreme. In the early 1920's, the conductor was apotheosized. Willem Mengelberg, arrived from Holland as the guest for Artur Bodanzky's orchestra, gave some luminous performances and at once became the object of hero worship generally reserved for cinema stars. Furtwängler, Stokowski, Koussevitzky, and Toscanini helped further to bring about the fetish of the conductor in the American concert hall. In this adulation for the conductor many concertgoers soon assigned a secondary position to the composer; Brahms, or Beethoven, or Wagner seemed less significant to them than the conductors interpreting these masters. Toscanini conducting a mediocre work would pack the house. A lesser conductor, but a fine artist in his own right, performing masterpieces saw half-empty auditoriums.

The conductor could do no wrong. Each little new trick introduced by some new director became a matter of major musical importance to music lovers. This man conducted without a score; that one, without a baton; a third, radically rearranged the seating of the orchestra men. . . . Even the distortion of musical compositions—in the attempt of a new conductor to cater to tastes dulled by a steady diet of sensationalism—was given applause. The astute and discriminating musician, of course, rebelled against this deification of the conductor, realizing only too well (as Daniel Gregory Mason did, when he wrote in a letter to the New York *Times**), "it vulgarizes the taste of audiences by making them value sensation above beauty; exaggeration and feverish seeking for effect above the moderation and balance that alone wear well." But the audiences were enchanted.

In recent years, we have arrived at a saner and more intelligent conception of the role of the conductor. We recognize that music is always more important than its interpreter. A sensational leader like Toscanini, Stokowski, or Koussevitzky still attracts large audiences, some of whom no doubt are attracted more by the performer than by the music performed. But, for the most part, in symphony halls throughout the country the composer has, at last, assumed his deserved place, far above that of the conductor who interprets him. The once prevalent vogue for guest conductors (which fed on the insatiable desire of audiences for new sensational personalities in front of their orchestras), has generally passed.† Most American orchestras know only one conductor, and that con-

---

* January 29, 1928.

† Not, unfortunately, in New York, where the financial success of the centenary season inspired the directors of the Philharmonic to resume its policy, launched that year, of bringing many different personalities to the head of the orchestra!

ductor retains his post over a period of many seasons. The fashion of the publicized prima donna conductor has also waned. Concertgoers are interested in good, intelligent, artistically fashioned performances; if these emerge from under the baton of comparatively unknown conductors, there will be applause and recognition—as were the cases with John Barbirolli in New York and Eugene Ormandy in Philadelphia. In the early 1920's, a Barbirolli or an Ormandy would have been ignored, obscured by the shadows of illustrious European personalities.

Not that the artistic importance of the conductor is minimized. Far from it! Audiences realize that he is no longer merely a human metronome. For many centuries, the only function of the conductor was to beat time: *Taktschlager,* the Germans called him. But in the nineteenth century, conductors like Karl Maria von Weber, Felix Mendelssohn, Richard Wagner, and Hans von Bülow asserted their personalities, and left their impress on the music they directed. Today we know that the conductor is a sensitive artist who can give life, vitality, sweep, and majesty to a musical work. He is the indispensable factor in every great symphonic concert: for conductorless orchestras have long ago proved an absurdity both in the Soviet Union and in New York. We have learned that while the art of conducting is the most complex, it offers the highest artistic awards in the entire field of musical interpretation. Toward this field many great artists aspire when they feel that they have exhausted the possibilities of their own instrument. Once, when Pablo Casals was mountain-climbing he injured one of the fingers of his right hand. "Thank God," he thought, "I won't have to play the cello any longer." He already had in mind the new world of conducting into which fate was thrusting him. Fortunately for those who have been moved by his incomparable artistry on the cello, Casals' finger recovered. But, eventually, Casals paid less and less attention to his cello and more and more to the baton—until the Revolution in Spain brought his remarkable orchestral activity in Barcelona to an untimely end. Koussevitzky was the world's greatest double-bass player, and Georges Barrère the world's first flutist when they exchanged their instruments for a baton. José Iturbi and Ossip Gabrilowitsch were world-famous pianists. All these artists (and many others) partially abandoned their own instruments (even in cases where they relinquished a field in which they had proved their right to a sovereign position, for another in which they probably could only be second-raters) because, in directing an orchestra, they were given artistic self-expression of incomparable richness.

Nor, on the other hand, is there any longer a tendency to overemphasize the powers of the conductor. We know that the conductor is no fabulous musician who can make the C-major scale sound like Beethoven's *Eroica*. Bad music remains bad music even with Toscanini guiding the performance. But it has now become an almost everyday experience of concertgoers that a piece of music which sounds flatulent or attenuated with a lesser conductor can suddenly acquire charm and character and artistic purpose when shaped by the hands of a great interpreter. In the same way, a bad orchestra remains a bad orchestra whether led by Koussevitzky or by an amateur. (Gustav Mahler's dictum that "there are no bad orchestras, only bad conductors" should receive only discriminating interpretation.) A skillful conductor can conceal some of the defects in an orchestra; and a great conductor can make the musicians under his baton surpass themselves. Where there are too many gaps, however, neither the science nor the art of the conductor can create an integrated organism. Your everyday music lover also knows that one and the same orchestra can sound differently on alternate weeks with different conductors. A great leader can bring an orchestra to greatness; a poor one can make the very same orchestra sound much like an amateur ensemble. The centenary season of the New York Philharmonic Symphony Orchestra brought a parade of conductors to the head of that organization. It was then forcefully revealed to subscribers how, with different men directing, the orchestra actually acquired a different character. Mitropoulos made the orchestra dynamic, brilliant, showy; Bruno Walter brought to it a touch of the lyric and the poetic. Under Toscanini, it once again proved itself one of the greatest orchestras of all time. With several other conductors—why mention names?—it suddenly became slipshod, and its performances were tired and lackadaisical. What is true of the New York Philharmonic is true of every other orchestra. Each time it comes into contact with a new conductor it changes its colors chameleon-like, and acquires an altogether new appearance.

II

What, then, is this strange alchemy which can make a conductor convert orchestral dross into gold?

One can dissect a conductor, as the biologist dissects the frog, and learn some of the anatomical qualities which go into the making of greatness.

The ear, first of all: a conductor obviously must have unusual aural sensitivity to musical sound, to tone colors, to different shades and tints of orchestral texture. A Toscanini can detect, even while a full orchestra is blaring *fortissimo,* that a flutist has given the wrong accentuation. A Koussevitzky can perceive, through the labyrinth of a musical score, that a rhythmic pattern is not in exact design. A conductor whose hearing is not quite so acute is likely to tolerate a performance which is not fastidiously correct in details.

Then comes the brain. The conductor must have a comprehensive musical training which embraces a working knowledge of most instruments of the orchestra. To this he must add a good memory. A conductor must know the music he is directing thoroughly, every note of it, for only then can he give specific directions to his performers.

Finally, the conductor must have that innermost sensitivity which comes from the heart. He must feel the emotional qualities of the music he is directing keenly and spontaneously, if he is to impress these emotional qualities on his men.

But ear, brain, and heart—important and indispensable though they are to the conductor—are not everything. There are any number of wonderful musicians who have these three attributes. A friend of mine is a case in point. He has perfect pitch: His ear is so sensitive that he can tell the speed of a moving train by the pitch sounded by the wheels on the tracks. His knowledge of musical scores is so exhaustive that he rarely consults the printed page. He is a profound musical scholar. He adores music, feels it in every fiber, and reacts to it emotionally. Yet he is not a great conductor (though he has conducted frequently); he is not even a good conductor.

If a knowledge of the score, and musical training and equipment were the essentials of conducting, then, surely, composers would be the ideal interpreters of their own works. The concert world has had sufficient experience in hearing Stravinsky, Ravel, and Richard Strauss conduct their own music to realize that this is not the case. Strauss, as a matter of fact, is a remarkable Mozart conductor, yet in the direction of his own

8

music he is generally accepted as only a third-rate performer.

Evidently we must search beyond anatomy in our dissection of the great conductor. In our search we come to an element difficult to describe, but the presence of which is electrically felt: an element which, for want of a better word, we may speak of as "personality." I am inclined to consider a magnetic personality as important to a conductor as is scholarship, and much more essential than either perfect pitch or a photographic memory. Without such a personality, no conductor can hope to achieve greatness. Toscanini, Stokowski, Koussevitzky, Mitropoulos have the capacity to galvanize the men who play under them, and the audience as well. No sooner do these conductors come on the stage than one feels the contact of some inexplicable electric currents. The very atmosphere suddenly becomes highly charged. In such an atmosphere, a performance becomes cogent and dynamic, bursting with vitality.

Genius has not only the capacity of creating great art; it is often capable of producing great art in others. It has not only the power of being inspired, but also that of inspiring. A minor orchestra under a great conductor will sound like a major one; and even a major one will outdo itself in the presence of genius. Soloists have frequently confessed that playing under Toscanini or Koussevitzky made them achieve heights which they formerly thought unattainable. In the opera house, singers have frequently surpassed all previous efforts, driven on to new artistic peaks by the irresistible drive of a new conductor.

Genius with the baton, as in every other field, is the capacity to take pains. A great conductor who hears the score vividly with his "mind's ear," must be unsparing of himself and of others in his attempt to bring his conception to life. He must remain dissatisfied with his preparation until the details have been scrupulously absorbed by the orchestra, until he has not only concentrated on the general effect but also laid stress on every accent, nuance, shading. A lesser conductor is likely to become fatigued, mentally and physically, before he has achieved his goal. He is tempted to be more easily satisfied with results. A great conductor is as meticulous and as unyielding in the rehearsal of a work he has performed a hundred times as in that of a new work; one of the truly infallible signs of conductorial genius is the capacity to approach a thrice-familiar score with freshness and enthusiasm, as though it were an altogether new creation. Too many conductors, directing the Beethoven Fifth Symphony or the Tchaikovsky *Pathétique* or the Brahms First, for the hundredth time, have lost their capacity to respond to this music. In earlier years they had performed these works magnificently; but after two or three decades they are capable only of tired and listless performances. Too many conductors are at their best only in the performance of new works, into the preparation of which they can hurl themselves with herculean energy and painstaking care. Toscanini or Koussevitzky or Bruno Walter, however, will direct a classic of which they have long since learned every note by heart as if the music had been written the night before, as if every effect in the score came to them as a new discovery. At one time, Stokowski, rehearsing the Schubert *Unfinished Symphony*, felt that the violins were taking a beautiful theme too mechanically—as a result of their lifelong association with it. Because he was able to retain his freshness for this music, Stokowski recognized the stilted quality of the playing; and he remedied it by having each violinist perform it individually, and criticizing his execution.

Some great conductors succumb to staleness; it is the one

10

weakness in their artistic make-up. I recall, for example, a rehearsal of the Beethoven Seventh Symphony conducted by the late Felix Weingartner in Salzburg. In his time, Weingartner was undoubtedly one of the greatest of Beethoven interpreters. But old age did not bring to Weingartner (as it brought to Muck and Toscanini) richness and wisdom and maturity; only weariness and exhaustion. The rehearsal I attended proved that Weingartner had lost all enthusiasm or interest in the symphony, and to such an extent that he disregarded (or did not hear) the most obvious errors in rhythm, and the most flagrant violations of tempo. At one point, his concertmaster, Arnold Rosé, was compelled to rise in his seat and behind Weingartner's back to beat the proper time values furtively to the other men so that the performance might remain cohesive.

III

For what end does the great conductor strive in his performance? Obviously, to recreate in a living performance what a composer has put down on paper. On the surface this may appear a childishly easy assignment: the notes are there; all the conductor has to do is to read these notes correctly. But there are subtleties and complexities involved in bringing life to the printed page, and it is in these that the conductor becomes hopelessly enmeshed unless he has science, art, and personal magnetism to assist him.

There are questions of tempo, of accent, of retards and accelerations, of dynamics which can only be suggested in the score, and concerning which each conductor must decide for himself in the light of what he feels to be the intentions of the composer. Here musical scholarship, taste, even intuition might serve the conductor in the choices he makes. After all, there is no one set interpretation. The Tchaikovsky *Pathétique* conducted by Koussevitzky and Toscanini becomes two strangely different works; yet each is correct as far as the notes on the page are concerned. It is a question of musical style. Koussevitzky gives stress to the emotional impact of the music, highlighting the melodic material, and permitting himself the luxury of a sentimental handling of tempo and phrasing. Toscanini, who is impatient with Tchaikovsky sentimentality, gives a more impulsive reading: the tempi are accelerated; the proportions of the music are given expanse; in the movement and sweep of the Toscanini reading, the heart-moving emotion of the music is slighted. In place of sentiment, we have drama. Which is the correct interpretation?—*Chacun à son gout.*

In questions of tempo and dynamics, too many conductors—because they lack the imagination, and the independence of true genius—lean heavily on tradition. This has been particularly true of the German school of conductors. Wagner's music should be conducted in this-and-this manner because (so one *Kapellmeister* will insist) Anton Seidl conducted it that way, and Hermann Levi before Seidl, and Wagner himself before Levi. But tradition, as Mahler once pointed out astutely, is only a lazy man's excuse for not thinking for himself. Too often it leads a conductor to perpetuate the sins of his predecessors. One example will illustrate this point. In 1930, Toscanini was invited to Bayreuth to conduct two Wagner music-dramas. As the first foreigner to invade the sacrosanct Germanic halls of the Wagnerian shrine, he was the object of great antagonism. This antagonism reached something of a fever point after his performance of *Tannhäuser* because certain pages of the Venusberg music were played at an unheard-of pace. The critics growled; competitive conductors called the interpretation scandalously out of tradition. Finally, Toscanini invited a few critics to his apartment. There he took the disputed passage, pointed out the metronomic markings in the score, and with the aid of a metronome convinced even the most doubting of these Thomases that it was he who was right, and not a generation of Wagner conductors.

But more than questions of tempo and dynamics must be answered by the conductor. There is the problem of orchestral balance. The orchestra, after all, is composed of many different parts: strings, woodwinds, brass, percussion. These different parts are, in turn, divisible into other classifications: the strings into violins, violas, cellos, basses; the woodwinds into flutes, clarinets, oboes, and bassoons; the brass into trumpets, horns, trombones and tuba. To blend these different components into a sonorous whole calls for sensitivity of ear, immaculate taste, and a complete mastery of the potentialities and weaknesses of every instrument in the orchestra. With Toscanini (as with Mahler before him) balance is achieved with such supreme skill that the music is always transparent; it is possible to detect even the subsidiary voices of the orchestral choir. With Koussevitzky and Stokowski the balance is adjusted so that the orchestral tone becomes sensuous and brilliant.

Then there are questions of style. Obviously Mozart is not to be performed in the manner of Tchaikovsky; nor Tchaikovsky in the manner of Beethoven. A conductor must understand the manners and idioms of different composers and must have the technique with which to express these idioms. To play Mozart with feeling for its sensitive architectonic construction and its classic style, Beethoven and Brahms with Germanic breadth and expansiveness, Debussy with a richness of color—this calls for taste, a grasp of historic perspective, and sound musical judgment.

13

Frequently, what may seem to the layman an insignificant interpretative task may prove formidable to a conductor. There are numerous conductors who can play, say, the *Rites of Spring* by Stravinsky with extraordinary effect; yet many of these same conductors are completely incapable of recreating a beautiful melody for strings with simplicity and purity, with sensitive phrasing, with an exquisite sense for line and color. To perform a Rossini melody in the manner of Toscanini calls as much for the resources of a conductor's art as to interpret a complicated modern score; sometimes I am inclined to think that it is an even greater achievement. I recall visiting a conductor's class at the Berkshire Music Center where the young men (all of them unusually gifted) were called upon to direct an orchestra in difficult works by Hindemith, Stravinsky, and Schönberg. They went through the task with unbelievable skill and self-assurance, revealing that they knew the music well, and that they knew precisely what they wanted from the orchestra. One of these young men, whose performance was particularly striking, was also asked to rehearse a Haydn symphony. He suddenly lost control of himself. He knew the Haydn music, and yet he was incapable of projecting the lyric pages or achieving sensitive balances.

It does not take an intricate work to reveal the gifts of a conductor. Let him conduct an air with a simple accompaniment, and you will know whether he is a man of genius. With an ordinary conductor, all the notes will be there; but with a master, the notes become part of a beautiful texture, and one recognizes that in the design each single note has a definite role. The melody suddenly acquires wings and soars.

Beyond these considerations (and there are others) there comes into prominence the intellectual background of the conductor. "To know Beethoven," Bruno Walter has said, "you must also know *Hamlet* and Goethe." Like every artist, the conductor must draw repeatedly from the well of his own experiences and backgrounds when he is interpreting music. The richness of these experiences and backgrounds will, in turn, influence the depth and maturity of his performances. A provincial mind cannot recreate Beethoven or Wagner without betraying its narrowness and limitations. A conductor who is a great musician—that and nothing more—can never hope to rise above a certain degree of competent mediocrity. It is no accident that the greatest conductors of all time, from Mahler and Muck to Toscanini and Bruno Walter, are men of extraordinary cultural equipment. In speaking the majestic accents of music, these conductors consistently reveal the enormous span of their interests. Dimitri Mitropoulos stressed this very point when he remarked: "The conductor in himself is nothing. It is the infinite amount of culture back of him that is the conductor. First he must have a sensitive and carefully trained musical mind. Then, he must have something to say to his people."

IV

To know a conductor one must have seen him at work during rehearsals. For a conductor to convey his conception of a musical work to his men is often a soul-searing assignment. He calls every resource at his command to assist him in conveying his own vivid impressions to his musicians. Frequently, musical terminology is not explicit enough in describing the wishes of the conductor. Stokowski will give a talk on metaphysics or religion to set the mood for his men. Before rehearsing a Balinese composition, he brought a pagan icon to the stage and set it in front of the orchestra. Toscanini, in explaining the fluidity with which a certain phrase was to be produced, dropped a handkerchief. ("Like this the music should sound," he cried, "like this dropping handkerchief!") Still another conductor might walk up and down the stage in the manner of a robot to interpret a rigidly rhythmic page of music. The description or analysis of exact mood, color, and tone quality which a conductor hears so clearly within him sometimes defies the science of a conductor's technique. He must make his explanations to his men through histrionics, gestures, speeches. It is finally understood and assimilated by the orchestra often only as a result of sweat and tears on the part of the conductor.

It is, therefore, to be expected that in this process the conductor's temper should become short, his humor bitter, his orders dictatorial, his vocabulary lewd. Some conductors (Sir Thomas Beecham is one) maintain their equilibrium amazingly, and go through a rehearsal with good mood and bright humor. But most conductors are martinets who treat their men harshly. Toscanini has heaped the most vulgar expletives on his men. Stokowski and Koussevitzky are merciless in their criticisms, and devastating in their denunciations. There are hot words—and a great deal of anguish. Once Toscanini left the platform, went to the corner of the stage, sank into a chair and started weeping like an insulted schoolgirl. Another conductor once jumped from his dais and attacked an offending reed player with blows of the fist. Stokowski once dismissed one of his veteran performers in the heat of a rehearsal.

When they yield to humor it is usually coated with acid. "This is no sty," cried Stokowski to his reed players. "You are squealing like pigs!" "Madam," said one conductor to a soprano whose intonation was painfully inexact, "will you please give the orchestra your *A?*" When an oboe player,

16

upon being instructed about the phrasing of a passage, re-marked, "Any fool can see that," his conductor answered, "I'll have to take *your* word for that, sir!" Occasionally—but this is comparatively rare—it is the musician, and not the con-ductor, who has the last word. In California, Klemperer was rehearsing a Beethoven concerto with Artur Schnabel as soloist. Schnabel was offended by some of Klemperer's tempi and, be-hind his back, signalled to the men the tempo he preferred. He was caught in the act by the conductor, who looked down on Schnabel haughtily and exclaimed: "Herr Schnabel, the conductor is *here!*" He was pointing to the platform as he spoke. "Klemperer is here!" "Ah," answered Artur Schnabel sadly, "Klemperer is there, and I'm here. But where is Bee-thoven?"

The wonder of it is that for all his evil temper, vile tongue, and ruthless manners, a truly great conductor is adored by his men. To work under him is not easy, to tolerate his attitudes not pleasant. Yet Muck, Mahler, Toscanini, and Koussevitzky —perhaps the four most domineering leaders in baton history— have also been among the most worshipped. No one knows the true worth of a conductor as does the musician who plays under him; and no one displays such schoolboyish and humble adoration for true genius as your everyday orchestral musician. The man in the orchestra knows when he has participated in an inspiring performance, knows when the leader in front of him has made him soar to heights. When confronted with genius, the musician becomes idolatrous. More than once has a bitter and stubbornly fought rehearsal ended with the musicians rising spontaneously in their seats and cheering their conductor. The heat and the bitterness of the battle are forgotten. What re-mains unforgettable is the victory of having a musical com-position emerge into a palpitant work of art.

17

V

Fashions in conducting have come and gone. To too many of these have audiences been tempted to ascribe exaggerated importance. There was a time, about two decades ago, when it was fatal for a new conductor to make a debut conducting from a score. One leading orchestral manager explicitly instructed all his conductors that they were to direct every work from memory. Conducting from memory is, of course, of inestimable value to a director: it was Hans von Bülow who first insisted that "a score should be in the conductor's head, not the conductor's head in the score." But it can be of value only if the conductor is so familiar with every marking on the printed page that to consult it is superfluous. He is, then, free to concentrate his attention on his men, and by doing so is often in a better position to master them completely than if he divides his attention between them and the printed page. But a performance from memory in which a score is only half-learned is far worse than a scholarly performance from score. Carelessness, superficiality, and confusion are inevitable results. There were times when a conductor's memory lapsed so badly that he was forced to beat time haphazardly until he could recover himself; in the interim the performance lapsed into chaos. Ten years ago or so, when every other visiting conductor felt it was his duty to conduct from memory, irresponsible performances were so prevalent that these conductors were frequently described by their men as "guess conductors."

Very often, a conductor who knows his score comprehensively prefers to have it in front of him even though he does not consult it during the performance. It reassures him, puts him at his ease, knowing as he does that it is there ready for consultation if his memory suddenly becomes capricious. Tosca-

18

nini has frequently said that conducting from memory is an unnecessary strain for a conductor with good eyesight.

A great deal of public attention has been focused on the question of gesturing. A conductor's gestures are important in enunciating the rhythmic pattern and in directing the phrase, in giving important cues, and occasionally in drawing a beautiful effect from the orchestra. There are times when an especially eloquent gesture on the part of the conductor will evoke a particularly eloquent response from the orchestra. Karl Muck's dynamic beat—as decisive as a hammer blow—produced chords from the orchestra shattering in their effect. Furtwängler used to make his orchestra sing by raising his face toward the ceiling, lifting his hands shoulder level, and then swaying his body slightly backwards. Stokowski produces a luscious lyric line from the violins with a majestic sweep of the left hand. Toscanini draws a poignant passage from the orchestra by pressing the thumb of his left hand on his heart, while his right continues tracing circular movements.

When a conductor is master of his baton technique—his right hand clearly enunciating the beat, while the left outlines the phrase—he is capable of conducting a good performance without the benefit of a single rehearsal. His gestures are capable of transmitting his wishes to his men. If he is a great conductor he can actually give a good account of himself and his orchestra even if they are performing together for the first time, each unfamiliar with the idiosyncrasies of the other. There have been numerous conductors, as a matter of fact, who preferred to do their detail work at the actual performance, feeling that it afforded opportunities for greater spontaneity. Nikisch was such a conductor; Stokowski is another.

Good baton technique calls for the most sensitive physical and mental coordination. Nicolai Malko, the conductor, pointed this out when he said in an interview: "If his coordination is out for the minutest fraction of a second, if his reflexes are not in perfect working order, the performance will suffer. . . . To train his body should be one of the conductor's tasks, since during the performance he can express himself to the orchestra solely through physical movements, facial miming, and all the intricacies of what may be called 'sight signals.' . . . In order to make this physical activity the manifestation of imaginative agility, the conductor needs a body that is responsive to instantaneous demands. More than other musicians he must rely on physical or motor consciousness. A violinist or pianist has always his instrument under his hand. The conductor must establish the same control at a distance."*

Another conductor, Leon Barzin, gives an interesting example of how the lack of perfect coordination in a conductor can result in a defective performance: "A well-known conductor was having theme trouble, as it is called in radio parlance. His programs were excellently performed—all except his theme, that musical bit that serves as a label to identify a particular program or orchestra. The conductor appealed to a fellow musician to watch closely to see if the source of the trouble could be located. The diagnosis was simple. Throughout the program the conductor's coordination was perfect and the performance of his orchestra was a natural reflection of his capability. But in playing the theme he would invariably 'throw' his knee before his stick, with the result that part of the orchestra would respond to the signal of the knee while the remainder of the orchestra would follow the stick."

Mr. Barzin then goes on to comment: "Coordination means control from the tip of the toe to the very end of the stick, so that no motion of any part of the body may confuse the musical

---

* In an interview with Ludwig Wielich in *The Etude*, February, 1941.

content of the chore. . . . A definite sign of a conductor's lack of coordination is his need to explain all his meanings through speech rather than through his stick during rehearsal periods. There is no question that a certain amount of speech is needed. But if you talk to your violin all day it will not play the passage for you. You must create the sound, the precision, the interpretation. So should the baton. It saves a great deal of time. The average orchestral musician is a sensitive human being, who reacts to the slightest motion, even that of a muscle, if it is intended to convey a musical message." *

The corybantic gestures of Sir Thomas Beecham, with his ecstatic motions of the body and elaborate patterns of the stick, have a decided effect on the orchestra. Yet, in the final analysis, the most effective conducting is that which employs the simplest means. A conductor's gestures are meant for the orchestra, and not for the audience. Those conductors who bear this in mind find that simplicity is often more eloquent than complexity. Some conductors can give the most minute instructions with their eyes. Some conductors magnetize their men with abrupt, decisive beats with the wrist. Generally speaking, the greater the conductor, the simpler and more economical the motion— though, to be sure, there are exceptions. Muck used to strike the beat with short, crisp strokes of the baton; at times his motions were so sparing that they were not perceptible to the audience. Toscanini merely uses a broad circular motion of the right arm, while frequently his left is static, resting on his hip. Conductors like Stokowski and Koussevitzky (though permitting themselves indulgences at random passages) utilize comparatively simple and clear rhythmic patterns, and most restrained movements of the left hand, sparing cues. Many

---

* "Facing the Conductor," by Leon Barzin in *Be Your Own Music Critic,* edited by Robert E. Simon, Jr., Doubleday, Doran & Co., 1941.

21

conductors do not move their bodies at all while conducting. But each conductor must evolve his own gestures, those which are most natural for him, and which best express his personality.

Stokowski, Coates, Mitropoulos, and Rodzinski have in recent years set the fashion of batonless conducting. Actually, a Russian conductor, Vassily Safonov, preceded them in this. But conducting without baton can never acquire a widespread vogue with conductors because the experience of a century has taught them that tempo and rhythm can be articulated more precisely and graphically with a stick than with bare hands.

It was not until 1820, in England, that the baton first came into prominence—with Spohr. Before that, varied were the means conductors used to beat time! In ancient Egypt, a musician would clap his hands to designate the beat. In ancient Greece, he wore a special leaden shoe with which he would stamp out the time in regular intervals. In later centuries, some time-beaters favored a handkerchief tied to the end of a rod; at the Sistine Chapel a roll of paper was employed; at the Paris Opéra, Lully used a heavy walking stick which he used to pound on the floor. Some conductors, who beat time while playing their instruments in front of their orchestras, conducted with movements of the head. Not until 1807 did a musical theorist insist that a wooden rod, or baton, was the most effective instrument for the hands of the conductor. And not until 1820 was the baton emancipated. In that year Spohr, on a guest appearance with the Royal Philharmonic Orchestra of London, amazed his musicians by drawing out of his pocket a little stick and beginning to direct them with it. "Quite alarmed at such a novel proceeding," wrote Spohr in his autobiography, "the directors protested against it, but when I besought them to grant me at least one trial they became pacified. . . . I . . . could not only give the tempi in a very decisive

22

manner, but indicated also to the wind instruments and horns all the entries, which ensured to them a confidence such as hitherto they had not known. . . . Incited thereby to more than attention, and conducted with certainty by the *visible* manner of giving the time, they played with a spirit and correctness such as, until then, they had never before been heard to play. Surprised and inspired by this result, the orchestra, immediately after the first part of the symphony, expressed aloud its united assent to the new mode of conducting, and thereby overruled all further opposition on the part of the directors. . . . The triumph of the baton as a time-giver was decisive." And it has remained decisive up to the present time.

Some other conductor (was it Furtwängler?) began in this country the style of directing an entire symphony or suite without permitting applause between movements. Since a symphony is usually composed of different movements which have no direct relation to each other, the value of having it performed without a breathing space for applause appears to have questionable artistic merit. But the fashion seems to have caught on with the public, and it is rare these days to find an audience bold enough to give vent to its emotions at the end of a movement with handclapping.

One of the more regrettable fashions adopted by numerous conductors is that of violating the original intentions of the composer by altering tempo, rhythm, by deleting a few bars here and there, by exaggerating dynamics, etc., for the sake of giving a "new" or "individual" reading. Hans von Bülow was one of the most notorious of these violators; he would consider it a part of his day's work to revamp completely an entire movement of a symphony according to his own tastes. In the hands of a truly great interpretative artist such revisions are usually in good taste, and a musical work may profit by such treatment. But, needless to state, such a practice is open to unfortunate abuses. In the 1920's, when conductors were competing with each other for the admiration of a volatile public, "individual" readings were an almost everyday experience. Even such a reputable and self-effacing musician as Mengelberg was soon guilty of them. But most great conductors realize that simplicity is usually the greatest virtue of a musical reading. Stravinsky was perfectly justified in writing: "I have a horror of . . . *interpretation.* The interpreter of necessity can think of nothing but *interpretation,* and thus takes on the garb of a translator, *traduttore-traditore;* this is an absurdity in music, and for the interpreter it is a source of vanity inevitably leading to the most ridiculous megalomania."* A great performance is one in which the composer's intentions are fully realized, and not one in which the personality of the conductor clashes with that of the composer. To speak what is in the score—no more, no less—is still the supreme achievement of the great musical interpreter.

VI

One vogue which seems mercifully on the decline is that of the prima donna conductor, who, incidentally, is no twentieth century phenomenon, nor a product of American commercialism. During the past century there lived in Europe several outstanding conductors who were the last words in baton showmanship. Some of our present-day symphonic leaders may frequently indulge in quixotic behavior to attract the limelight of attention. But even the most eccentric of their antics pales into insignificance in the face of the vagaries of one Louis Antoine Jullien. Jullien brought spectacle and his-

* *Stravinsky: An Autobiography,* Simon and Schuster, 1936.

trionics to orchestral conducting at a time when the art was still in its infancy. In doing this he anticipated the twentieth century prima donna by several decades. Born in France in 1812, the son of a bandmaster, he began his music study in the Paris Conservatory where he was the despair of his professors because he would frequently bring in cheap dance tunes as serious composition exercises. He left the Conservatory abruptly and became a leader of dance music at the Jardin Turc. Financial insolvency forced him to escape one lonely midnight to England. There, fortune smiling on him, he was able to procure an engagement as conductor of popular summer concerts at the Drury Lane Theatre. In 1842, he became conductor of orchestral concerts at the English Opera House where he achieved his greatest triumphs. And from this time on his eccentric story begins.

He had a flair for the spectacular which impelled him from the first to increase his orchestra to gargantuan proportions (actually augmenting its size to twice that of any existing orchestra anywhere) and to feature at one of his earliest concerts two symphonies in succession. This flagrancy likewise inspired him to adopt a dress which made him the most distinct figure on any concert platform. His clothing was tailored with meticulous perfection; his hair showed the fastidious care of a coiffeur; his long black moustache was waxed into rigidity. A brightly colored velvet coat was always thrown open to reveal an elaborately embroidered shirtfront. He rarely wore a cravat, permitting the graceful lines of his neck to rise Shelley-like from an open collar. Jewels sparkled on his fingers. During his performances he stood on a crimson platform etched in gold. In front of him was a hand-carved music stand also gilt stained; behind him, an ornately decorated velvet chair which, in its elaborate splendor, resembled a throne.

Jullien was soon the most talked of figure in London. Notoriety and publicity inebriated him, fed his ego, inspired him to follow one extravagant idea with another. Before long, he introduced at each and every concert a quadrille of his own invention. At a climactic passage, he would seize the violin and bow from the hands of his concertmaster, or would tear a piccolo from the breast pocket of his velvet jacket and (swaying elaborately as he accompanied the ecstatic motions of his body with exaggerated grimaces of the face) he would play with the orchestra. At the end of the performance he would dramatically sink into his velvet throne, overcome by exhaustion.

Before he conducted music of Beethoven he would have a pair of kid gloves brought to him ceremoniously on a silver platter. Before the eyes of his public he would put on these gloves with great dignity and begin to direct the sacrosanct music. For other important music he used a special jeweled baton. And he would always direct the music with such flourish and elaborateness that a contemporary newspaper—the *Courier and Enquirer*—was tempted at one time to make the facetious comment that Jullien "used the baton to direct the audience."

Jullien died insane, in Paris, March 14, 1860.

Hans von Bülow, famous contemporary of Wagner and Brahms, often considered the first of the great modern conductors, also blended histrionics with artistry. Volatile by temperament, unpredictable in his whims and moods, eccentric in mannerisms, strongly addicted to self-display, and profoundly gifted as a musician, Hans von Bülow was essentially a twentieth century prima donna conductor, born fifty years too soon.

In his conducting, von Bülow always glorified himself as a personality. His gesturing was extravagantly elaborate, di-

rected more at the audience than at his players. His interpretations of the classics invariably wrenched effects from the
music in order to emphasize strongly the great individuality of
the conductor—effects which caused such conductors as Weingartner to wring their hands with pain.

Circus tricks were always evident at von Bülow's concerts.
When he repeatedly had his orchestra (his orchestra, mind
you, not himself) perform classical symphonies entirely from
memory, it was purely a stunt to electrify his audiences, with
no resultant musical value. Von Bülow never succeeded in
immersing himself in his art sufficiently to forget that an audience was behind his back. In a particularly effective passage,
he would turn sharply around while conducting in order to
notice his audience's approval. And, like a famous conductor
of our time, he was addicted irremediably to making speeches
before his performances; too frequently, it was not clear what
caused the speech or what its essential message was.

One example will suffice. At a concert in Hamburg, which
took place shortly after the death of Wilhelm I—a concert
in which von Bülow conducted a Beethoven symphony, and
Johannes Brahms was piano soloist in his own concerto—von
Bülow suddenly turned around to the audience, immediately
before the performance, and inexplicably elaborated upon the
genius of Felix Mendelssohn, somewhat irrelevantly comparing
that composer to Kaiser Wilhelm. Then, just as mysteriously,
he heaped praise upon the genius of Johannes Brahms. "Mendelssohn is dead; the Emperor Wilhelm is dead," von Bülow
whined at the end of his oration. "Bismarck lives; Brahms
lives." Then, impetuously, he wheeled sharply around, and his
baton descended for the opening bars of Beethoven's Eighth
Symphony.

Artur Nikisch—the incomparable Nikisch he was called by

his admirers—was one of the greatest conductors of his generation, perhaps of all time. But Nikisch was also a prima donna. He was as meticulous about the elegance of his appearance on the platform as he was about the quality of his performances. Before he stepped on the stage he was careful that his tight-fitting clothing should reveal the graceful outlines of his body to best advantage. And he was scrupulously fastidious that the elegant movements of body and exquisite hands, the latter encircled at the wrists by lace cuffs that puffed somewhat foppishly out of the sleeves of his dinner coat, should present a picturesque sight to his audiences.

Nikisch knew the value of showmanship. He was one of the first conductors to utilize the then sensational practice of conducting entire programs from memory. He was the first conductor to treat his audiences with rigid discipline, and would severely upbraid them, in beautifully polished phrases, when they disturbed the music by moving in their seats or rattling a program. At one concert, he stopped a Bruckner symphony in the middle of a passage to scold a noisy woman in the front row.

When, in 1912, Nikisch toured throughout America with the London Symphony Orchestra, he experienced unprecedented triumphs. Newspapers spread his picture across the front pages, speaking of him as the "$1,000 a night conductor." His shock of brown hair, his poetic eyes, even his fingertips were rhapsodized in prose and poetry. Legends were created about his phenomenal memory and profound musicianship. He was stopped on the street by sentimental admirers who would kiss his hand; and at the concert he could not escape from the adulation of a mob that wanted to embrace him. He found himself a legend. People flocked to his concerts not so much to hear the music as to watch him. This strange adulation drove at least one critic to express resentment. "In the highest form of instrumental art (except chamber music where, thank God! there is still a bit of holy ground!)," wrote Henry E. Krehbiel in the New York *Tribune*, "as in the hybrid form of opera which chiefly lives on affectation and fad, it is the singer and not the song that challenges attention from the multitude. We used to have prima donnas in New York whose names on a program insured financial success for the performance. . . . For prima donna . . . read the conductor, and a parallel is established in orchestral art which is even more humiliating than that pervading our opera house."

The year when the above paragraph was written was 1912. It might very well have been published in yesterday's paper about some of our present-day conductors.

VII

There are conductors who can fool some of the audiences some of the time. But there has never been a conductor who could fool his orchestra any time. The orchestra has the capacity to sniff out a faker or a genius before a conductor has been many moments on the platform. Orchestra men frequently tolerate complete ignorance on the part of an inexperienced conductor in the mechanics of conducting, because beyond such ignorance they recognize a spark of true talent. There have been occasions when a concertmaster gently took a novice aside and then and there gave him instructions in the elements of baton technique; the rest of the orchestra waited tolerantly for the instruction to end, and did not permit itself to be prejudiced against the conductor. On the other hand, in the presence of sham, orchestra men can be fiercely intolerant. On one occasion a conductor in place of giving the violins

explicit directions as to dynamics, lapsed into prose-poetry.
"The music should sound as if you were playing on top of a
high mountain, overlooking a bank of clouds. You are fanned
by the winds. . . ."

The concertmaster interrupted him roughly: "Look, just
tell us whether you want the music played loud or soft." Orchestra men will tolerate elaborate lectures on various and at
times unrelated topics during rehearsal hours from a Stokowski
or a Koussevitzky, but in a mediocre man this conduct is insuf-
ferable.

However, there are times when even a great conductor over-
steps the bounds, and in trying to impress his erudition upon
his men tries their patience severely. A case in point is the
famous Klemperer-Labate incident which took place during a
New York Philharmonic rehearsal.* Mr. Klemperer had repeatedly rehearsed a certain passage, and each repetition was
preluded by a lengthy discourse. Finally Labate, the first
oboist, crisply interrupted with "Mister Klemps, you talka too
much!"

There was the time a young and highly publicized conductor
came to serve as guest for one of the great American orchestras. His first few moments on the platform were particularly
impressive. He was playing new music, yet he was rehearsing
from memory. Besides this, in correcting a passage, he could
actually recite every note on the page. Was this another Toscanini? But, after a brief period, there was something about his
directions which indicated that, though he could recite the
notes by rote, he did not always have a clear idea what the
music sounded like. To test him, one of the reed players performed entirely different notes than those written in his music.

* From *A Smattering of Ignorance,* by Oscar Levant, copyright, 1939, 1940,
reprinted by permission from Doubleday, Doran and Company, Inc.

The young conductor continued beating time with his stick, oblivious of what had actually taken place. From that moment on, it was bank holiday for the players. They realized that the young musician tried to palm off a freak memory for conductorial genius; that, actually, he did not have the least conception of what was in the music he was conducting. They interpolated their own phrases into the work, changed the tempi, inserted strange dissonances. One of the violins turned his music sheet upside down and played the music accordingly. Through it all, the conductor smiled beatifically, and after the rehearsal was over praised the men for their wonderful cooperation. The interesting epilogue to this strange story is the fact that it actually took the critics and audiences a few concerts to realize what the orchestra men had learned in a half hour.

VIII

Conductors of major American orchestras earn between $20,000 and $60,000 for a season's work. (Toscanini and Stokowski used to receive as much as a $100,000 a season, but these two were isolated examples.) To earn this income, a conductor puts in a full quota of a year's hard work. His tasks, of course, include the direction of the concerts and rehearsals; but this is only a fraction of his duties. He must find the time to hear young artists either as possible soloists for his concerts or as candidates for some available orchestral posts. He must see interviewers. He must serve on numerous committees for musical and charitable endeavors in his city. Then there are the social functions without which, unfortunately, no conductor's life in America seems complete. The conductor of a great orchestra must be the affable guest at numerous teas, luncheons, cocktail parties, and dinners during the course of a season, functions which tax his energy and consume his time. There have been conductors in New York (and no doubt elsewhere as well) whose careers were permanently shattered because, jealous of their time, they refused to yield to social formalities.

There are few conductors who do not find that the supposedly free months of vacation are as strenuous as the active season. It is then that the conductor must study scores continually, hundreds of them, in order to keep in contact with all the new music that comes to his desk, and to refresh his memory with old scores. To plan a full schedule of concerts requires herculean preparation.

During the season, work at rehearsals and concerts severely taxes the nervous and physical resources of a conductor. It is harrowing work, sapping the energy, trying the nerves. The conductor must find extended rest periods, moments of complete relaxation through the cultivation of hobbies, interims of complete quiet and seclusion, if he is to devote himself successfully to his task. Conductors usually refuse to see many people on days of concerts. They spend a great part of the time in bed. Most of them eat sparingly on such days (if they eat at all); and they do not turn to a substantial meal until after the performance.

The concert is over; rehearsals for the next performance in all probability begin the very next morning. A conductor, during the season, finds little breathing space between one performance and the next, unless he takes brief leaves of absence. The life of a conductor, therefore, is one of continual drive, continual expenditure of nervous energy, continual intense concentration, continual self-criticism and self-annihilation (as well as criticism and annihilation of others).

No wonder, then, that they are usually a hypersensitive and hyperthyroid lot, full of temperamental moods and passions, volatile, nervous, and easily upset from their equilibrium!

IX

Up to a few years ago, America has been quite content to purchase the conductors for its orchestras from Europe. Audiences preferred it that way: a conductor without a foreign name, a Continental manner, a European background had small chance of making an impression. But even before the outbreak of the Second World War, the trend in conducting has been away from importations and more and more toward home grown products. Growing musical maturity of our audiences has made them more partial to genuine talent, and less concerned with European glamour. Eugene Ormandy, an American-trained conductor, succeeded Stokowski with the Philadelphia Orchestra, and was a success. Frank Black, Alfred Wallenstein, Howard Barlow—American born as well as American trained—have become the three leading conductors over the radio.

We have gone a long way in developing our own conductors and finding a place for them in our orchestral world. But we have not gone far enough. Unfortunately, whether or not a talented, well-trained American musician finds an opportunity to show his talent as a conductor is still too much a matter of chance. A young American conductor, even if he has all the talent in the world, must have social backing, or money, or important connections, or else must be a favored son of destiny, before he can find even a minor place for himself. There is, up to the present time, no opportunity in this country (as there was in Europe before 1939) for apprenticeship in small opera

houses and with lesser orchestras whereby aspiring conductors can begin at the bottom and work their way up, acquiring on the way valuable experience, maturity, training.

A young conductor developed this very theme in a revealing letter to the New York *Times**: "I know a great many young conductors, but I don't know a single one who would not want to live in any part of the country, who would not be willing to work to his utmost capacity in every possible field, who would not prefer years of economic difficulties to a secure job (not conducting) in New York, if he were given the opportunity. . . . I have written to almost every city in the United States which has no orchestra but which might be able to support one. Those few which answered at all were entirely in the negative. . . . I know the young American conductor wants to go where he can start from the bottom, where he will have to work hard and long before his work will show results; he is neither lazy nor incompetent. But those who don't happen to have friends simply cannot know where to turn. There are always some local musicians ambitious enough to make it impossible for an outsider without friends to do the work only an outsider would be capable of doing. We would be happy to be chor-repetiteurs, to play the cymbals, to draw the curtains or collect music if that would get us anywhere. We all would be glad to work with school or college orchestras, poorly as they play."

With the exceptions of Stokowski, Stock, Damrosch, and Ormandy, our great orchestras are conducted by musicians who received their training and experience in Europe. Men like Monteux, Rodzinski, Mitropoulos, Bruno Walter, Goossens—and numerous others—developed their talent with smaller

---

* May 3, 1942 (Moritz Bomhard). Subsequently, Mr. Bomhard explained that "the last two sentences, in particular, refer to statements in Mr. Olin Downes' article in the *Times,* claiming that only in Europe conductors were willing to be chorrepetiteurs, play cymbals, etc. . . . My letter was in answer to something which might almost be called a challenge. . . ."

musical organizations in Europe. Then, proving their talent, they were given opportunities to establish their reputations. Europe, with its opera house and orchestra in practically every city of any dimensions, used to offer the aspiring conductor endless opportunities for apprenticeship once he finished his schooling. Europe, however, can no longer be the training ground for our conductors. Henceforth—I suspect for many years to come—we must depend exclusively on our own capacities to develop conductors. We must no longer leave the emergence of conductors to chance. We must find an agency —preferably through the organization of smaller orchestras and opera houses throughout the country—whereby every young American musician with talent can be given the opportunity to cultivate that talent.

We have already made some progress in this direction. It is estimated that there are today about 2,000 semi-professional and amateur orchestras in this country. The scope of these orchestras is, of course, limited, and does not offer conductors the opportunity for growth and artistic expansion which a professional symphony orchestra, with a regular series of seasonal concerts, can. But it is the nucleus for an agency to develop our conductors. Naturally such an agency must now wait for happier and more peaceful days. But its realization is essential if we are to continue as the greatest center of orchestral music in the world.

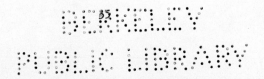

Paragon

1

Arturo Toscanini

Toscanini has become a legend in his own lifetime. His career is built around such monumental outlines, his musical achievements have been so fabulous, and his artistic importance assumes such epical stature that it is difficult in speaking or writing of him not to envelop him in legendary glamour. Tales about Toscanini are without number. They highlight his incredible memory, his aural sensitivity, his artistic integrity, and his interpretative genius. The curious thing is that most of these tales are not the inventions of imaginative admirers, but are based on fact. But beyond his musical greatness is the stature of the man himself: his dignity, idealism, and priestlike consecration to the highest ethics, his humility and self-effacement, warmth of heart and understanding—qualities which set him apart from most musicians. Once in a long while is musical genius of a high order married to a personality of such scope and richness. Such a marriage results in a Beethoven; and in Toscanini.

If he is the greatest musical interpreter of our time, it is not only because of his incomparable musical equipment. Important though that is, and in some respects without equal among conductors, it does not tell the whole story about Toscanini. His greatness as an artist arises from the majesty of the man himself. He has bigness and nobility, honesty and courage, sincerity and depth; and these human qualities are expressed in his art.

39

He has been the outspoken foe of Fascism because from the very first he saw in it the debasement of human dignity. Most other musicians in Italy scrambled to join the Fascist bandwagon. Toscanini refused even to pay lip service to the movement. At one time he received the blows of young upstarts because he refused to preface one of his concerts with the Fascist anthem. At another time, he was ordered by Mussolini to cooperate in a screen production of a Verdi opera; his stormy refusal was heard halfway round the world and forced even the dictator to seek cover and forget his orders. Eventually, Toscanini's undisguised disgust with Fascism made him a virtual prisoner at his home, as an enemy of the state. Only his world fame saved him from the fate of a Matteoti. He was permitted to leave the country (which he vowed never again to revisit as long as Fascism held it in bondage) only after he had promised never to give public expression to his anti-Fascist sentiments. (Mussolini knew with whom he was dealing: Toscanini would be bound to his promise by his implacable honor, even if it were given to a thief.)

To leave Italy, perhaps forever, was a cruel blow to Toscanini. The Italian sun, its climate, its food and wine, its geography, its people, and its language were inextricable parts of his being. He was happiest at his home on the beautiful Borromean Island near Stresa. There the Italian sun warmed his blood. Italian scenery—it is one of the most beautiful spots in the entire country—filled his eyes. To deprive himself of these pleasures and necessities was not an easy sacrifice to make. Yet from the first Toscanini knew that some day he would have to make it, and he made it willingly rather than be silent witness to a despotic regime.

In the same way, he spoke his mind openly against Hitler and the Nazis in 1933, vowing never to step on German soil as long as the forces of oppression were dominant. Somewhat later, in Salzburg (before Germany took over Austria) there was talk of banning the broadcast of the Bruno Walter performances as a concession to Nazi diplomats. Because Toscanini announced that he would have nothing to do with Salzburg if these broadcasts were prohibited, the ban was lifted.

When Wilhelm Furtwängler came to Salzburg for a few guest performances, he was welcomed warmly by his fellow musicians. But Toscanini could not forget that Furtwängler was also a representative of the Nazi government, and for this reason refused to have any contact with him. The two musicians, however, were thrown together at a banquet held at the Town Hall by the Landeshauptmann. Furtwängler approached Toscanini and congratulated the Italian maestro for his magnificent performance of *Die Meistersinger*. Toscanini greeted this praise icily, then added firmly: "I wish I could return your compliment. But I have always thought that a man who gives his assent to a system that persecutes every independent-minded man and woman cannot interpret Beethoven's symphonies truly. For you Nazis have banned all manifestations of spirit, leaving nothing but forced rhythms and an excessive display of strength. And that is precisely what you did the other day with Beethoven's Ninth Symphony, extinguishing all that is noble in it and unduly accentuating the loud and what you would probably call the 'dynamic' passages. But, sir, the Ninth is the symphony of brotherly love, mind you. Don't forget that it was a German, too, who wrote those words *'Seid umschlungen, Millionen'* and a German who put them to music. How can one conduct such an appeal to mankind and remain a Nazi?"*

---

* From *Splendor and Shame*, Otto Zarek, 1941. Used by special permission of the publishers, The Bobbs-Merrill Company.

Toscanini abandoned Bayreuth in 1933, and Salzburg in 1938, because he would not be part of the Nazi system. What it meant for him to renounce first Bayreuth, then Salzburg, where he had been permitted to make his wonderful music under the happiest of auspices, only those who know Toscanini well have realized. It was a loss second only to that of his own native land. But Toscanini did not hesitate in his choice: He would demonstrate to the world that he was the implacable foe of tyranny.

Toscanini is a good business man, and can drive a merciless bargain for his services. Yet his generosity is fabulous. He is aloof, and difficult to approach, except to the one who has a worthy favor to ask. He undertook to conduct the Palestine Symphony Orchestra (composed of refugees from Nazi Germany) without a salary; more than that he even stoutly refused to accept traveling expenses. He was tired and ill at the time, but he kept his word and made the long and arduous trip to Palestine to fulfil his promised engagements. He directed the public performances of the NBC Orchestra at Carnegie Hall only on the condition that the receipts be distributed to charity. He gladly conducted this symphonic group in several radio concerts to promote the sale of Defense Bonds. At Bayreuth, and later in Salzburg, he donated his services, because he knew that the payment of his fee was impossible at either place; and he worked harder there, without compensation, than he ever did in America with the Philharmonic and the NBC Orchestra at staggering salaries.

Many years ago, in Italy, there was a festival of Verdi operas. Toscanini was asked to cooperate. He said he would be glad to do so; but out of veneration for Verdi he could not possibly accept compensation. (This incident had an amusing epilogue. Another Italian conductor, violently envious of Toscanini's fame, was also asked to cooperate. This conductor said that he would, but only on one condition: He wanted to be paid a higher fee than that received by Toscanini. "You may pay me only one lira more than Toscanini gets," said the conductor, "but I *must* get a better price than Toscanini." To his amazement, the management accepted the offer. When payment was made him, it consisted of a check for one lira—and it was only then that the conductor learned that Toscanini had offered his services without charge.)

Toscanini has the expansiveness of the Latin heart. Much has been written about his tyrannical rule over his orchestra men; but much more could be said of his attachment for them, his warmth of feeling for them when the day's work is over. When he took the New York Philharmonic on a tour of Europe in 1931 he acted to the men as a father to his children. The hardship of travel only made him the more gentle and solicitous. He looked after each one of them personally, was concerned over their health, appetites, and comfort. One of the orchestra members fell ill aboard the liner. Toscanini stood watch at his bedside until recovery took place. When Toscanini toured South America with the NBC Orchestra he once again revealed his extraordinary capacity for affection. When he was told that one of his men had been killed in Rio de Janeiro by an autobus, he wept like a child, remained in his suite, refused to see anyone or eat anything. When he recovered from his grief, he raised a subscription for the musician's widow, to which he himself contributed a thousand dollars. A few hours before the steamer docked in New York, on the return journey home, Toscanini sent his men a touching personal farewell message: "You have never played so well, or so inspiredly. We have never been so linked before. We must be proud of what we have done. While writing I feel sad at heart, and it will always be so when beautiful things come to an end."

His generosity and tenderness are only two facets of a many-sided personality: another is humility. There is an anecdote told about Thomas Mann that when the great writer visited Hollywood, one of the scenario writers there met him, and abased himself by calling himself a worthless hackwriter in comparison to an artist like Mann. Mann later told of this incident to a friend and commented sadly: "That man has no right to make himself so small. He is not that big."

Toscanini's humility is the smallness of the truly big man. He is altogether incapable of understanding why he is made so much of. "Toscanini, he is nothing," he will say again and again with obvious conviction. He thinks of Beethoven and of Wagner, and in all honesty he feels that his own contribution, in comparison with their gargantuan achievements, assumes pygmy stature. "To write that score—that takes genius." He cannot see why he should be adulated for a routine job of interpreting other people's music. He does not even know what is so extraordinary about his work.

There is an almost childlike simplicity about him. He does not try to conceal his feelings; he wears his heart on his sleeve. He cries and he laughs as the emotion strikes him. He yields to momentary whims, like a child. To ask for a pianissimo from his orchestra he once fell on his knees, clasped his hands in prayer, and cried: "Pianissimo, please!" In trying to explain his conception of a musical work he postures, acts, burlesques. "Like this the music should sound," he might say, "like a mother rocking her baby to sleep," and he proceeds to rock his hands in cradle-fashion.

When a beautiful performance emerges from under his baton, he is supremely happy—nothing in the world gives him so much joy. His face beams, his eyes glisten, he cannot control his lips from breaking into youthful smiles. He even breaks into a raucous high-pitched song. Many times he does not even know he is singing. Once, he sharply interrupted a rehearsal and cried: *"Who* is making that noise?"

He never looks upon himself as the cause for this glorious music-making. He is never tempted into self-congratulations. He praises his orchestra, calls his men the greatest combination of instrumentalists in the world. *They* are responsible for such a magnificent performance. He lavishes adulation on the composer. It is *he,* after all, who is responsible. But nowhere in his calculations does he himself enter. That he, too, had a share in this is to him incomprehensible. It is for this reason, that he flees from applause, and abhors public demonstrations to him. In the old days, when he was more a victim to his tempestuous emotions, he would escape from the opera house in the middle of a performance, and run through the winter streets without coat and hat, mumbling to himself as he ran, because an ovation to him had shattered the artistic atmosphere he was trying to create. Today he is more quietly tolerant of applause, and accepts it with less protest; but he is still obviously uncomfortable, and would be much more contented if his work passed unnoticed.

My choice story of Toscanini's self-effacement is the one which I was the first to describe in print. It is now famous; but it is so illustrative that I cannot resist the temptation to repeat it, even at the danger of telling a thrice-told tale. Toscanini was rehearsing Beethoven's Ninth Symphony with the New York Philharmonic. He gave his musicians such a new insight into the music that, when the rehearsal ended, they rose to their feet and cheered him. Desperately, Toscanini tried to arrest their ovation, waving his arms wildly, crying to them to desist. When there was a lull in the ovation, Toscanini's broken voice could be heard exclaiming—and there were tears in his eyes as he spoke: "It isn't me, men. . . . it's Beethoven! . . . Toscanini is nothing."

But all this is when performances go well. When they go badly, Toscanini suffers acute mental and physical pain. He has stormed from the concert platform after a poor perform-ance, rushed like a stabbed bull into the artist's room and there given vent to his rage. No one can come near him at such moments. He is inconsolable. Once at a New York concert a bad note was struck at the end of a piece of music. That bad note was like a hammer blow on his sensibilities. He fled from the stage outside into the street and wandered through the thick of the traffic conscious only of his pain and that sour note. At last, a few of the orchestra men caught up with him, pushed him into a taxi, and brought him back into the concert hall. A few minutes later he calmed down; and the concert could proceed.

I have seen him walk from rehearsals in Bayreuth and Salz-burg, his face contracted, his eyes piercing. He is oblivious of people in the street, of where he is and whither he is going. He is conscious only of the fact that a rehearsal did not go well. At such rehearsals, while he is giving shape and design to a performance, he undergoes the most penetrating agony. His temper is cyclonic. He will abuse his men with violent har-angues, forgetting to whom he is talking or how, conscious only that the music has not been fully realized. He cries his invectives in Italian, because the language is so rich in profanity. Once when he did so, he realized that the musician he was ad-dressing did not understand a word of Italian. He desperately searched for adequate words in English to express his seething emotions. At last, he burst out with: "You bad, bad man!"

Once he was particularly vituperative to a trumpet player. After the rehearsal, the concertmaster went to Toscanini and discreetly reminded him that since the trumpeter was himself a very great artist, would it not be appropriate for Toscanini to apologize for his harsh, stinging words? Toscanini saw the point and magnanimously agreed. Meekly he approached the trumpeter and offered his apologies. "But, you know, you didn't play the phrase correctly," Toscanini added. Suddenly, Toscanini remembered how the phrase had been played by the musician. Blood rushed to his face, his eyes blazed. He forgot his apology and good intentions. Once again he exploded into invective. "You see," said Toscanini when he recovered, "God tells me how the music should sound—but *you* come in the way!"

He expresses his rage by kicking his stand, or more often by breaking his baton into pieces. Once he was conducting with a baton that was made of particularly pliable wood which would not break. Toscanini tried again and again to break it but failed. His rage mounting, Toscanini drew a handkerchief out of his pocket and tried to tear it. That, too, refused to yield. Finally, he took his alpaca coat off his back, and proceeded to tear it to shreds. When he was through, he felt relieved, and quietly asked the men to begin the phrase all over again.

"It is easy to understand," once wrote Stefan Zweig in a particularly revealing essay,* "why none but his intimates are allowed to attend these rehearsals, at which he knows he will be overcome by his insatiable passion for perfection. More and more alarming grows the spectacle of the struggle, as Toscanini strives to wring from the instrumentalists the visioned masterpiece which has to be fashioned in the sphere of universally

* Introduction to *Toscanini*, by Paul Stefan, Viking Press, 1936.

audible reality. His body quivers with excitement, his voice becomes hoarse, his brow is beaded with sweat; he looks exhausted and aged by these immeasurable hours of strenuous toil; but never will he stop an inch short of the perfection of his dream. With unceasingly renewed energy, he pushes onward and onward until the orchestra has at length been subjected to his will and can interpret the composer's music exactly as it has presented itself to the great conductor's mind. Only he who has been privileged to witness this struggle for perfection hour after hour, day after day, can grasp the heroism of Toscanini; he alone can estimate the cost of the super-excellence which the public has come to expect as a matter of course."

This savage pursuit after perfection is part of the struggle of every great artist. Yet few artists pursue it so relentlessly, so remorselessly as Toscanini. His integrity and idealism are such that anything short of the full realization of his conceptions costs him indescribable pain. He has time and again bolted from symphony halls in horror at hearing symphonies he loves performed unimaginatively by conductors. "Swine, swine," he will cry, as he rushes from the concert hall as if it had suddenly become a place of desecration. And he is as severely critical of himself as of others. He has been known to rehearse a work, then abandon it before concert time, because he finds himself incapable of giving life to the music he heard deep within him. After conducting some works at rehearsals, he will sometimes go to a corner of the stage and beat his fists at his temples, and whine. He does not reprimand the orchestra, for he knows it is doing the best it can; he is castigating himself for his shortcomings. He used to avoid recording his performances because when he heard the records he was horrified that the actual performance ran so far afoul of his intentions. Recently, he was listening to a radio performance of the Beethoven Seventh Symphony, and during the entire performance he annihilated the conductor for his ineptitude in certain passages. That the broadcast was of records, and that the conductor of the recorded version was Toscanini himself, only plunged him into greater despondency.

*

There are many wonderful qualities to a Toscanini interpretation, which can be uncovered through musical analysis. There is the distinctness of his performances: his balances are achieved so sensitively that always, even in complicated *brio* passages, there is a lucid transparency in the orchestration. Constantly we hear all the different voices which go to make up the orchestral choir.

Then there is the electric, dynamic exposition of dramatic pages: the beats are incisive, the chords are like the stinging lashes of a whip, the playing of the men is tense and precise. On the other hand, in lyrical pages, he draws a song from the throat of the orchestra incomparable for purity, serenity, and simplicity.

Beyond this, there is his methodical exactness: one recognizes that every note in the score is given its due and assigned its appropriate place in the complicated pattern of the symphony or overture. With Toscanini one is aware of an almost scientific correctness in the performance.

Finally, there is *style:* Toscanini's amazing flexibility and versatility enable him to perform the works of many different composers in the manner best adapted to their idiom. Toscanini's Schubert in the *Unfinished Symphony* has simplicity and movement; his Brahms has spaciousness; his Mozart and Haydn are refined; his Wagner is dramatic, orgiastic in color and dynamics; his Beethoven has stateliness; his Debussy, delicacy.

Nature is his ally in his work, having endowed him with the most sensitive pair of ears, and the most fabulous memory in music. To hear him rehearse a complex modern work, and to see him interrupt a particularly climactic passage because the flutist, say, did not play a few notes staccato, is to realize that nothing takes place in the orchestra that escapes his hearing. His memory is equally formidable. It is well known that, since the beginning of his career, he has directed every performance without written music—compelled to do so by his myopic eyesight. It can be said that virtually the entire known symphonic and operatic repertoire has been photographed on his memory which is so exact that the slightest markings on the printed page linger with him for decades. A violinist once approached him for advice on the playing of a certain passage in a late Beethoven quartet. Toscanini confessed that he had not seen the music since 1896, but after a few moments of silent thought, brought back to mind the passage in question and gave the violinist the advice he was seeking. At a rehearsal of a Vivaldi concerto grosso, Toscanini insisted that a certain passage for violins should be marked staccato. Discreetly, the concertmaster approached him and, with music in hand, showed Toscanini that there were no such markings on the printed page. Toscanini still insisted that he was right, even though he confessed that he had not looked at the score for many years. The following day, the maestro brought to rehearsal a more authoritative edition of the music than the one used by the orchestra, and proved that the markings were as he had said. One of the famous anecdotes about Toscanini's memory concerns the time a bassoon player came to him saying that his instrument was broken and could not sound E-flat. Toscanini thought a moment, then said: "That's all right. You can rehearse with us. The note of E-flat does not appear in your music today."

When presented with a new score, Toscanini will take it to bed with him and read it from cover to cover. After he has read it several times, the music is indelibly engraved on his memory. He can be given a new score on a Friday afternoon, yet the following Monday morning he comes to rehearsal and begins working on the music from memory. Once he did this with a work of Ernest Schelling, with Schelling playing the piano part. During the rehearsal, Toscanini corrected the composer in a specific passage, pointing out to him that he was not playing the piano part as it was written in the manuscript.

His ear and memory offer only a partial explanation for a Toscanini performance. His sense for style is no less significant—and this arises from an extraordinary musical erudition and scholarship. In casual conversation, Toscanini has made comments on music history and backgrounds which have amazed even musicologists. His knowledge of every phase of music is encyclopedic. He knows what a composer's intentions are because he is familiar with everything about the composer, his background, his times, his materials.

He has the infinite capacity of genius for taking pains. A fleeting passage which would escape the notice of most conductors would be subjected by him to the most intensive preparation. I recall in Salzburg a rehearsal of the chorus in *Die Meistersinger,* when Toscanini spent several hours on a few bars in search of transparency and preciseness. When he conducts a symphony, every note is scrupulously adjusted by him into the texture of the whole. When he rehearses an opera he works with the solo singers, with the chorus, orchestra, and even the stage-director—always fastidious about the minutest details—until he has been able to create an integrated performance.

With his scholarship and thoroughness is combined an infallible instinct. He *senses* the way a work should sound, even though the markings on the page do not give him the specific indications. He has an interpretative sixth sense; composers have said so for decades. Once he conducted a Verdi work in which, of his own volition, he inserted a slow and subtle retard in one of the passages. At the end of the performance, Verdi rushed up to him and said with amazement: "How did you know I wanted a retard in just that place? I was afraid to mark it that way in the score because I thought that conductors would tend to exaggerate it. But you played it exactly the way I heard it inside of me!" Frequently, in playing a modern work, he has altered a rhythmic phrase, made slight revisions in the orchestration, or readjusted the dynamics, only to have the composer confess that that is the way he had always felt that his music should be, but was unable to get it down on paper. Once a young American composer brought his score to Toscanini. Toscanini read the music through, stopped at a certain passage, and said to the composer. "That isn't what you want to say. If you changed the instrumentation here as follows, I am sure it would be closer to your original intentions." The composer confessed to me that that very passage had puzzled him for a long time, and not until Toscanini had designated the remedy had he been able to arrive at a satisfactory artistic solution. Puccini used to say that "Toscanini conducts a work not just as the written score directs, but as the composer had imagined it in his head even though he failed to write it down on paper."

A Toscanini performance reflects the interpreter's unashamed adoration for the music he is performing. There is a famous quip told about the orchestral musician who is making faces while performing. "You see," he explained, "I just don't like music." Unfortunately, this might apply to innumerable conductors. They don't like the music they conduct. They've either grown tired of it, or else they never took to it in the first place. Toscanini can bring his incomparable freshness of viewpoint, enthusiasm, and vitality to everything he directs because he loves the music with the intensity of a music student hearing his Beethoven symphonies and Wagner music dramas for the first time. He has been known to burst into weeping while listening to a radio performance of *Tristan und Isolde* or a Beethoven symphony. "It is so beautiful, I cannot help it," he explains. After years of conducting he is as thrilled by a stroke of genius in a Beethoven symphony or a Richard Strauss tone-poem as if he were coming into contact with it for the first time. There is something essentially schoolboyish about his adoration for the music masters. He owns a valuable collection of manuscript letters by Mozart and Verdi, some manuscript scores, and other mementos of great composers. These items have a holy aura for Toscanini. In their presence he is as humble and as reverent as a high priest before a shrine. Such love for music can only result in the warmth and sunshine of his interpretations, in which the interpreter speaks from a heart overbrimming with his emotions.

There remains to mention Toscanini's culture, which is ever betrayed in the majesty of his conception and the purity of his tastes. Toscanini approaches musical interpretation not only with a prodigious musical equipment and training, but also with the mellowness that comes from a highly cultured background. He reads voraciously; he is a passionate admirer of Goethe, Dante, Shelley, and Shakespeare; he has read everything Shakespeare has written, and committed much of it to memory. He is a lover of great painting. He is interested in history and politics. When he speaks through his music, he speaks with the language of a highly cultured individual.

His is one of the great musical careers of history. He was born in Parma on March 25, 1867, and was a student of the cello at Parma Conservatory. Even as a child his memory was exceptional. He learned his lessons by heart after going through them once, always playing for his teachers without consulting the music. Once a teacher questioned him about his memory. Young Toscanini, to prove his capacity, took pencil and paper and wrote down the full orchestral score of the *Lohengrin* prelude.

He was graduated with highest honors. For the next few years he played the cello in different Italian orchestras. One of his assignments was with the orchestra of a wandering opera company which traveled in South America. It was with this assignment that he had his rendezvous with destiny.

The opera company was directed by a Brazilian conductor, Leopaldo di Miguez, who was not popular with the company. When the troupe reached Rio de Janeiro, Miguez suddenly withdrew from his post a few hours before the scheduled evening performance of *Aïda;* at the same time he made public his grievances against the opera company in the newspapers. A substitute Italian conductor, Superti by name, stepped to the platform that evening, but met such a wave of antagonism on the part of the audience that he was compelled to take cover. Obviously still another conductor, more acceptable to the audience, would have to be found. But where—at this last moment? Suddenly, some of the musicians in the orchestra thought of the lean, nervous, wiry cellist, Toscanini, who had long since amazed them with his prodigious memory and ear. They suggested to the director that Toscanini be given the baton—and because the director was desperate the suggestion was accepted.

But Toscanini could not be found; and Toscanini could not be found because just that evening he was playing truant from work to have a rendezvous with an attractive South American woman. Smoking or drinking have never been Toscanini's vices; but women—that is a different story. "I kissed my first woman and smoked my first cigarette on the same day," he has said. "I have never had time for tobacco since." He had met this beautiful woman in the afternoon, and immediately forgot that he had a performance that evening. Fortunately, one of the musicians in the orchestra knew of the incident, and rushed to the home of the beautiful *senorita*. Toscanini was there, and Toscanini would not abandon his love idyll. "Love is more important than music," Toscanini cried. But the musician finally won Toscanini over with his pleas and arguments, and regretfully the young Italian abandoned his lady for the sake of his initiation into conducting.

Toscanini was nineteen years old at the time. As he was pushed towards the conductor's platform, his obvious nervousness (or was it his youth?) made an impression on an audience grown so much more restive by the prolonged delay; its resentment was temporarily pacified. There was an electric quality to his brisk movements as he raised his baton. The audience watched him tensely, noticed, for example, that he did not attempt to open the score in front of him. The baton descended with an incisive movement of the wrist; and the performance began.

That he conducted the entire performance from memory—a mere youngster who had never before held a baton in hand—was in itself a miracle to that audience. But there was a greater miracle still; the performance itself. Such a vital reading, so beautifully projected, was not to be heard frequently in Rio de Janeiro. Some swore that they had never before heard an *Aïda* such as this. The audience rose to its feet to acclaim the young conductor. Toscanini was on his way to greatness.

It is not difficult to mark off the milestones of his epical career. The first was the debut in South America. The second: La Scala.

After this debut, Toscanini took over the conductor's post with the touring opera company and during the remainder of the tour conducted eighteen different operas—and all from memory. Back in Italy, he directed operas in different opera houses over a period of several years, receiving an ever-rising choir of praise. At last, La Scala called him. He was only thirty-one years old, and already he was principal conductor of one of the leading opera houses of the world.

The Toscanini era at La Scala—from 1898 to 1909—was historic. If there was something extraordinary in a young man taking over the artistic direction of a world-famous opera house, it did not appear so to Toscanini himself. He took over command without any show of self-consciousness, and proceeded to assert his will. The La Scala company knew they were dealing with an irresistible force before which they had to yield if they were not to be crushed.

He knew what he wanted; and he was intransigent. He instituted vigorous rehearsals, the like of which La Scala had never before known—working singers, orchestra, chorus and himself to the point of exhaustion. The thoroughness with which he prepared each opera inspired awe in some quarters, blasphemy in others. He worked demoniacally for perfection of execution, and was not satisfied until it was realized. Besides this, he overhauled the repertoire, introducing German operas by Wagner, Gluck, and Weber, as well as representative works from the Russian and French repertory. A great era had come to La Scala, and it had come because of the indefatigable, insatiable, untiring young conductor.

The third milestone was the Metropolitan Opera House,

where, in 1908, he was engaged together with Giulio Gatti-Casazza, general manager of La Scala. Toscanini arrived in America already a famous conductor. But after his first performances (who had ever heard of a performance of *Götterdämmerung* conducted from memory?) he became subject for adulation usually reserved by audiences for the prima donna. He ruled at the Metropolitan, as he had ruled at La Scala, with a firm hand. He castigated temperamental singers with his acid humor. "Madame," he said to one lady who insisted that *she* was the star of the show, "stars are only found in heaven." Upon another occasion, a pampered soprano insisted upon showing her vocal powers by holding a note much longer than the score specified. Toscanini rudely interrupted her with the orchestral close. At one time, the singers came to Gatti-Casazza with wails and lamentations that Toscanini was abusing them beyond human endurance. "What can I do?" asked Gatti-Casazza. "He abuses me, too."

His reign at the Metropolitan brought about one of its glorious epochs. It was the high artistic mark in the history of that operatic institution. There was no doubt but that when Toscanini was in the conductor's seat, the operas of Wagner, Mozart, Gluck, or Verdi were reborn—fresh, vital, electric. The critics were effusive in their praises; and the audiences, idolatrous.

In a violent fit of temper, Toscanini withdrew from the Metropolitan in 1915. The true explanation for his resignation has never been offered, though many spurious excuses were given at the time. But it is strongly believed today that Toscanini left because his artistic integrity had been offended. He had not been given enough rehearsals; he did not get the full cooperation of the singers, many of whom sulked because of his dictatorial rule. With him departed a great age of operatic performances which, unfortunately, has never again returned to New York.

From 1920 to 1929, Toscanini was back at La Scala, as artistic director. Those were wonderful years for La Scala! Toscanini was in full control, and with Toscanini in full control there was opera-making unequalled anywhere else in the world. Music lovers from every part of the globe made pilgrimages to Milan to hear his performances, and, having heard them, felt that they had been given an unforgettable artistic experience.

From this time on, the milestones in Toscanini's career grow even more numerous. He came back to America in 1926 as a guest of the Philharmonic Symphony Society and was given a thunderous acclaim. He remained ten years with the Philharmonic which, under his direction, became the greatest symphonic ensemble in the world. His farewell performance in 1936 was an eloquent tribute to his popularity. From early morning, on the day of the concert, queues stretched from the box-office, waiting patiently until the evening for an opportunity to enter the hall. There, later that evening, the tumult and the shouting were the expression of an enamored public for their best-loved musician.

Meanwhile, in 1930, he came to Bayreuth, the first foreign conductor ever to perform there. He gave incandescent performances of *Tannhäuser* and *Tristan*. In 1931, he was back at Bayreuth, this time for *Tannhäuser* and *Parsifal*. Renouncing Bayreuth in 1933 because the swastika now hung high over Germany, Toscanini associated himself with Salzburg. It was because of his presence at the Mozart shrine—and its magnificent performances of operas and symphony—that the Salzburg Festival became from 1934 to 1938 the greatest center of music-making in the world, and the most glamorous.

58

In 1937, Toscanini returned to America to direct for the radio public the NBC Orchestra which had been organized expressly for him by the National Broadcasting Company. For the next few seasons, Toscanini conducted symphony concerts over the air before the largest audiences ever known to hear an orchestral performance—several millions for each concert. With this same orchestra Toscanini went on a good-will tour of South America in 1940. It was for Toscanini a sentimental journey, for he was returning for the first time to the country in which he had made his debut. In South America, Toscanini received the greatest ovations, and the most moving manifestations of reverence and adoration, ever given to a musician.

*

It has been a hero's life; and it has received a hero's acclaim. Yet there is something tragic about Toscanini. He has never been a happy man. He had left La Scala in a fit of temper first in 1908, then again in 1929. In much the same violent mood he abandoned his posts with the Metropolitan Opera House in 1915, and with the New York Philharmonic in 1936. It would be a mistake to look upon this as a manifestation of prima-donna temperament. He did not foresake one post after another because he was searching for the adventure of grazing in new pastures. He was driven away (often at the cost of personal suffering) by his savage artistic conscience which dictated that nothing short of perfection must be tolerated. As long as he was given full control over the artistic policies of an orchestra or an opera house he was capable of remaining at his post and giving himself unsparingly to his assignments. But when there were obstacles placed in his way—complaints about long and expensive rehearsals, for example, or grumbling criticisms of his programs—he could work no longer.

"Toscanini, the insatiable, the captive of his longing for perfection, is never granted the grace of self-forgetfulness," wrote Zweig. "He is consumed, as with undying fires, by the craving for ever-new forms of perfection."

That craving for perfection has sent him searching from one post to another, from one land to the next. In fleeting periods he clutched it with both hands; at such times he was blissfully happy. But perfection, in an imperfect world, is elusive. He who would seek it must know crucifixion. Toscanini has been crucified not once but many times. He was crucified when he had to bid permanent farewell to his native land, and again when he had to exile himself from Bayreuth and Salzburg where his artistic dreams came closest to achieving realization. He was crucified each time he had to confess, through his resignations, that perfection was not to be achieved by him.

And yet, despite (who knows? perhaps because of) all these elements of tragedy that have punctuated his life, Toscanini's career has been one of the most triumphant of our age.

The Showman Conductor

1

Leopold Stokowski

When orchestral concerts were still in their infancy in this country, about a century ago, audiences came to the concert hall more for the circus stunts that accompanied each performance than for the music itself. Haydn, Mozart, and Beethoven were only incidental attractions (if they were attractions at all). What drew the audiences was the eccentricity of a conductor like Jullien who, visiting America in 1853, delighted them with his *bizarrerie.* The audiences of the time might listen patiently to masterpieces. But the music they really liked was a number like *The Railroad Gallop* (during the performance of which a toy locomotive would run around the stage puffing smoke); or *The Fireman's Quadrille* (firemen in regulation attire would march upon the stage during the playing of the music, pouring actual water on a simulated fire); or, toward the close of the century, the *Anvil Chorus,* in which the orchestra was supplemented by a group of stage smithies pounding on anvils.

Such theatricalism has gone out of our symphonic music. Another brand, more subtle perhaps but no less superfluous to the performance, has entered with several conductors, of whom Leopold Stokowski is unquestionably the most celebrated.

He conducted without a score in front of him at a time when such a feature was comparatively rare in this country. (When he first did this, about thirty years ago, a kind old lady was tempted to remark: "Isn't it a shame that the wonderful Mr.

Stokowski can't read a score? Imagine, how great he would have been if he only knew how!") When conducting without music lost its novelty, Stokowski began directing without a baton. At the very same time he discovered that there was poetry and drama in the motion of his hands. He has since been tireless in his efforts to draw the attention of his audiences to them. When directing Alban Berg's *Wozzeck* at the Metropolitan, he meticulously adjusted the lighting in the opera house so that his moving hands might throw grotesque and impressive shadows on the walls and ceilings. In his appearances on the screen, his hands have always monopolized the attention of the camera. Very recently, at a Carnegie Hall concert, he had a beam of light playing on his fingers.

He has given more than passing attention to his appearance on the stage, to the way his clothing drapes his attractive figure, to the effect of his gestures on his audiences. He has yielded on numerous occasions to the temptation of making little speeches from the platform. Sometimes he tried to explain a controversial piece of music. Sometimes he has severely taken his audiences to task for their apathy to modern music; and then, on another occasion, he lashed them verbally for rising out of that apathy to hiss a new work by Schönberg. Most often he has lectured them about their bad concert manners, about talking and chewing gum during the performance, about coming late and leaving early. Once he even went to the length of giving his audience an object lesson. He performed a *Fantasie* by Lekeu, during the performance of which one musician after another straggled late upon the stage. During the rest of the program, which included some songs by Brahms and a Wagner number, the men wandered about the stage, then rambled off noisily.

He has brought adventure into the symphony hall. At one

concert he tried to dispense with lights, at another with applause. He eliminated the office of the concertmaster, feeling that every first violin should have the same responsibility. He has shifted the seating arrangement of his orchestra again and again. He has introduced new and unorthodox instruments into the orchestra, such as the Thereminvox (ether music) and the Hammond tone-sustaining piano. He has given a concert in collaboration with the Clavilux, an instrument that throws colors on a screen, in an attempt to fuse color and music into a new artistic expression. He has performed the most radical music of our time, that of Stravinsky and Schönberg and Edgar Varèse. Once he attempted the introduction of quarter-tone and eighth-tone music at a regular concert. He was probably the first great conductor to give serious consideration to jazz. When conducting the NBC Orchestra in 1941, he inaugurated intimate concerts for the audience attending the broadcast, in which he informally rehearsed new and old music when the broadcast period had ended.

His Youth Concerts in Philadelphia also struck a novel note. He had the children plan the programs, arrange the publicity, draw the advertising posters, and write the program notes. Once he rocked Philadelphia to its very foundation by having the young people rise and sing the *Internationale!*

He has always planned unusual effects, and has usually cloaked them in a charming garb of spontaneity. His pretty speeches, for example, (supposedly inspired by an actual incident in the hall) were frequently prepared beforehand. There is an illustrative incident concerning the opening night concert of a summer series by the Philadelphia Orchestra which reveals a characteristic Stokowski maneuver. At the conclusion of the concert, the manager begged Stokowski (who was in the audience) to step on the stage and direct his orchestra in one number. Stokowski leaped on the platform and led his men in an electrifying reading of the *Blue Danube Waltz*. That the orchestra should suddenly sound so beautifully under Stokowski, even in an unrehearsed number, brought home to the audience the magic of this great conductor. Only the men of the orchestra knew that two weeks earlier, at the last rehearsal for the regular season, Stokowski suddenly decided to prepare the waltz, and prepared it with the most meticulous care as to details. This rehearsal proved bewildering to his men at the time, for they knew that the waltz was not scheduled for the closing concerts of the season.

That he is a great conductor, one of the greatest of our time, is not even disputed by those who condemn his antics most vehemently. For more than three decades, he has brought great music to the American symphony halls, and from time to time this music has been presented in performances of incomparable majesty. But great music has not been the exclusive attraction at the Stokowski concerts; dramatics, novelty, adventure have been music's partners. The result? Crowded houses whenever Stokowski steps on the platform; brilliant audiences; adulation and fame such as no other conductor in our time has enjoyed, except perhaps Toscanini; front-page attention. Stokowski has been the source of news, the subject for anecdotes, and the center for controversy.

Over a period of more than thirty years Stokowski has been the stuff from which news is made. He has known how to direct the limelight of attention upon himself and his art. Through these many years nothing and no one has succeeded in obscuring him from public attention. When, as conductor of the Philadelphia Orchestra, he went on a leave of absence, he remained the focus of attention by going to the Orient for the purpose of studying Oriental music. (Was it coincidental

66

that this leave of absence took place at the same time that Toscanini had returned to America and was receiving a thunderous
acclaim?) When he retired as the musical director of the
Philadelphia Orchestra he even eluded the obscurity that usually
accompanies retirement. As the founder and director of the
American Youth Orchestra which toured South America as a
gesture of good-will, the front pages belonged to him. Besides,
he now associated himself with the cinema and, therefore, substituted a national fame for a comparatively localized one.

For a musical personality who has enjoyed more publicity
than any other in our time, a great deal of contradictory information has gained general credence. His name is *really*
Lionel Stokes some say (was he not born in London?). Others
insist that he was really born in Poland (do not his name and
accent betray him?). There are those who feel that he is a
modest and self-effacing artist. For years he has featured on
his programs beautiful orchestral transcriptions of music by
Bach without revealing that the transcriber was himself. When
the discovery was made, he explained: "It's Bach who is important, not his transcriber." On the other hand, others insist
that he is publicity-mad, on the alert for space on the newspaper's front pages with varied and sometimes quixotic ex-
ploits. Some believe he is a true artist concerned only with
the highest standards of his art: When he first came to the
radio he announced that he would perform only great music,
and that if great music was not wanted he would withdraw
from the microphone. Others will point out that he is Stokowski, concerned only with Stokowski: only an artist with a
touch of Narcissus-complex would permit the camera to hover
so lovingly and admiringly on his hands, his back, the crown
of his hair. Some feel he is a musician of unquestioned integrity: he has kept his concerts on a high plane of artistic excel-

lence from the moment he began conducting. Others criticize
him for his lack of artistic integrity: conducting for a soloist
like Kate Smith; collaborating with Bob Burns and his Bazooka,
and Mickey Mouse; permitting such a desecration of a masterpiece as that of the Beethoven *Pastorale Symphony,* converted
into a Bacchanalian orgy in *Fantasia,* without his veto.

Actually, a complete picture of Stokowski must include all
of these contradictory qualities. Stokowski is Stokowski, which
is to say he is a genius and a charlatan in one, a great artist
and a circus performer. There are many who lament the fact
that a part of his make-up should be the cheapness and vulgarity
of a vaudeville entertainer; they feel that if he were less the
tricky showman he would be all the greater as an artist. Such
jeremiads are silly. One might just as well lament the fact
that New York is a city of noise, dust, and skyscrapers. That *is*
New York; that is its individuality. Stokowski's theatricalism
is not only a source of his weakness but actually even a source
of his strength. What we admire in Stokowski's conducting,
upon analysis, is that which we deplore in his personality: his
wonderful sense for the dramatic. Only an artist conscious of
his audience and of his effect upon that audience can bring
such sweep and passion, such breathtaking climaxes, such a
sense for the theatre as Stokowski does. He is a master in the
handling of orchestral sonority. He is a dramatist, conscious
of timing. He is not a poet in the sense that Bruno Walter is;
or such an exquisite stylist as Toscanini. The more gentle
and elegiac moments are not for him. He does not play Haydn
and Mozart well; his slow movements too often lack quiet and
serenity. Music in his hands lacks repose and contemplation.
But it becomes an exciting experience. Where music profits
from such treatment, Stokowski is a remarkable interpreter.
But that is because the blood of the showman is in his veins;

because he feeds on the limelight; because an audience stimulates him. Were he less a showman, a great part of his ability would not be there.

*

He is as much an enigma to the musicians who play under him as to his audiences. There are those who have worked with him for many years who feel that he is a stranger to them. He is not a conductor who radiates warmth and affection. He never calls his men by their first names, and most of them he does not even know by their last. If he passes them in the street he is just as likely as not to pass them by without a sign of recognition. At rehearsals he is cold, methodical, ruthless. He comes to the stage without a single word of greeting (he has been known to begin a rehearsal after an absence of many weeks without so much as a formal salutation to the orchestra), and begins working on the score in front of him without a moment's delay. He treats his men with dictatorial firmness in which compassion has no part. He brooks no nonsense. In the face of incompetence he is not explosive; he is merely acid, with a humor that cuts the offender like a knife-blade. Yet when things go well—even very well—he does not yield to praises.

Occasionally, there is a smile on his lips, and sometimes he ventures a jest. But such moments are not frequent at Stokowski rehearsals. Even when such a lighter moment arrives, he suddenly changes face and, without the least warning, reverts to severity.

He is equally volatile in his relationship with the musicians. If he is kind to a musician at one moment, he can become cruel a moment later, and without warning. He has been known to treat some player acidly week in and week out. Yet, unexpectedly, he speaks well of him, or goes out of his way to do a

69

secret favor for him. He has also been known to reveal attachment for certain musicians and then expel them at the slightest provocation. Generally, he dislikes intensely any musician who caters to him and who tries to win his favor, and he will become fond of the one who dares to criticize him openly without mincing words.

Though he works his men to tears, he never prepares a composition so painstakingly as Toscanini or Koussevitzky. He is more concerned with the general effect for which he is striving, and lets the minutiae of a performance take care of themselves. He believes implicitly that one quality every great performance must have is freshness and, after working out the general outlines of a composition, he prefers to leave some of the details to the actual performance. A rehearsal of a well-known symphony is frequently sketchy, with only spasmodic pages touched upon. Even a complex modern work, played for the first time, is frequently rehearsed by him not note for note but in random passages. For this reason, perfectionists will criticize many Stokowski performances severely. The violins may sometimes slight a difficult passage. There is often a lack of precision and exactness which so many other conductors demand. But, it must be confessed, something important takes the place of technical perfection: Some of the soaring moods achieved by Stokowski, when he carries his orchestra to dizzy heights of eloquence, are the result of spontaneity.

There are times when he will preface the rehearsal of a specific work with a long speech; more often than not, the speech will not be concerned with the music itself, but with metaphysics, religion, ethics, or literature. His message may appear irrelevant at the moment it is delivered, but it usually has some relation to the music he is about to rehearse. He is trying to set a mood for his men; to prepare their mental stages (so to speak). Then, after he has had his say, and has worked out the general outlines of a piece of music, he will take a seat in the back of the empty hall, and listen to its performance at the hands of an assistant. After making important notes, he returns to the stage and puts on the finishing touches.

His capacity to make an orchestra *sound*—the luxuriant orchestral texture he achieves—is one of his greatest gifts. He proved this once and for all when he organized the American Youth Orchestra and made it imitate the tone quality of the Philadelphia Orchestra. During rehearsals, he is continually experimenting with sonority. He is a master in the blending of tone qualities. He makes the most subtle adjustments between different sections of the orchestra. He is assiduous in working out different blends of sounds. Many of his rehearsals are merely exercises in sonority. But when he has finished his experiments, the orchestra under him produces a tone, the beauty and richness of which is the envy of so many other conductors.

*

He owes his inexhaustible energy to methodical living. When he was still the conductor of the Philadelphia Orchestra, he budgeted his time carefully. He would rise early in the morning, eat a sparing breakfast, and then walk to the Academy of Music for the morning rehearsal. When there was no rehearsal scheduled for the morning, he would spend his time reading scores. Afternoons (once again when there were no rehearsals) would be allocated to interviews, business appointments, personal contacts. Evenings usually were spent quietly in the company of a few friends, or in reading. When there was a concert, Stokowski would take a nap in the later afternoon. Just before the concert, he would relax in the hands of a masseur.

He has always had the hypochondriac's fascination for diets, exercise, and healthful living. He takes walks regularly, and always indulges in the milder forms of setting-up exercises. He is almost an ascetic when it comes to food, his meals usually consisting of raw fruits, raw vegetables, and juices (though there was a time when he believed strongly in heavy meat diets). He never drinks coffee, smokes, or indulges in intoxicating drinking. He dislikes parties and elaborate social functions. Reading, spending silent hours in quiet contemplation (almost after the fashion of an Oriental), listening to music—these are his favorite diversions.

His career has been all of one piece and pattern: the traits (praiseworthy and otherwise) which today make him one of the most glamorous of living conductors were there even when he was an unknown musician. He was born in London on April 18, 1882. His name has always been Leopold Stokowski. His father was Polish, and his mother, Irish—neither one of them professional musicians. As a boy, Leopold studied the violin and piano, revealing sufficient talent to attract the interest of a patron who financed his academic education. The study of music he later continued at the Royal College of Music with Stanford and Davies, supporting himself during this period by assuming any and every assignment which might earn him a shilling. At one time, he even served as hack pianist in a cheap London music hall. His pleasure came in playing the music of Bach, his favorite composer from the very first. He played Bach continually, and acquired a truly comprehensive knowledge of that master's music.

In 1903, Stokowski received his first dignified musical post. He was appointed organist of the St. James's Church in Piccadilly. From here he was invited to New York to assume the organ post at the fashionable St. Bartholomew Church. He was a very good organist; we have evidence of that from many who heard him. He played Bach magnificently, and with fine dramatic instinct. His music made churchgoing an exciting emotional experience. He immediately found a clique which was fascinated by him and which spoke ravishingly of his musical gifts. The musical Stokowski of later years was slowly growing out of embryo.

He spent his summers in Europe studying conducting. Finally, in 1908, he was given an opportunity to direct a few summer concerts in London. A few months after this, a great opportunity came his way. The orchestra in Cincinnati, after a moribund period, had been reorganized. It was searching for a young and energetic leader who might vitalize it. Some far-sighted patrons thought of the brilliant and appealing organist of St. Bartholomew, and felt that his personality might go well in Cincinnati. Stokowski was offered the post; and he accepted eagerly.

Stokowski's career in Cincinnati is of interest not because he proved himself at once to be a great conductor (which was not the case!), but because he proved himself at once to be Stokowski. He took over the command of the orchestra with a firm hand, always threatening dismissal for his musicians if his slightest wish did not become law. He inaugurated programs which were incredibly progressive for the time (including an All-American program!), refusing to consult the tastes of his public, or the opinions of his critics. He even began to make little speeches to discipline his audiences for their lack of manners. As early as 1911, he was upbraiding his audience for fumbling with its programs. "Please don't do that! We must have the proper atmosphere. . . . I do not want to scold you or to appear disagreeable. . . . We work hard all week to give you this music, but I cannot do my best without your

73

aid. I'll give you my best or I won't give you anything. It is
for you to choose." (Many years later, when first appearing
before the radio microphone, he used almost the same words:
"We'll play the best music, or we won't play anything. If you
do not like our music, say so, and we won't give any more
radio concerts.")

He made his concerts in Cincinnati such a reflection of his
own dynamic personality that, when he announced his resignation in 1912, he caused a panic in Cincinnati music circles. It
seemed unthinkable to have symphony concerts without Stokowski. Every effort was made to keep him. Stokowski had
explained that he was going because he could not get the full
cooperation of his men. At one of his last rehearsals, a
spokesman for the orchestra arose and swore for all the men
that if Stokowski would reconsider his decision he would never
have any further cause for complaint. The directors of the
orchestra came to him with promises of every kind: his every
wish would be catered to; there would be all "necessary adjustments." ("Adjustments!" stormed Stokowski, "what cannot
be adjusted is the loss of my enthusiasm, which enthusiasm is
absolutely necessary in the constructive work of building an
orchestra!") Subscribers wrote appealing letters.

But Stokowski remained adamant. Did he already have the
contract for the Philadelphia Orchestra in his pocket? Probably—for his excuses for resigning sound feeble and insincere.
In any case, that spring Stokowski brushed the dust of Cincinnati from his shoes. During the summer, he fulfilled a few
engagements in London. The following fall, he was in Philadelphia in his new post.

The Philadelphia Orchestra was not only a step East for Stokowski (geographically an important direction for an ambitious conductor, because most of the great orchestras of America

were at the time in the East), but also a step upward. Cincinnati had proved valuable practice ground. Stokowski had acquired experience. He knew all the tricks of the trade. To that repertoire of tricks he was now prepared to add quite a few of his own.

*

In 1912, the orchestra centers in America were Boston, New York, and Chicago. Philadelphia was still a musical suburb. Its orchestra had been founded in 1900 by an admirable artist, Fritz Scheel—friend of Brahms, Tchaikovsky, Rubinstein, and Hans von Bülow. Scheel conducted four excellent concerts in 1900. His success inspired the formation of the orchestra on some permanent basis. In 1901, the Philadelphia Orchestra Association was organized, and in 1903 it was incorporated. Its aim was the presentation of the best in symphonic music in an annual series of subscription concerts.

Fritz Scheel remained the conductor of the Philadelphia Orchestra until 1907. He was a musician of taste and discrimination who refused to pamper his audiences by offering salon numbers (as so many other conductors did at the time throughout America). His programs were always musically sound, sometimes even adventurous. In 1903, he directed a cycle of Beethoven symphonies. In 1904, he invited Richard Strauss to conduct three concerts devoted to his own works. He was a receptive host to the works of living composers, giving American premières of music by Dvořák, D'Indy, Sibelius, Rimsky-Korsakow, Glazunov, and Converse. His stubborn refusal to descend from the high standards he had set for his orchestra resulted in small audiences and enormous deficits: he used to say with more good humor than malice that he was grateful a conductor performed with his back to the audience so that he could forget how empty the hall was.

75

Scheel was succeeded by Carl Pohlig, a competent musician, but a rather colorless personality. Pohlig had his admirers in Philadelphia. But out of the city—during the tours of the orchestra—he was treated coldly. He was not the man to encourage large audiences to come to his concerts. He was altogether incapable of directing attention to his orchestra or to himself. His programs were in good taste, but without unusual interest. His own personality lacked positive qualities. Under his direction, the Philadelphia Orchestra continued its rather unexciting existence, accumulating more deficits than prestige. In Boston and New York, the Philadelphia Orchestra was looked upon rather condescendingly as a small-town orchestra with a small-town conductor.

It was at this time that Stokowski (with his ever wonderful sense of timing) entered on the Philadelphia musical scene. To audiences long accustomed to undramatic concerts, the appearance of Stokowski promised adventure. His electrifying career in Cincinnati had been well publicized. Here then was the man to remove the drabness to which symphony concerts had succumbed and to bring to them a touch of glamour.

His first concert, on October 11, 1912, saw a crowded auditorium. Extra chairs had been placed within the orchestral rail. The atmosphere was charged. The audience awaited its new conductor with nervous anticipation. Then, as the critic of the Philadelphia *Public Ledger* reported, "Stokowski came forward with bowed head, evidently pondering the content of his musical message. Those who went forth to see a hirsute eccentricity were disappointed. They beheld a surprisingly boyish and thoroughly businesslike figure who was sure of himself, yet free from conceit, who dispensed with the score by virtue of an infallible memory, and held his men and his audience from the first note to the last firmly in his grasp."

76

The critic spoke the enthusiasm of the entire audience when he discussed Stokowski's conducting. "The new leader has been surprisingly successful in welding the several choirs into a single coherent entity. They played yesterday with a unity of purpose—particularly among the first violins—not usually attained until mid-winter. They brought out the full value of the lights and shadows. The climaxes were duly accentuated, the pianissimos with the utmost delicacy and refinement were contrasted with the full-throated polyphony." Mr. Stokowski's conducting is after the order of Nikisch, whom he frankly admires. . . . His gestures are graphic, the arcs and parabolas he describes tell of a kind of geometrical translation going on in his mind, whereby he visualizes the confluent rhythms in outward action. . . . There is from the first to the last no languor or slackened moment; he directs with a fine vigor and intensity that mounts to ecstasy yet does not lose its balance or forget its sane and ordered method."

Stokowski's debut was a triumph; there was no question on that score. At the end of the concert, a huge laurel wreath was laid on his platform. Stokowski stood within the wreath and motioned to his men to rise and receive the tributes of an audience which had risen to its feet.

And from that moment on, the history of the Philadelphia Orchestra was the history of Leopold Stokowski.

*

Some years ago, Pierre Monteux, disappointed at the apathetic reception given him by audiences when he served a short term as guest with the Philadelphia Orchestra, remarked poisonously that in Philadelphia only conductors who were tailor models were appreciated.

It is quite easy to cast a slur on Stokowski because he has been fastidious about his tailoring, his appearance on the stage,

77

the graceful lines of his gesturing. It is also easy to speak venomously of his numerous attempts at sensationalism, and to condemn some of his performances for their greater concern with general effect than with technical accuracy. Many great composers of our time grumble at the way Stokowski interprets their music only because of his carelessness about technical details. One of the greatest of living masters (he has asked me not to mention his name) once complained to me at great length about Stokowski. "It's very exciting what he plays, but it just isn't *my* music." An American interviewer once questioned Sibelius about Stokowski. "He is a very fine man, I am sure," Sibelius was quoted as saying, "a very interesting man, and interested in many things—but not, I think, in music." In short, a case can be built against Stokowski. But to do so is to forget that other arguments can be summoned, of equal if not greater weight, to prove that he is also a genius.

We must remember that if he is a sensationalist, he is also one of the most dynamic figures in the music of our times. His concerts have never been guilty of stagnancy. Over a period of several decades he has kept them alive, important, experimental. If Stokowski has been egocentric, consciously striving to direct attention upon himself, he has also succeeded in making symphonic music attractive to large audiences. The hall was full when first he stepped on the platform in Philadelphia, and it remained full for the next thirty years whenever he conducted. If Stokowski is more concerned with the effect of his performances than with minutiae, he has also proved himself capable of giving performances searchingly poetic, performances built on heroic lines with heroic proportions, performances of luminous quality, aflame with the sparks of his personality.

He built the Philadelphia Orchestra into one of the great

orchestral ensembles of all time, and he built it because he has
been ruthless and uncompromising. He had hardly arrived in
Philadelphia when he came to grips with the authorities. He
insisted on a sufficient number of rehearsals, and in the proper
hall, regardless of expense. He won this battle, just as he was
destined to win every other battle, because he was intransigent.
At his first rehearsals he immediately asserted his will over his
men. He gave his orders imperiously, with the tone of a leader
who is accustomed to being obeyed. He electrified his men;
he crushed them with his acid criticisms. Pohlig and Scheel
had been demanding musicians; but their rehearsals, in comparison with the Stokowski workouts, had been Sunday school
outings. Stokowski was ruthless in his dismissals of men who
had outlived their usefulness to the orchestra. He worked his
men severely, driving them with the force of his cogent personality, until they produced the kind of music that satisfied
his discerning ear and exacting tastes, the kind of music that
pleased his passionate love for beautiful sounds. During these
workouts, an orchestra was being transformed, an orchestra
which soon matched the great orchestras of the world in lumi-
nousness of tone, virtuosity, and beauty of sonority.

Philadelphia now joined Boston, New York, and Chicago as
a leading center of symphonic music, not only because its orchestra had been shaped into greatness, but also because its
programs were so experimental. From the first, Stokowski was
a passionate advocate of the modern composer, and during a
period when the modern composer was not tolerantly listened
to. Stokowski closed his ears to the groans of his audiences
and employers, and with the stubborn heroism of a true pioneer
performed the music he felt deserved a hearing. In 1916, for
example, Stokowski proposed to perform, for the first time in
America, the gargantuan Eighth Symphony of Gustav Mahler,

79

which called for a large orchestra and a chorus of a thousand voices. The directors of the orchestra refused to consider Stokowski's plan at first, because they insisted that there was simply no audience for Mahler's music, and then because such a concert would entail the expenditure of $14,000. Stokowski remained firm, and the directors were finally compelled to yield. They raised the money not only for nine Philadelphia performances, but (also at Stokowski's insistence) an additional $12,000 for a New York presentation. Incidentally, in this clash between Stokowski and directors, it was Stokowski who proved that his judgment was sounder than that of his adversaries. The performance of the Mahler symphony proved an unprecedented triumph for the Philadelphia Orchestra; it might well be said that it marked for the first time the success of this orchestra in New York, and the prelude to its international reputation. Beyond this, the performances as a whole brought in profits.

From 1916 on, the Philadelphia Orchestra energetically gave voice to new music. To survey the list of American (or world) premières by the Philadelphia Orchestra is, in a measure, to view a cross-section of musical creation in the twentieth century; but for Stokowski, many of the great works of our time would have had to wait indefinitely for their first American hearing. Sibelius (symphonies no. 5, 6, 7), Schönberg *(Kammersymphonie, Die Glückliche Hand, Pierrot Lunaire)*, Scriabin (symphonies no. 3 and 5, the *Divine Poem)*, Elgar *(Enigma Variations)*, Chausson (symphony in B flat), Rachmaninoff (symphony no. 3, Piano Concerto no. 4), Manuel de Falla *(El Amor Brujo)*, Prokofieff *(The Age of Steel)*, Stravinsky *(The Rites of Spring, Les Noces, Oedipus Rex)*, Szymanowski (symphony no. 3, Piano Concerto), Shostakovitch (symphonies no. 1 and 3), Alban Berg *(Wozzeck)*, Carlos Chavez *(H.P.)*—

these are only a few of the many important composers of our time to have found recognition in Philadelphia. And American composers? Certainly few conductors have done such yeoman service for our native musicians, even at a time when the American composer was the *bête noir* of our symphony halls. Ernest Schelling was performed by Stokowski as early as 1912; Daniel Gregory Mason in 1916. Other American composers— like Samuel Gardner, Henry Hadley, Charles T. Griffes, Josef Hofmann, John Alden Carpenter, Leo Ornstein, Edgar Varèse, Aaron Copland, Arthur Farwell, Wallingford Riegger, Henry F. Gilbert, Abram Chasins, Efrem Zimbalist, Roy Harris, Harl McDonald—have found representation on Philadelphia programs.

*

What has helped to make Stokowski such a vital force in the music of our times, and such a devoted apostle of the new, is his restless intellect which is ever groping for new spheres for musical expression. Once again, we would be unjust to the man if we were to say that it was his vanity which led him continually to search for new worlds to conquer. It would be more accurate to point out that he has an insatiable intellectual curiosity which makes him restlessly search out new avenues. The same intellectual hunger which has driven him for nourishment to different philosophies and cultures (Confucian, Buddhist, Christian), which has brought him to metaphysics, philosophy and literature, has also brought him to scientific research, in which he is by no means a mere dabbler. He was one of the first great conductors to turn seriously to phonograph recording; the year was 1919. Once associating himself with recorded music, he made a study of the science, and the Victor Company has attested to the fact that the present high standards of orchestral recording owe a partial debt to Stokowski's indefatigable researches. In 1929, he interested himself in radio broadcasting. At once he began to experiment in the control room, and to work over mechanical problems of orchestral transmission. He has helped to evolve (we have the word of radio engineers for this!) a more successful method of sending symphonic music through the air. Then, having conquered the air-waves, he entered the world of the cinema, once again spending time and effort in the laboratory. Those who have heard and seen *Fantasia* know how successfully he has solved the problem of lifelike reproduction of orchestral music on the screen, a problem which before this had defied the solutions of trained scientists with many years of study and experiments in sound films to their credit.

*

Stokowski's name, and that of the Philadelphia Orchestra, had become so synonymous over a period of many years that when, in 1934, he announced that he was through as principal conductor, the music world refused to believe its ears. The Philadelphia Orchestra without Stokowski?—as fantastic as Romeo without Juliet, relativity without Albert Einstein, evolution without Charles Darwin. What caused Stokowski's decision at that time remained a mystery. Perhaps he felt that his audiences (and the directors of the orchestra) were beginning to take him too much for granted. There had been some attempt on the part of the authorities to urge him to popularize his programs by sacrificing the moderns for the classics. A volcanic eruption was necessary, he may have felt, to shake them out of their complacency. If he wished to strike terror he succeeded only too well, for immediately the directors came to him with the offer of "music director"—a post quite apart from that of conductor—which placed full dictatorial powers over the organization into his hands without the power of outside veto. This offer cemented the breach—but only temporarily. In 1936, Stokowski again announced his resignation, promising to return each season for a few guest performances. In 1941, he severed his last ties with the orchestra he had brought to world prominence.

What brought about Stokowski's permanent withdrawal from Philadelphia where his very word had become law? It is probable that not even Stokowski can offer the answer. One can make guesses and draw assumptions. Stokowski is too restive to remain permanently in a world he has conquered completely. He had acquired a role of first importance in American symphonic music; not even the triumphs of Toscanini—which threw so many other conductors into a shade—could detract from the lustre of Stokowski's fame. He had achieved with the Philadelphia Orchestra the highest position to which he could possibly aspire. Having accomplished all this, he began to search nervously for untried fields of musical activity, for new triumphs in virgin territory. Hollywood attracted his roving eye. Hollywood offered him a fabulous new kingdom through whose agencies he could perform for millions, through whose resources he could evolve new directions for music. Did he have a Hollywood contract in his pocket when he resigned from the Philadelphia Orchestra in 1936? The answer is not important. What is important is that Stokowski had visited Hollywood, had spoken to some of its leading personalities, and had recognized that there was a place for him there.

His first film appearance took place in the *Big Broadcast of 1937*. He caused many sinking hearts when he insisted upon playing, not some sentimental Tchaikovsky melodies, but two compositions of Bach, including the G-minor fugue. The G-minor fugue for consumption by the nation's factory-workers, stenographers, newsboys, merchants? Hollywood shook its

83

head with skepticism. It yielded only because, as always, Stokowski was intractable. The Bach music, and Stokowski, took the country by storm. His second screen appearance, in which he performed a speaking as well as a conducting part, was with Deanna Durbin in *100 Men and a Girl*. He conducted a movement from a Tchaikovsky symphony, as well as works by Mozart and Liszt. Then Walt Disney asked him to cooperate in the making of a Mickey Mouse short retelling the fable of the Sorcerer's Apprentice. Stokowski was to conduct the orchestra in the music by Paul Dukas. But once Stokowski associated himself with Disney, he was dissatisfied merely with the role of conductor. He convinced Disney that they could produce something important and revolutionary, not only with Dukas' music but also with the works of other music masters. The story goes that when Stokowski first broached the subject to Disney, suggesting that they make a film of Bach's Toccata and Fugue, Disney politely told Stokowski to leave the story angle to the scenario department and to concern himself only with the music—mistaking Toccata and Fugue for a pair of storybook lovers like Romeo and Juliet, Troilus and Cressida, or Heloïse and Abelard. At any rate, Stokowski's voluble enthusiasm and irresistible personality won over Disney. They worked out a script together, discussed the animation, analyzed the accompanying music. For three years, Stokowski was a familiar figure in the Disney studios. At the same time, he was working out a new method of recording the music for the screen. The result was the two-million dollar *Fantasia* which gave pictorial interpretations to such musical masterpieces as Stravinsky's *Rites of Spring*, Beethoven's *Pastorale Symphony*, Moussorgsky's *Night on Bald Mountain*, Bach's Toccata and Fugue in D-minor, Tchaikovsky's *Nutcracker Suite*. How in the world can you expect to appeal to the masses with esoteric music by Bach, Stravinsky, Dukas, and Beethoven, and with a revolutionary film, *sans* plot or coherence, the various sections of which are tied together only through the smart remarks of a master of ceremonies (Deems Taylor)? Hollywood cynically asked this question. But *Fantasia* attracted more than a million customers at two-a-day performances in New York alone in a period of less than a year. And after its national distribution it yielded fabulous profits.

*

And still Stokowski continues to make history. From certain points of view perhaps his most remarkable achievement has been the formation of the All-American Youth Orchestra, in the spring of 1940. Convinced of the richness of musical talent among the very young, Stokowski boldly decided to gather the best of this talent into a great symphony orchestra. Fifteen thousand young musicians received auditions in every State, and from this number 560 were chosen as outstanding. Stokowski then traveled from one end of the country to the other, listening to the 560 young musicians. From their ranks he selected the eighty-odd who he felt deserved to join his orchestra. The average age of this unusual symphonic group was eighteen, but there were two members who were only fourteen years old. After giving a few preliminary concerts in the United States, Stokowski (with funds provided largely out of his own pocket), took his orchestra on a good-will tour of South America. Then he gave numerous concerts throughout the United States, and made phonograph recordings. Perhaps nowhere else have Stokowski's rare gifts and powers as a conductor been so eloquently proved as with his Youth Orchestra. In a bewilderingly short time, and with material of comparatively inexperienced orchestral players, he fashioned a symphonic ensemble that deserved ranking with the greatest American orchestras. One survey actually placed the Youth Orchestra as the seventh leading symphonic organization in this country. That this is no exaggerated praise each music lover can learn for himself by listening to the recording of music from *Tristan und Isolde* which Stokowski made for Victor with the Philadelphia Orchestra and comparing it with the same music Stokowski performed for Columbia records with the Youth Orchestra. It is sometimes difficult to recognize which is the Philadelphia Orchestra and which is the orchestra of youngsters. Higher praise than this can be given to no conductor. Stokowski has proved Mahler's adage that there are no great orchestras, only great conductors.

2

Serge Koussevitzky

Russian children usually enjoyed playtime by simulating soldiers or noblemen. But when Serge Koussevitzky was a child he would pretend he was an orchestral conductor. He would line up two rows of empty chairs in the living room. Then he would re-enter the room, bow stiffly to an imaginary audience and, with stick in hand, would proceed to direct a symphony while singing the principal parts at the top of his voice.

The child is father to the man. To see Koussevitzky stepping imperiously on the stage and, with sovereign air, proceeding to direct a concert—his audience and his orchestra both in the hollow of his hand; to see him at a rehearsal, arriving in a cape which is removed from his shoulders before he steps to his platform—to see him at such moments is to realize that, in conducting, his temperament finds fullest expression. He was born for the baton. He was meant for giving orders to other musicians, and being obeyed; he has the inflexible will of a despot. He was meant for the limelight. He has always been conscious of his audience, has directed his gestures and bodily movements as much to the public gaze as to his men's eyes, and (like Stokowski) has been fond of his tailor, always presenting a suave and well-draped figure on the stage.

From childhood, Koussevitzky aspired to the conductor's stand: that was the goal he set for himself from the first. Born in Tver, a town situated near Moscow on the banks of the Volga, on July 26, 1874 (his mother died while he was still an infant), he showed such unusual musical talent that he was designated for a musical career. His father, a professional musician, gave him his first music lessons. Serge was only seven when he had his first experience as a conductor, called upon to direct one of his own compositions. Directing an orchestra proved much more exhilarating to him than hearing his own music acquire life; he knew at once that he preferred interpreting other people's music at the head of an orchestra to creating his own. He was nine when he joined the string section of an orchestra, and only eleven when he began to serve as a regular substitute for the permanent conductor (for the child never lost sight of his ambition). At fourteen, he was the regular conductor of an orchestra associated with a theatrical troupe.

Young though he was, he realized that his native town offered him few opportunities for that musical growth necessary before he could become the conductor of an important orchestra. He ran away from home with only three rubles in his pocket, came to Moscow, and there applied for a scholarship at the famous Philharmonic School. The only scholarship open was for the double bass, which Serge accepted eagerly.

Graduating with high honors, he concertized on his double bass first throughout Russia, then twice in Germany. He was acclaimed the foremost virtuoso of the double bass since Dragonetti (to hear Koussevitzky play that instrument is to forget that it is the most awkward member of the orchestral family; it suddenly acquires finesse, and a wide gamut of artistic expression). He also filled several posts, including one as professor at the Philharmonic School, and another as a double bass player in the Imperial Orchestra. But the life of a virtuoso and teacher —even that of a world-famous virtuoso—was not for him. He had not forgotten that he wanted above everything else to be a conductor. To help him realize this dream, he went to Germany for the necessary preparation. He studied at the *Hochschule*. He spent his free hours poring over orchestral scores and committing them to memory. He haunted the symphony halls of Berlin. Artur Nikisch, conductor of the Berlin Philharmonic, became his idol—Artur Nikisch with his exquisite laces trimming his wrists, his beautiful stage manners, his prima-donna readings! No doubt the baton personality of the later Koussevitzky evolved slowly at these Nikisch concerts, where the young musician's adulatory eyes were focused on the master's platform behaviour, and his ears drank in the master's brilliant performances. Would we today have had an altogether different Koussevitzky if his idol in those days had been Karl Muck instead of Nikisch? It is likely—for, without a doubt, as young Koussevitzky marked down the details of Nikisch's interpretations in his scores, and as he studied the minute details of Nikisch's conductorial technique, he had found his model, the imitation of which influenced him profoundly in his most impressionable years.

*

In 1905, Koussevitzky married Natalie Oushkoff, the daughter of a wealthy landowner. They had met four years earlier at a Koussevitzky double bass concert: She was in the audience and Koussevitzky had noticed her from the stage. They did not meet until two years after this, at which time they became attached to each other.

It is said that when Koussevitzky's father-in-law came to him inquiring what he wished for a wedding gift, Koussevitzky unhesitatingly asked for a symphony orchestra. And a symphony orchestra he received! At last, Koussevitzky had the funds with which to bring his life-long ambition to realization. But before he did so, he went to Germany on an extended honeymoon. In Berlin he made his official debut as conductor (in 1906). Then he made guest appearances in London, Paris, and Vienna. He now satisfied himself that he was ready for a full assignment. He gathered seventy-five of the best musicians available in Russia, brought them to Moscow, and there moulded them into his own symphony orchestra.

Koussevitzky had ideas and ideals; courage to fight for unpopular music causes; independence from set formulas. Freed from constraining pressure by box-office or directors—answerable only to his conscience—he was determined to make his concerts different. They would provide great music to audiences, but beyond this they would exert an influence on orchestral music in Russia, a land which still lagged behind Germany and Austria in music. The advanced vanguard of Russian composers (Stravinsky and Prokofieff, for example) were not in favor, while other Russian composers (like Scriabin and Moussorgsky) were misunderstood; Koussevitzky would fight for them. (As a matter of fact, he had already founded a publishing house in Moscow devoted exclusively to the publication of new Russian music.) The modern composers of Europe were virtually unknown to Russian audiences; Koussevitzky would be an indefatigable propagandist for all that was new and interesting in modern European music. He worked to bring attention to young conductors and instrumentalists, by inaugurating popular Sunday evening concerts in which young, unknown conductors took over his baton, and young soloists were featured. But Koussevitzky in championing the new would not slight the old. He would launch monumental festivals devoted to representative works of one composer: a festival to Beethoven, another to Bach, a third to Tchaikovsky. These festivals were destined to become the principal artistic events of the Moscow and St. Petersburg seasons.

90

He did these things with his orchestra, and in doing them he was perhaps the greatest single influence in the musical development of Russia during the first part of the twentieth century. But this is only one half of Koussevitzky's contribution to his native country. To electrify cosmopolitan cities like Moscow and St. Petersburg with dynamic music-making did not altogether satisfy his missionary ardor. The other half is a saga of its own. Shortly after founding his orchestra, Koussevitzky was fired with the ambition of bringing great orchestral music to people who had never before heard a concert. He chartered a steamer, and for four months traveled along the Volga with seventy-five musicians. They stopped off at little villages and hamlets, gathered in the public square (or any other available open space) and there gave free public concerts of music by Beethoven, Tchaikovsky, Brahms for hard-faced peasants who begrudged the moments they stole from work at the soil to hear these strange performances. Most of the audiences who came to his concerts had never before heard a symphony concert; to most of them many of the instruments in the orchestra appeared as fantastic curiosities. They came to the concert driven by peasant inquisitiveness. They lingered on, enchanted by the sounds they heard. There was no pretense or pose to their enthusiasm. They came, they heard, and were conquered.

That first summer, Koussevitzky traveled about 2300 miles, giving hundreds of concerts at a personal outlay of more than a hundred thousand dollars. That tour was so successful that Koussevitzky made two others. Before he was through, he had created communities of sincere music lovers all along the banks of the Volga, where his name now assumed legendary stature. During long winter nights, mothers would tell their children about this strange benefactor who would come to their little village in the spring, bringing with him a veritable army of musicians and the most wonderful music in the world.

The outbreak of World War I brought these Volga expeditions to an end. Koussevitzky confined his musical activities to Moscow and St. Petersburg. With the outbreak of the Revolution, Koussevitzky, in recognition of his leading position in Russian music, was appointed director of the Russian State Orchestras. But he was not happy in the new order. Bureaucratic red tape consistently interfered with his artistic efforts. He chafed under restrictions and prohibitions. Besides, the times were not propitious for music-making—at least, for the kind of music-making to which Koussevitzky had been accustomed. There was starvation, suffering, the painful process of social and economic readjustments. In 1920, therefore, Koussevitzky left Russia and came to Paris.

*

The Paris period of Koussevitzky's career was no less brilliant. He who up to now had been Europe's propagandist to Russia now became Russia's propagandist to Europe. He organized his own publishing firm (just as he had done in Moscow) to provide an outlet in Europe for the music of modern Russians, which otherwise, would have been ignored. He founded his own orchestra again, the Concerts Koussevitzky. Through his lambent performances, he gave Paris a rigorous introduction to the art of Moussorgsky and Rimsky-Korsakow, Scriabin and Miaskovsky, Prokofieff and (though here Paris surely required no education) Stravinsky. Paris had been receptive to Russian art ever since Diaghilev first brought it, in its many different aspects, to the attention of the French intelligentsia: Russian painting in 1906; Russian symphonic music in 1907; Russian opera in 1908; finally, the Russian ballet in 1909. Paris, therefore, responded to Koussevitzky's concerts with élan. His performances of Moussorgsky's *Boris Godu-*

nov and *Khovantchina* at the Paris Grand Opera in 1921 were the season's most publicized artistic events. But Koussevitzky was not only the apostle of Russian music in Paris. He was here, as he had been in Russia, the passionate sponsor of every form of modern musical expression. He even paid Paris the flattery of giving world premières of new French works ignored by the French themselves—work like Honegger's *Pacific 231* and Debussy's *Sarabande et Danse* (orchestrated by Ravel).

He was very much the man-of-the-hour in Parisian music circles when, in 1924, he was invited to become the permanent conductor of the Boston Symphony Orchestra.

*

The year in which Koussevitzky conducted an orchestra for the first time (it was the seventh year of his life) was the year in which was born the orchestra with which his name is inevitably associated.

In Boston, in 1881, America's first great symphony orchestra was created. There had been symphony orchestras in America before the Boston organization came into being: the New York Philharmonic Orchestra, for example, was forty years old in 1881. But orchestras in America knew a precarious existence. Because they depended on box-office returns, they frequently catered to public taste which was not particularly discriminating at the time. Even an orchestra like the New York Philharmonic never knew whether it would survive from one season to the next. There were other problems as well. The musicians of the orchestra did not draw a living wage from their work, and had to supplement this activity by performing at balls, weddings, and beer halls. If a more profitable engagement presented itself, a musician did not think twice about skipping a rehearsal or even a public concert. Such a situation was not likely to provide concerts of high artistic attainment.

Then there arose a benefactor in Boston who supplied the answer to America's orchestral problem. He was the banker, Henry Lee Higginson, a student of music in Vienna before he became a colonel in the Civil War. In Vienna, he had heard the famous Philharmonic orchestra, and he was determined to create a similar organization in his native country. From his own pocket he provided a guarantee fund of a million dollars with which to create an orchestra in Boston modeled along the lines of the Vienna Philharmonic. Such a guarantee provided annually a $100,000 budget for the orchestra (the annual budget of the New York Philharmonic at the time was $7,000!). This was the first attempt in America to subsidize an orchestra along such generous lines. It was the first attempt to make the existence of an orchestra independent of box-office receipts, the first attempt to pay the musicians a living salary capable of making them free to devote all their time to the orchestra.

Colonel Higginson was determined to maintain the standards of his orchestra on the highest possible plane regardless of public reaction. For the first three seasons, he engaged George Henschel of London as conductor, a discerning musician who immediately brought to America European standards of orchestral music-making. Then from 1884 to 1889, the orchestra was under the firm, disciplinary hand of Wilhelm Gericke, a taskmaster who could be depended upon to create an integrated orchestral organism. It was under Gericke that the Boston Symphony began to acquire technical fluency and artistic stature. The orchestra achieved virtuosity; its different choirs were sensitively adjusted. When Artur Nikisch came to conduct the orchestra in 1889 he (who had already directed some of the greatest symphonic organizations in the world) was so delighted by the Bostonians that he exclaimed: "All *I* have to do now is to poetize!"

94

Nikisch's poetic temperament and immaculate taste brought refinement, sensitivity and new artistic vistas to the great orchestra. His four years created a new peak for orchestral music in America; performances such as these—fastidiously prepared, and projected with such romantic ardor—had never before been heard in American symphony halls. The audiences in Boston at once took to Nikisch, were delighted by his magnetic personality and his charm, and were moved by his warm, personal readings. But their enthusiasm soon cooled—strange to say, for it would appear that Nikisch was precisely the personality to create a permanent impression on audiences of the late 19th century which searched for dramatics in their music. Nikisch's stay in Boston was made further disagreeable by frequent clashes of temperament with the men of the orchestra, and particularly with the directors. Finally, Nikisch bought back his contract for $5,000 and escaped to Europe.

Emil Paur succeeded Nikisch, holding command for five years; he was followed by Wilhelm Gericke, on a return engagement, who now remained at his post until 1906. In 1906, the brilliant young Wagnerian conductor, Karl Muck, came to Boston; and with him arrived one of the great epochs in the history of the Boston Symphony Orchestra.

Muck was the opposite artistic pole to Nikisch. Nikisch was the romanticist, guided more by emotion and instinct than by the brain, unafraid to give freedom to his feelings in the music he conducted. Muck was the disciplined classicist, with an amazing capacity for analysis. Every Muck performance revealed the fastidious study and dissection that went into its preparation. Nikisch was the poet of the baton; Muck was its scholar. Nikisch sought at his concerts spontaneity; Muck sought complete and comprehensive rehearsals with nothing

95

left for the concert but to designate the essential cues and time values.

Muck was, undoubtedly, one of the truly great conductors of all time. He may have had some objectionable personal qualities: He was arrogant; he had a stinging tongue; he treated his men with the merciless severity of a Junker officer. But he was the master of every phase of the conductorial art, and an interpreter of supreme attainments. It was to be expected that with him the Boston Symphony Orchestra would reach the heights; it is doubtful if there were many other orchestras at the time, anywhere, on a level with it.

Karl Muck left in disgrace in 1918, unjustly suspected of being a German spy. It is not my intention to discuss the Muck affair; I have written about it frequently, and have helped (I hope) to clarify the issue somewhat.* In any case, Muck went. His successors—Henri Rabaud and Pierre Monteux— were not capable of maintaining the glory of the orchestra. Henri Rabaud failed because he did not have the necessary capacities and gifts; Monteux—who is a remarkable conductor, even if he is not a Muck—because the failure of a general strike in the orchestra to establish a union resulted in wholesale resignations, and Monteux was compelled to work with an orchestra that had become a skeleton of itself.

Monteux remained until 1924. Frantically, the directors of the Boston Symphony searched for a conductor who had the authority, experience, skill, and temperament with which to reorganize the orchestra, and to restore to Boston that orchestral prestige and honor it had once known. They decided on Koussevitzky, the man who had made orchestral history in Russia and France. And with that choice came another great epoch for the Boston Symphony Orchestra.

---

* See *Music Comes to America*, by David Ewen. Thos. Y. Crowell Co., 1942.

It may sound like a characterization conveniently contrived for our present purpose to say that Koussevitzky's art combines qualities of a Nikisch and a Muck. Yet this is its aptest description. While Koussevitzky was most strongly influenced by Nikisch, after whom he patterned himself in his early years, there is more than a touch of Muck in him.

Like Nikisch, Koussevitzky is a romanticist. He loves a beautiful melodic line, which he draws lovingly from the strings. He is not ashamed of feeling deeply, and expressing his feelings in rubatos and dynamics. His Tchaikovsky is unashamedly sentimental, just as his Beethoven is poignant. He is also like Nikisch in his conviction that a conductor's duty is to interpret the music, not just to pay strict conformance to what is printed on the page. He does not hesitate to change tempi, to make deletions, to revise scoring or to alter dynamics if he feels that the music profits by such treatment. Once he wrote to Sibelius that he was forced to play a movement from one of the symphonies in a completely different tempo than that which was designated in the score. "That's the way I feel the music," he told Sibelius, "and that's the only way I can play it." ("The right tempo," answered Sibelius generously, "is as you feel it.") The very great interpreter—whose taste and judgment are discerning—can afford such indulgences, which with lesser artists can only spell ruin. Von Bülow, Mahler, and Nikisch more often than not actually brought out new, brilliant and eloquent qualities in the music they conducted as a result of their discriminating revisions. And Koussevitzky has done so too.

But Koussevitzky (and this is at least a partial explanation of his unique powers) is not a slave of his emotions. Though he permits his feelings to express themselves, it is he who is their master. Such discipline comes from his scholarship, from

97

his capacity to analyze. Like Muck, Koussevitzky does not begin conducting a score until he has studied it with microscopic thoroughness, horizontally and vertically. He spends many hours each day in his comfortable, sun-baked study, poring over manuscripts and printed scores on a specially constructed music stand which is on the table in front of him. He reads the score through from beginning to end, as if it were a novel, gathering general impressions, and acquiring the basic conception of the work. Then he rereads it a second time, now permitting his eye to travel vertically so that he can concentrate on harmonic details and on the orchestration. If a certain construction puzzles him, he rushes to his piano (which is near at hand) so that he might gain an aural impression of it. But he does not often enlist the piano, blessed as he is with an extraordinary facility for score reading. (About a decade ago, a very silly rumor gained circulation that Koussevitzky did not know how to read a score. The source for this libel was the fact that Koussevitzky had in his employ a brilliant pianist who often played through a new work for Koussevitzky a few times before Koussevitzky began to study it for himself. Not until Koussevitzky had dismissed his assistant were these rumors dispelled.) When he has read a score through several times, he begins to mark up every bar and phrase for the exact effect he wishes to achieve. Then, and only then, will he feel himself ready to begin rehearsing.

This scholarly zeal is apparent in his performances; only Toscanini is more concerned with details than Koussevitzky. Besides scholarship, his temperament and will exert the most powerful influences on his performances. His readings are vivid, flaming with personality, throbbing with a sort of nervous excitement. They have intensity. They have a wonderful rhythmic continuity. They have a gorgeous palette of orchestral colors. His Ravel *Daphnis et Chloé*, (second suite), for example, remains a miracle of orchestral painting, the subtle tints and hues of which no other conductor seems capable of reproducing. His performances are powerfully dramatic, each emotional effect built up with extreme skill. In music calling for such interpretation—as in Scriabin, Ravel, Sibelius, Moussorgsky, Debussy, or Stravinsky—Koussevitzky is truly incomparable. In other music, he is frequently admirable, but for other reasons: for the spaciousness of his design, his breadth and sweep and majesty, his musicianship and understanding. If there are flaws to his artistry, it is that in some music—say by K. P. E. Bach or Mozart—he overbuilds his effects beyond the requirements of the work. He can control his intensity and passion, but he sometimes fails to suppress his love of color and his profound feelings for beautiful sounds.

He is one of the great living masters of orchestral technique. His capacity to subject the men who play under him to his will is responsible for their mechanical perfection and unanimity of spirit. The orchestra is as pliable under his fingers as the double bass; he plays on it with an infinite variety of touch and nuance; he seems to have no difficulty in making it express everything he wishes. Carping tongues have attempted in the past to minimize his extraordinary powers over an orchestra. They say that when a man can buy the best instrumentalists available regardless of price, when he has conducted one and the same organization for almost twenty years until his smallest idiosyncrasy is known to his players, when, finally, he holds over the heads of his men the whip of a possible immediate dismissal, it is to be expected that he should be in masterful control. Such arguments were eloquently answered in the spring of 1942 when Koussevitzky arrived in New York to

guest-conduct the New York Philharmonic Orchestra. He
completely subjugated that orchestra to his purposes (and after
only three days of rehearsals) as if he had had a lifelong association with it. The orchestra, which only four days earlier
had sounded stodgy and tired, acquired under Koussevitzky a
new lease on life and seemed electrified.

*

If Koussevitzky could accomplish such a miracle for the New
York Philharmonic in a few days, it is understandable that he
should have rebuilt the Boston Symphony, over a period of
several years, into one of the two or three great orchestras of
the world. The moment he took command, he remained fa-
natically true to his mission of creating a perfect symphonic
ensemble. Men had to be dismissed ruthlessly; America and
Europe had to be combed for the finest instrumentalists pro-
curable. The orchestra had to learn that the conductor would
have no compassion for mediocrity. Koussevitzky was despotic at rehearsals. The players learned to be alert and sensitively responsive to his slightest wish.

But in bringing back to Boston the orchestral grandeur it
had known with Muck, it was not enough to create a wonderful ensemble. Koussevitzky did more than this. He restored
glamour to the conductor's platform, the glamour of his historic career, and that of his magnetizing personality. He also
made Boston one of the great centers of music-making in the
country, if not in the world. His stubborn support of the modern composer has persisted in this country even in the face of
a disinterested public. There were times when, before the
performance of a new work, members in the audience would
haughtily rise from their seats to leave the hall; other times
when they met the completion of a performance of some new
work with frigid silence. But Koussevitzky felt he had a mis-

sion to perform, and he performed it courageously and with determination. New music from every part of the world has kept the Boston Symphony programs vital and energetic; new music from America as well—for from the moment Koussevitzky assumed his Boston position he immediately became something of a godfather to American composers.

*

Not the least of Koussevitzky's many brilliant achievements has been the development of the Berkshire Symphonic Festival, one of the great music festivals in this country. The Berkshire Festival was created in 1934 on an estate in Stockbridge, Massachusetts. Not until two years later, when Koussevitzky came on the scene to dominate musical activities, did it achieve national importance. The festival now moved to new grounds, Tanglewood (Hawthorne's Tanglewood) near Lenox. There, an open-air shed was built in 1938, and in 1941, additional small theatres were constructed for the performances of chamber music and opera.

Koussevitzky's personality is, of course, the unifying force in Tanglewood. It has attracted to the festival grounds each August music lovers from every part of the country (about 10,000 of them attended each concert). Koussevitzky's incapacity to yield to complacency, or to be artistically static, promises much for the future of the festival. Having established symphonic and choral music on a permanent basis, he now speaks of adding performances of opera and chamber music to the regular festival repertoire. If there is to be an American Salzburg, it could not be in more progressive hands than those of Koussevitzky.

In the summer of 1940, Koussevitzky brought a lifelong dream to realization in Tanglewood with the opening of the Berkshire Music Center. For years, Koussevitzky had aspired to create a center where music students, teachers, and professional musicians could gather, teach and study, and exchange experiences and ideas. It was a music school along new and revolutionary lines that Koussevitzky was thinking of, where study would be less formalized, where students rubbed elbows with teachers even after school hours and profited by contact with them, where there would be continued and uninterrupted music-making by teachers and pupils.

Three hundred students from every part of the country gathered at Tanglewood in the summer of 1940 for the first session of the new Center. They received a new experience in music education. Instrumentalists were taught by the first-desk men of the Boston Symphony, then gathered into chamber music ensembles and into two orchestras. Young conductors received training from Koussevitzky himself, and were given an opportunity to work with actual student orchestras. Young composers, besides working in classes conducted by Copland and Hindemith, could come to these teachers any time during the day, on the grounds of the school, for advice and criticism. Vocal instruction comprised choral training and regular appearance in opera performances; also, from time to time, in impromptu renditions of old choral *a cappella* music. There were lectures frequently on aesthetics and music history, and concerts each evening in which the students participated as performers and audience. Thus, from morning till night, the students at the Berkshire Music Center live in an atmosphere of music.

*

Koussevitzky, who appears to be of such dominating stature on the stage, is actually short, and slight of build. He has been eloquently described as resembling a "diplomat of the Napoleonic era." His face reveals strength in the eyes, the downward swoop of his eagle-like nose, and the assertiveness of his chin. His complexion is ruddy.

He speaks with great gusto, in a thick Russian accent, and with extraordinary capacity for enthusiasms. His remarks are usually studded with superlatives. He is as likely to talk about the German philosophers (Nietzsche or Schopenhauer) as about music. He loves to participate in intellectual parlor talk. As he discusses a subject, he gestures violently to emphasize a point he is making.

He has apparently unlimited energy and drive. When he strolls, it is with a brisk step. He is always in a whirlwind of activity, and he thrives on it. At rehearsals he is particularly a dynamo. From the moment he begins work, his rehearsals move in an uninterrupted flow. As the orchestra plays, his body weaves into contortions, his baton slices the air. He cries out his instructions. "No! No!" he will shout, and then sing his conception of the music. "Legato!" his cry will pierce through the thickness of the orchestral sonority. "Sing!" he will plead with the violins. "Music must always sing."

At rehearsals, Koussevitzky is the born schoolmaster, his baton the schoolmaster's rod. The men must keep their noses to the grindstone every moment. Once one of the players was apprehended whispering to his neighbor. Koussevitzky shouted: "Don't spik! I say, don't spik! If you spik, I go right home."

He will dismiss veteran performers for what appear to some musicians to be excusable and casual mistakes. At one rehearsal, he was infuriated by a few sour notes from a wind player. Then and there Koussevitzky dismissed him from his job. The musician rose from his seat with all-too apparent disgust. As he passed by Koussevitzky he exclaimed: "Nuts to you, Mr. Koussevitzky!" Koussevitzky answered emphatically: "I'm sorry! It's too late to apologize!"

3

Dimitri Mitropoulos

Dimitri Mitropoulos, who succeeded Eugene Ormandy as the permanent conductor of the Minneapolis Symphony Orchestra, is a virtuoso among conductors. He plays on his orchestra as Horowitz plays his piano, with bravura and dash. He gives the immediate impression of a technique that recognizes no problems: the orchestra responds to his touch as if it were a keyboard. There is a suggestion of the flamboyant about his gestures. Slight of figure, solemn as a monk when he steps on the stage, he does not at once betray the dynamo that is in him. But once the music soars under his hands, he becomes transfigured. Every part of his body moves rhythmically with the music. His arms sweep through space; his fingers seem to pluck each sound out of the very air. His face reflects each mood of the music he conducts: Now it is contracted with pain, now it is brightened by an expansive smile.

Like every virtuoso, Mitropoulos magnetizes his audiences not only with a flashing display of pyrotechnics, but also with his personality. He has the Toscanini magic of discharging electric sparks the moment he steps on the stage. The orchestra and the audience come under his control, as if under a spell. Even through the radio, his dynamic presence is felt. It is possible to dislike Mitropoulos, but to remain indifferent to him is out of the question. Those who do not react favorably to his interpretations will not deny that the man carries you away with his strength and passion and will.

The virtuoso in him seeks tirelessly for effect, sometimes even to the disadvantage of the work at hand. Mitropoulos is brilliant; he is cogent; sometimes he is overpowering. If he often yields to the temptation of overdramatization, he never fails at the same time to make an exciting impression. That he is a conductor of genius is obvious to anyone who has heard him, even at his worst. At his best, when the music and the conductor's personality are as one, he is of Toscanini stature: I do not remember ever having heard, for example, a Mahler First Symphony such as he has given us, nor did I ever suspect it could sound that way.

He has musical scholarship, and a memory of such retentiveness that he is even able to rehearse without a score. He has temperament. He has a complete command of the orchestra. But before he can become one of the truly great conductors of our age—and he gives every indication that with the proper discipline and growth he might become one—he requires greater mellowness and sobriety. He is too high-pitched, too nervous for a great part of the repertoire that calls for a certain degree of detachment. Virgil Thomson recognized Mitropoulos' vulnerability as an artist when he reported that the conductor was "jittery, overweaning, exaggerating . . . careless about sonorities and indifferent to the musical meaning and proportion so long as he could make the music seem to stem (à la Stokowski at his worst) from his own personality."

He has to discipline his temperament, to keep his reservoir of vitality and strength on tap. Perhaps he will succeed in doing this with the greater ripeness that comes with age; if so, he will rise to heights achieved by few conductors of our time. But even with his faults he is an arresting personality and a

---

* Quoted by permission of the New York *Herald Tribune.*

stimulating artist: a concert directed by him is a vivid and unforgettable aesthetic experience, to excite and fatigue and
sometimes to inspire, the listener.

*

Dimitri Mitropoulos was first intended for the church. Two
of his uncles were monks; his grandfather (on his father's side)
was a priest; his granduncle, an archbishop in the Greek Orthodox Church. Dimitri—born in Athens on March 1, 1896
—felt the call of the cloth from childhood on. He would visit
his uncles at their monastery atop Mount Athos and his childish
imagination would be aroused by the serenity and beauty of
the setting. He wanted to follow in the footsteps of his family
—but for one obstacle. He loved music passionately, and was
determined to study it. A church life—that is, with the Greek
Orthodox Church—forebade the use of musical instruments at
the services. Mitropoulos had to decide, therefore, between
religion and music; and he chose music. "I didn't become a
monk only because they wouldn't permit me even to have a
harmonium."

He began to study the piano when he was seven, and attended the common schools and high school. Since the church
had been decided against, his father tried to induce him to
study for a career as marine officer. But Dimitri was determined, now more than ever, to concentrate on music. At the
age of ten he had mastered the piano and vocal scores of *Faust*
and *Rigoletto,* and less than four years later he had memorized
most of the famous operas in the repertoire. He entered the
Athens Conservatory in his fourteenth year. For the next six
years he specialized in piano and composition. Composition
appealed to him particularly. He wrote many works in many
different forms, often sacrificing hours from the piano to write
his music. In 1919, he finished an opera, *Beatrice,* on a French

text of Maeterlinck. This work so impressed the Conservatory directors that they decided to give it a handsome production. Camille Saint-Saëns was in the audience and, recognizing the talent of the composer, wrote a long and effusive piece about it for a Paris newspaper. More than this, he arranged a scholarship for Mitropoulos whereby he could study with Paul Gilson in Brussels, and Ferruccio Busoni in Berlin.

Completing his studies, he was appointed assistant conductor at the Berlin Staatsoper. Once he began conducting he knew that he had found his musical *métier*. The piano, even composition—for both of which he had shown such decided talent —were now abandoned, because "I knew that I could do only one thing, if I were to do it well." He conducted in an impressive manner. His rehearsals betrayed a searching intellect, as well as his amazing knowledge of the repertoire, particularly amazing for a man who never before held a baton in hand.

He was back in Athens in 1924 to become permanent conductor of the Athens Symphony Orchestra. He developed rapidly both in technique and artistic refinements. Before long, word passed out of Greece that here was a definite musical find. In 1930, Mitropoulos was invited to Berlin for guest performances with the celebrated Philharmonic where he gave a magnificent account of himself. In 1934, he made his Paris debut, conducting the Orchestre Symphonique (a concert in which he performed the Prokofieff Third Piano Concerto while directing the accompaniment). In the same year, he also conducted in England, Italy, and the Soviet Union; in 1935, again in Italy and in France (in France he conducted several new French works with the Lamoureux Orchestra); and from 1934 to 1937 he directed a three-month symphony season at Monte Carlo. All this while he retained his post with the Athens Symphony directing a series of concerts each winter. The last time he left Athens was on the day Nazi Germany invaded Poland.

Those who played under him in Europe spoke rapturously of his capacities. Inevitably, such high words of praise reached the ears of important musicians in America. One of them, Serge Koussevitzky, decided to invite Mitropoulos to America. In 1936, Mitropoulos served a brief guest engagement with the Boston Symphony Orchestra. He played (if memory serves) the *Symphonia Domestica* of Richard Strauss and the First Symphony of Mahler, putting his best foot forward. He was a sensation. Olin Downes, who was on a visit to Boston at that time, spoke with excited accents about the new conductor. "He is more than a kindling virtuoso. He showed a microscopic knowledge of four strongly contrasted scores, and his temperament is that of an impetuous musician. Mitropoulos addressed himself with complete comprehension and with blazing dramatic emotion."

The following year, Mitropoulos returned for another set of guest appearances with the Boston Symphony. It was rumored at the time that Koussevitzky was planning to retire, and that he was grooming Mitropoulos as his successor. In any case, Koussevitzky must have finally decided to continue at his post indefinitely, and he encouraged Mitropoulos to find a permanent post elsewhere. Mitropoulos did not have to look for a long time. Invited to conduct a few guest concerts in Minneapolis, he made such an overwhelming impression that the directors knew at once that they had found a successor to Eugene Ormandy, who had resigned one year earlier to go to Philadelphia.

In 1940, Mitropoulos was a guest conductor of the New York Philharmonic. The tempestuous acclaim accorded him —one critic remarked that the "subscribers became so enthusiastic they did everything but steal the goalposts"—encour-

aged the Philharmonic directors to offer him a permanent post
with the orchestra. Mitropoulos thought it over, and decided
that he did not wish to abandon Minneapolis where he found
his berth comfortable; but he offered to come for guest performances whenever invited to do so. During the Philharmonic centenary season in 1941-42 he was back in New York,
and once again he was given a magnificent hand. He was also
called to participate in the 1942-43 season. There are those
who say that the Philharmonic post can be his whenever he
wants it.

*

Mitropoulos had sacrificed the church for music. To music
he has devoted himself with an almost priest-like consecration.
The same singleness of purpose which made him abandon his
composition when he decided to become a conductor, has now
made him exile other interests and pursuits from his life and
to make everything subservient to his art. His life is as ascetic
as if he had accepted monasticism. "When I accepted the
Minneapolis post, I asked the directors if they wanted as perfect a musician as possible, or a society man who was a bad
musician. They said they wanted a good musician. So I took
the job on the promise that I would not be involved in social
formalities. They have never bothered me."

He lives in Minneapolis in almost austere seclusion. He
occupies a dormitory room at the University which is bare except for a piano and the essential pieces of furniture. Here he
lives alone—he has never married because he did not wish
anyone or anything to divert him from his complete absorption
in music!—devoting himself endlessly to his music studies, and
to contemplation. His life is bald and unpretentious. He is a
disciplined smoker, and never partakes of hard alcohol. His
meals are the last word in simplicity; he has been compelled to

109

select the simplest foods because his work places such a strain on him that it tends to bring on indigestion. He is a vegetarian for fourteen days, adding a touch of variety to his diet by eating chicken on the fifteenth. His clothing, away from the concert platform, is also undemonstrative: he prefers baggy trousers, a polo shirt, and a sweater as his daily costume.

Though he has some diversions—mountain climbing, motoring, and fishing particularly—he finds little time in which to indulge in such pleasures. When he has spent a particularly hard week of work and concentrated study, he finds relaxation on Sundays by visiting one motion-picture house after another, from noon until midnight. Generally, he is retiring, shy, and introspective; he does not care for the company of people. He is in dread of social functions and parties and formal celebrations. His dream is to retire alone on some beautiful island (he found one near Alaska which struck his fancy) with books and music.

He looks very much the priest, with his deep-set eyes which have a spiritual quality, and his ascetic sunken cheeks. He is, as a matter of fact, a deeply religious soul. He wears a crucifix inside his shirt, and a medallion of the Virgin Mary on the lining of his coat, and is never without these holy symbols.

His work severely taxes his strength and nervous energy. One explanation for his Spartan life is that it has been dictated by necessity; only by conserving his energy and strength carefully can he give the best of himself to music. His elaborate gesturing on the platform is particularly fatiguing: when a concert is over he will see no one, but rush to his room, and there collapse in bed. The next morning, however, he is fresh again, ready to begin his studies anew, and to undertake a new week of rehearsals. He has wonderful recuperative powers, which are aided by his capacity to sleep soundly.

At rehearsals there is about him a military air which reminds one that he was once in the Greek army. He has said that he does not like being a dictator, that he prefers treating his men as "colleagues." But he has a firm hand and an authoritative manner that tolerate no levities. He has no difficulty in commanding respect, for his prodigious scholarship is always a matter of awe to the men who play under him: without consulting a score at any time, he can tell you how many notes are in any bar of a Hindemith symphony or a Ravel concerto.

He is an internationalist, and to such a degree that when Italy invaded Greece in 1940, and momentarily made Mitropoulos a political as well as musical hero in this country, he pointedly performed some modern Italian works on his programs. Not that Mitropoulos did not ally himself heart and soul to the Greek cause; but he wished to make it clear that he felt it was the political leadership of Italy that had sinned, not Italian culture, or even the Italian people.

4

José Iturbi

José Iturbi's merits as a performer were proved long before he took up a baton. As a pianist he received an immediate acclaim in this country at his debut performance in 1928, following his sensational concerts in Europe. The clarity of his style, his subtle use of color and dynamics, his adaptability to different idioms from Mozart to Manuel de Falla, brought him to the front rank of living pianists.

From childhood on he seemed destined for a virtuoso career. Born in Valencia, Spain, on November 28, 1895, he began piano lessons in his fifth year. By his seventh birthday, he was already helping to support his family by performing in Valencia's leading cinema theatres, at neighborhood balls, and then in public recitals. In between his many assignments, he studied the piano, first in local schools, then in Barcelona with Joaquin Malats. A lucrative café-house position in Valencia interrupted his studies. While back in Valencia, he attracted the attention of a journalist who raised a subscription to enable Iturbi to abandon work and to return to study. This subscription—fourteen hundred pesetas—enabled Iturbi to go to Paris to enter the Conservatory, from which he was graduated in his seventeenth year.

His studies completed, he went to Zurich where he acquired a post as pianist in a fashionable café. There he was discovered by the director of the Geneva Conservatory who engaged him as head of the piano department. Iturbi held this post for four years, then decided to venture into the concert field. He was extraordinarily successful in Europe, almost from the very first; then proceeded to America where he met an even greater acclaim.

It was to be expected that the same good taste and comprehension of musical values which went into his piano playing would likewise feature his conducting once he had mastered the technique of the baton as completely as that of the keyboard. Yet, up to the present time—and it is a decade since he made his baton debut—Iturbi's work with orchestra has not measured up to his achievements with the piano; nor has it lived up to expectations.

It is not that he has failed to become a master of the orchestra. Almost from the first he proved that he takes to directing an orchestra with ease and command. His debut as conductor took place in Mexico in 1933 when he directed an orchestral concert at the Teatro Hidalgo in Mexico City. This was so successful that he was engaged for eleven additional performances. His work attracted the attention of the directors of Lewisohn Stadium concerts in New York who invited him to direct two special concerts. Further concerts with the Philadelphia Orchestra both at the Academy of Music and at the Robin Hood Dell, at the Hollywood Bowl and Lewisohn Stadium, and, during the 1935-36 season, with orchestras in Rochester, Detroit, and Philadelphia singled him out as one of the major dynamic baton discoveries of many years. I recall that after I heard some of his early rehearsals with the New York Philharmonic, I wrote that he was a "born conductor," with a "clear insight into the music he was rehearsing," and a "facility to transfer his slightest desires to his men without fumbling." I prophesied at the time a distinguished future for him. I thought that his future as a conductor might eventually throw into the shade his illustrious past as piano virtuoso.

I cannot say that my prophecy has thus far been fulfilled. In 1936-37 Iturbi was appointed the permanent conductor of the Rochester Philharmonic—an admirable organization which had been founded by George Eastman in 1923 and which had been permanently directed by Eugene Goossens from 1924 to 1931. Iturbi still holds this post. He has had every opportunity to develop naturally, profiting by his valuable experience as the sole conductor of a great orchestra. But that development has not taken place. On the contrary, Iturbi's performances have caused me greater and greater discomfort and anxiety; there are times, in listening to him, when I am tempted to feel that he shows today less promise, despite his greater self-assurance and poise, than he did a decade ago.

He has always had—he still has—extraordinary traits for a conductor: a fine memory, a sensitive ear, a mastery of a large repertoire, a capacity to excite his men and to arouse his audiences, an instinctive flair for baton technique. With such qualities he should have gone—and should still be going—far. That he has not done so has mystified me. His performances, particularly the more recent ones, too often leave the impression of awkward self-consciousness; each nuance and accent seems overcalculated; each climax, or rubato, labored. At other times, there appears an almost feverish search after effect. In short, what is so outstanding in his piano playing—the feeling of ease, spontaneity, and objectivity which he generates—is not to be found in his conducting.

*

The explanation for Iturbi's lapses as a conductor, lies, I suspect, in the fact that he has been guided by propulsions other than artistic from the moment he took to the baton. Instead of focusing both his eyes on the music, he has permitted one eye to stray toward his audiences, and another to Stokowski. He has made too conscious an effort to impress himself on his public as a magnetic personality. He has tried too painstakingly to "put himself over," even at the price of his natural growth as an artist. Perhaps he aspired, overnight, to become another Stokowski or Koussevitzky.

He conducts without a score, which is to his advantage in many scores in view of his retentive memory. But this has hardly been an advisable practice in so many other, and less familiar works, which he is compelled to feature throughout the course of a season. His treatment of many new works is almost cursory. Had he been more concerned with the quality of his performances, rather than with the effect they would have on his audiences, he would not have hesitated to use a score in front of him more frequently.

One can also grumble at his insistence on playing piano concertos while conducting the orchestral accompaniment. This is a picturesque stunt, but one which was discarded by Kapellmeisters two centuries ago because it was evident that no artist could fulfill two such exacting assignments at one and the same time. With Iturbi it has been noted that technical exactness, excellent balances, and precise coordination between piano and orchestra have frequently been sacrificed for this feat.

At the piano, he was—he still is—concerned almost exclusively with the soundest of artistic values. It is only since he has taken seriously to conducting that he has impetuously said things and done things which (in the manner of Stokowski) have brought him to the attention of the front pages.

How else can we interpret his extravagant indictment of women musicians made in 1937, except as a bid for newspaper space? Women, he announced in an interview, are physically limited from attaining the standards of men, and are limited

115

temperamentally besides. Could Iturbi possibly have been sincere, guided only by honest convictions, when he denounced the sex that had produced, in music, Myra Hess, Kirsten Flagstad, Wanda Landowska, Nadia Boulanger? . . .

In the same year, Iturbi cancelled a broadcast of the Philadelphia Orchestra because some of the music on the program was below his standards. That this was not exclusively the gesture of a highminded and idealistic artist was proved somewhat later when he found it to his advantage to play music by George Gershwin at his piano concerts; and one of the numbers to which he had objected on the program of the Philadelphia Orchestra was the exquisite "Summertime" from Gershwin's *Porgy and Bess!* A few years ago, Iturbi refused to conduct a concert of the Philadelphia Orchestra because the soloist at that concert was Benny Goodman, who had proved himself to be an admirable clarinetist in the serious repertoire. Iturbi felt that it was "beneath his dignity" to perform on the same program with a jazz artist. Once again this attitude of superior aloofness from any but the highest standards of art fails to hold conviction—particularly when it is remembered that it was not beneath Iturbi's dignity to appear several times as a guest artist with Bing Crosby, nor to announce to his nationwide audiences that he played "Swing" and that he "liked American jazz."

Of American Traditions

1

Walter Damrosch

Walter Damrosch has sold good music to America. That has been his greatest contribution as a conductor. He has never been—not even at the height of his career—a particularly inspired, or inspiring, performer. His standards too often were lax; his readings skirted the surface; his command of the orchestra, and its music, less than consummate. Yet he has been a force of incomparable significance with the baton; and—for all his inadequate performances—he has served music well.

Music has had, in the course of its evolution, many high priests to serve her reverently. It is doubtful, however, if it has ever had a salesman to compare with Damrosch. He has had the driving perseverance, and the instinctive capacity to understand the psychology of his public (the indispensable equipment of every super-salesman). More important still, he has had the glib tongue, the personal charm, the warm sense of humor with which to make friends and influence people. He has long had the custom of making witty little speeches to his audiences during his concerts. Through these speeches, audiences have come close to him, won over by his appealing manner. Once, when he directed a benefit concert in New York for the composer Moritz Moszkowski, in which sixteen pianists participated, he turned to his audience before the concert and mischievously whispered to it: "What they need here is not a conductor, but a traffic cop." Preceding one of his Wagner performances, he was suddenly tempted to reminisce publicly about his first experiences. "When I look at your young, shining, bright girlish faces, I recognize many who attended my first Wagner concerts fifty years ago." He has frequently taken his audiences into his confidence; sometimes, before conducting a particularly difficult modern work, he would openly confess that he was as puzzled by the music as the audience. Thus, from early in his career, he has sold himself to his public; and by selling himself, he has also succeeded in selling great music.

He began selling good music about sixty years ago. With the cogent drive of a bond salesman he began selling Mozart, Beethoven, and Wagner to audiences who previously thought that *Yankee Doodle* and *The Carnival of Venice* were the peaks of musical art. In the closing decades of the nineteenth century, and in the early years of the twentieth, he traveled with his orchestra, the New York Symphony Society, to parts formerly untouched by musical civilization, bringing with him a sample case of the representative musical masterpieces. How effective has been his salesmanship was proved again and again during the next decade when local orchestras sprang up in cities and towns he had visited.

In the early years of the twentieth century he decided that American audiences did not know the Wagner music-dramas as well as they should. Wagner, after a brief period of prosperity at the Metropolitan Opera House, was in eclipse in New York. After conducting a charity concert of *Götterdämmerung* in 1894, Damrosch was convinced that enthusiasm for Wagner had not completely vanished; that, given the proper impetus, it might reawaken. Convinced that it was his duty to continue the work his father had begun some years earlier—namely to fight for Wagner's recognition in America—he broached to the Metropolitan his plans for restoring the Wagnerian repertory. He met with deaf ears. Without hesitation he decided to found his own company with his own resources. He sold his home on Fifty-fifth Street and financed his own opera company. His first season netted him a profit of $53,000. But, as Andrew Carnegie had been astute enough to realize, American audiences were not succumbing to the spell of Wagner's genius half so much as to the novelty of hearing these operas. Carnegie, therefore, tried to dissuade Damrosch from launching a second season. "Such success as you have had rarely repeats itself," Carnegie told Damrosch. "You rightly divined the desire of the public for the return of the Wagner opera, but this current has drawn into it many people who have come for curiosity alone, and to whom Wagner is still a closed book. Many of these will not come a second time." The accuracy of his prophecy was emphasized when, during the second season, Damrosch lost $43,000. Only when Damrosch combined his Wagner presentations with the Italian and French repertory (enlisting the services of such stars as Melba and Calvé) was he able to keep his venture in good health. But as long as it remained alive, the Damrosch Opera Company promoted Wagner's interests. And the promotion of Wagner's interests was Damrosch's burning and unforgettable ideal as he continued to tour the country extensively, bringing the Wagner music-dramas to audiences which had never before heard them.

In much the same way, Damrosch sold modern music to New York audiences during a period when the modern composer was not given much of a hearing in this country. It is not generally recognized that composers like Stravinsky, Sibelius, Delius, Ravel, Elgar, and Honegger were first championed in this country by Damrosch.

Besides all this, he sold music to children through his morning educational concerts which he enlivened with his gentle and lovable introductory comments. He sold New York its leading concert hall; Carnegie Hall was built directly as a result of his encouragement and influence; and it was opened with a music festival conducted by Damrosch.

Today, his eightieth birthday behind him—and no less enthusiastic about his missionary work than he was fifty years ago—he is still a salesman for great music. Up until the fall of 1942, he sold the classics to some five million schoolchildren every Friday afternoon over the radio. His voice is known by youngsters throughout the length and breadth of the land. Not long ago, while visiting the West for a music educators' conference, he was invited by a school principal to address the children at a school assembly. Damrosch promised to come, but on the express condition that he would receive no official introduction. Damrosch came to the platform, facing some two thousand bright-faced youngsters who had been kept in the dark about the identity of their visitor. His first words, however, created a furor. All he said, in his soft-spoken and beautifully modulated voice, was: "Good morning, my dear children"—his radio greeting. Instantly, through the tumult of childish voices, could be heard the excited exclamation: "It's Papa Damrosch! It's Papa Damrosch!"

When the occasion demanded it, Damrosch has even been a successful salesman for himself. At one time, a famous guest conductor to the New York Symphony inspired one New York critic to remark how wonderful the orchestra could sound with a *good* conductor. Damrosch did not miss the implication. The next week he was back at the head of his orchestra. During the performance of the final movement of the symphony, the audience was startled to note that a chair was brought for Damrosch. Damrosch sat down, put down his baton, and listened to his orchestra complete the movement. Then Damrosch explained his behavior. "You see," he said simply, "I wanted to prove to you that my orchestra is so good it can play well without any conductor whatsoever!"

Recently he conducted the New York Philharmonic in a concert performance of his revised opera, *Cyrano de Bergerac*. The opera was rather attenuated, and somewhere along the middle of the second act the audience began to trickle out of the hall. Out of the corner of his eye Damrosch noticed the exodus. At the end of the second act, he turned around, and with disengaging simplicity, said to his public: "Please don't go home, yet. The best part of the opera is coming." In the face of such a plea, not even the most callous could leave his seat. The audience remained patiently, listened more attentively than it had done before this, and gave the composer-conductor a generous ovation.

*

For most people, eighty years may be a patriarchal age. Damrosch (who has never felt younger) feels that the calendar is lying when it speaks of him as an old man. Actually it is difficult to consider a man old who, in his seventy-fifth year, completed a new opera and saw it performed successfully at the Metropolitan Opera House; who, in his seventy-seventh year, appeared in a motion picture; who, one year after this, went into brief retirement to work intensively on his piano technique in preparation for his official debut in New York as concert pianist; who, when he was seventy-nine, completed an elaborate revision of an old opera and conducted it vigorously with the New York Philharmonic; and who, at eighty, wrote still another opera, and appeared as a guest conductor of the New York Philharmonic.

Damrosch may feel that he is yet too young to turn his eyes from the future—which he is still eyeing with great hope for the fulfillment of many important musical projects—in order

123

to contemplate the past. Retrospection, he may say, is a luxury for the old; and he is not old. Yet he must occasionally look back to his achievements with a feeling of warm satisfaction. He has personally seen America develop from a musically immature country—young, uninformed, sublimely innocent—into the greatest center of musical culture in the world. More than this: In this phenomenal evolution, he himself played a major—possibly decisive—role.

When Damrosch first decided to sell symphonic music to America, in the closing years of the nineteenth century (in those days symphony orchestras were few and far between; and audiences for good music—outside of a few large cities—were practically non-existent) he knew that it was a job to try even a stout heart. Damrosch realized that if he wanted to be a successful salesman for good music, in places where good music was unknown, he would at times have to sacrifice his artistic conscience and temperament, and adapt himself as resiliently as possible to his audiences. To be a successful salesman, Damrosch recognized, you must make your goods palatable; and you don't make them palatable if you persist in assuming (as so many visiting European musicians in America did at the time) a holier-than-thou attitude to your customers. Damrosch never lost his idealism in his struggles with his audiences. That was to remain intact through all the trials of his early career. But his idealism was blended with a sound practical sense that could make temporary concessions, and yield to momentary expedience. Had his artistic conscience been inflexible, the times would have crucified him. Fortunately, Damrosch was made of resilient fibre.

He was born in Breslau, Germany, on January 30, 1862, the son of Leopold Damrosch, one of the most distinguished musicians in Germany at the time. Richard Wagner was supposed to be Walter's godfather. Because he had christened another of Leopold Damrosch's sons, who had died in infancy, Wagner superstitiously refused to have his own unlucky star over Walter as well. Another godfather was chosen. When Walter was five years old, his father transported the family to New York, where he had been engaged to conduct the Arion Society. In America, Walter began his music study, first with his father, then with Von Inten, Boekelmann, and Pinner. There followed another period of study in Germany with Draeske and Hans von Bülow. Then, upon his return to America, almost before he could catch his breath, he was thrust into a professional career.

He began conducting in 1885, and in the same year undertook the first of his famous tours with his orchestra—to Louisville, Kentucky. Also in 1885 Leopold Damrosch died and passed on his various conductorial posts—with the New York Symphony, the Oratorio Society, and the Metropolitan Opera House—as an inheritance to his son. Young Walter was then twenty-three years old. At the time he was little more than a novice as conductor. Previous to his father's death, he had conducted a few concerts in New Jersey, and had assisted him in preparing symphony and opera performances in New York. Suddenly, the death of his father brought Walter the man-sized assignments of directing a major orchestra, a major choral society, and undertaking the entire German repertoire at the Metropolitan Opera House (which his father had launched a season earlier). Fortunately, working with his father had proved to be valuable preparation for these tasks. Without much experience to guide him, he took over his father's duties with quiet self-assurance.

As he carried on his father's many duties with the skill and self-confidence of a long-experienced conductor, he must have brought back to mind more than once his concert debut in America which had taken place many years earlier. He was a child at the time. Leopold Damrosch was rehearsing a performance of Schubert's *Der häusliche Krieg* with the Arion Society. The score called for a cymbal crash, and since to Leopold it seemed extravagance to engage a special musician for this task, he decided to recruit his little son. Painstakingly, he taught Walter how to crash the cymbals—and when. At the concert, Walter was so frozen by excitement and fear that, when the moment arrived for him to crash the cymbals, he simply could not move his hands.

It was a long road that stretched from this inauspicious concert debut to the assumption of full-time duties as a major conductor in New York—a road paved with uninterrupted study and fastidious preparation both in America and Europe. When, in 1885, destiny placed his father's burdens on Walter's shoulders, he knew that he could carry them. But he was inspired by a mission greater than merely doing his job well. He wanted to educate America to music. He wanted to transfer his own great love and enthusiasm for the wonderful art to the uninitiated American masses.

After his visit to Kentucky, he toured the South extensively. Then the West. Some of his trials would have broken a less determined spirit than his. In one place he met the open disgust of a manager because Damrosch confessed that his orchestra was unable to play popular ballroom music. In another town, his performance of a Beethoven symphony was interrupted in the middle by loud cries for *The Arkansas Traveler*. Gently, Damrosch complied with the request, played *The Arkansas Traveler*, then continued with the symphony from the point where it had been interrupted. When Damrosch visited Oklahoma with a performance of Wagner's spiritual music-drama, *Parsifal,* he was interrupted, immediately after he had directed the other-worldly prelude, by the local manager who rose to the stage with the momentous announcement: "I would like to announce that Stewart's Oyster Saloon will be open after the concert." Damrosch waited for the proclamation to end, then, unruffled, continued with his direction of the Wagner drama.

There were times when the necessity of conforming to train schedules compelled him to play a musical work faster than the tempo indicated in the score. Or else, he might find it expedient to omit a slow movement from a symphony in order to make the composition more digestible to untrained palates. Damrosch did all this without permitting his conscience to be pricked by remorse. Let others look upon music as a temple, which one must approach with reverence and on bended knee! To Damrosch, music was something to be loved with the intensity and adoration of a young man for his first sweetheart. Like the young lover, Damrosch was eager to introduce his loved one to everybody, everywhere, to shout her virtues from the housetops, until everyone heard him and her beauty was visible to the entire world.

*

He still loves music this way. Not even a professional career of more than sixty years has robbed him of his wonderful enthusiasm for, and excitement about, great music. Even today, a performance of music is for him the rarest type of pleasure he can enjoy; and in some seventy-odd years those ears of his have soaked in no small dose of music. Not that his is a one-track mind. He has always had an overabundance of enthusiasms. Today he still follows his many hobbies with his one-time zest. As a child he used to like building little pasteboard theatres for marionettes. As a matter of fact, it can be recorded that the first American performance of *Das Rheingold* took place in a theatre of his own construction: the characters were played by puppets, and the music was performed and sung by the exuberant young Walter at the piano. Today he still likes to build those little theatres, some of which are quite pretentious. He also likes to try his hand at carpentering and (during the summers) at gardening. He likes to play the genial host to his small group of intimate friends, and to his rather large circle of immediate relatives. He enjoys good food, liquor in moderation. He likes to paint on canvases, to read good books (history and biography particularly), to go to the theatre. He has an almost childlike passion for wearing elaborate costumes at fancy-dress balls.

But his first love is music. He is today studying the piano with the application and devotion of a young student preparing for a career. His taxing work at composition, and his duties as conductor of children's radio concerts, he considers as recreation. And, like a true busman on a holiday, he finds no greater pleasure than spending his evenings at a good concert or opera. He won't miss an important musical event in New York if he can help it; that dignified gray head of his is a familiar sight in the front row of every major concert performance in New York. He himself may have conducted a Beethoven symphony hundreds of times until every marking on the page is thrice familiar; yet even at this late day, when he hears an energetic and inspiring performance he is as speechless at the wonder of the composer's genius as he was in his student days. I remember meeting Damrosch aboard a ship on our way back from the Bayreuth Festival where we had both been to hear Toscanini conduct (I believe that the ship was the old *France,* and the trip took place in August, 1930). I asked him how he liked Toscanini's performance. Damrosch reacted as a schoolboy might. He closed his eyes, spoke with the rapturous descriptive phrases of a novitiate. It was difficult to remember, in hearing his rhapsodic flow of rhetoric, that here was a musician who himself had performed these music-dramas time and time again over a period of several decades.

After having served faithfully as principal conductor of the New York Symphony Society for more than forty years, Walter Damrosch decided to withdraw in 1926. It was not spectacular music that had been heard these many years at Damrosch's concerts: It would be overstressing a point to call Damrosch an excellent conductor. He knew how to arrange fascinating programs, and he had an extraordinarily wide repertoire. But he did not have the capacity to drive his men toward heights. He was too easily satisfied with the results he received. He may have known, when he retired, that there were now in New York far greater conductors than he; that he no longer had a place in the New York symphony scene. Or he may have felt that his life-work had been completed. He had set out to sell good music to the country, and, after forty years, had sold it successfully. As he himself remarked at the time: "Gradually symphony orchestras were founded in the cities which I had visited. Philadelphia, Rochester, Detroit, St. Louis, Omaha, Los Angeles, San Francisco no longer needed a visiting orchestra to satisfy their newly awakened desires for symphonic music. Excellent local orchestras under accomplished conductors amply supplied their artistic needs, and I began to feel that my work in that direction was over, and that I could do no more than repeat myself in continuing to perform to my own home audiences the works of the masters."

But that was only half the explanation for his retirement. The other, and the more convincing reason was that he had suddenly found a new love: the radio. The salesman in him had never died. He recognized immediately that science had brought him a medium through which he could reach a public of fantastic proportions, a medium which suddenly made his annual tours an obsolete method of carrying good music to the entire country. Other musicians at the time looked rather disdainfully on the radio. They spoke of it as "canned music," and made sport of the unholy sounds which emanated from the loud speaker. But Damrosch realized that he had acquired a powerful ally for his missionary work; and he did not hesitate to associate himself with it, in spite of the condemnations and sneers of other musicians.

He conducted his first radio concert in 1925 on an invitation by A. Atwater Kent—interspersing his genial remarks about the music between the numbers. The response he received took his breath away. Letters poured into the studio in grateful acknowledgment for the good music Damrosch brought to the radio. Immediately, the National Broadcasting Company engaged him to direct a series of twenty weekly symphonic broadcasts for the following year. In that year it was estimated that some ten million people heard each of his concerts; two hundred million heard the series of twenty broadcasts. "It was only then that I realized at least some of the possibilities which this opened before me. Audiences of millions at one concert, instead of three thousand at the concert hall; the greater proportion of these radio listeners absolutely virgin soil." Damrosch conducted another series of symphonic concerts in 1927-28, and the following two years he directed a third and fourth series for General Electric.

By 1931, Damrosch was once again made to realize that his work was done. Radio was no longer spoken of derisively by musicians. More and more serious artists were associating themselves with the new medium. Broadcasts of great sym-

WALTER DAMROSCH

THE LATE FREDERICK STOCK

phonic music—unheard when Damrosch first came to the air—were now an almost everyday event: the Boston Symphony, the Philadelphia Orchestra, and the New York Philharmonic were now broadcasting regularly. Men like Howard Barlow and Frank Black were conducting studio orchestras in regular broadcast periods. Damrosch had succeeded in selling great music to the radio.

He now decided to devote himself exclusively to an undertaking which he had launched in 1928, when he inaugurated a music-appreciation hour for schoolchildren over the radio. He had been selling great music to adults for more than forty years, building the concert audiences of yesterday and today. He would now sell great music to the audiences of tomorrow.

Unfortunately, Damrosch's Music Appreciation Hour became a victim of the Second World War. After fourteen years of uninterrupted broadcasting, it was suspended in the fall of 1942. The war has made heavy demands on the radio networks for time, and the directors wished to curtail Damrosch's program from a full hour to a half. Damrosch, feeling that his work could not be adequately accomplished in that time, regretfully parted company with NBC.

Knowing, as we do, Damrosch's irrepressible energy and enthusiasm, it is safe to say that he is not retiring his baton. He is too young for that; and he feels that there is still much for him to do.

2

Frederick Stock

With the exception of Damrosch, no other conductor still active with the baton has had such a long and uninterrupted career as Frederick Stock.* Stock, like Damrosch, is an inextricable part of American orchestral history. For thirty-seven years he has been the conductor of the Chicago Symphony Orchestra. His long reign has had regal dignity. He has never resorted to sensationalism to attract attention, nor courted publicity for self-aggrandizement. He has scrupulously avoided the fireworks of controversies. His career, therefore, has consisted in an important job well done by a man who always considered his work more important than himself.

Stock is a man of rare simplicity of character and modesty. At rehearsals, for example, he resorts to no unusual antics, nor succumbs to outbursts of temper: He is soft-spoken and even-tempered, knows exactly what he wants and gives his men precise instructions. He has extraordinary conductorial technique at his command which makes it possible for him to work methodically, and with a minimum of physical effort and mental strain. Temperament, he has—for his performances are always alive with character. But he has not the temperament of a prima donna. The humblest musician in the orchestra, up to its directors, knows that he may be firm where artistic standards are concerned, but that on all other matters he is easy to get along with. He is good-humored, pleasant company whether

---

* As this book was going to press, Dr. Stock died of a heart attack.

one rubs elbows with him in the living room or works under him at the concert hall. He does not provide material to warm the heart of a publicity director; as a matter of fact, he shrinks from publicity, stoutly refusing to have the limelight focused on him, always deflecting it from himself to his orchestra.

That Stock has remained the principal conductor of his orchestra over this long period reflects honor both to himself and to his audiences. To himself—because, without sacrificing integrity, without offering any attraction beyond that of great music performed with discerning musicianship, he has been able to hold the interest of his public. To his audiences—because through all these years they closed their ears to the siren calls, and shut their eyes to the dazzling glamour, of other, perhaps more electrifying, conductors. With symphony audiences throughout the country fluctuating in their adoration from one European conductor to another, and mostly for superficial considerations, Chicago audiences remained true to Stock—and for purely musical reasons.

Because he has not encouraged the publicization of his achievements, it is sometimes difficult to remember that his is one of the great conductorial careers of our time, and quite unique from certain points of view. He is the only conductor whose entire history is inextricably bound up with one orchestra. Even Stokowski, whose name was inevitably associated with the Philadelphia Orchestra, began his career in Cincinnati, and, after Philadelphia, continued it with the All-American Youth Orchestra. Stock first took up his baton in Chicago, and since then no other orchestra has known him as a permanent leader. Also, Stock, in his unassuming manner, has made the Chicago Orchestra one of the progressive musical organizations of the country. His programs have been models for taste, novelty, and sound musical interest. "I have spent

endless time pondering over the problem of program-making,"
he once confessed. "There has always been among all audiences a sharp cleavage between those who do not like to hear
the new in music . . . and those whose enthusiasm for the
new, the unfamiliar, knows no bounds. The lovers of the
classics . . . cannot easily be convinced that all this treasure
of beauty and grandeur was, at one time, new and unfamiliar.
. . . All things considered, one would be wise in practicing
conventionality in program-making, but beware of becoming
pedantic; introduce as many new works and repeat as many
unfamiliar ones, as the audiences will willingly absorb—and
then leave well enough alone."

He has been faithful to the old; and yet, from the very first,
he has been an advocate of the new. In a survey conducted by
Dr. Howard Hanson on the American orchestral repertory a
few years ago, the Chicago Symphony earned first place among
American orchestras in the wide and elastic range of its programs over a long period of years; it has presented under Stock
more works by a greater variety of composers than any other
orchestra—about 240 compositions by 70 different composers.
And Stock has also kept a watchful eye on the American composer. Early in his career he repeatedly performed American
music (he was the only regular conductor in America at the
time to do so) despite the groans of dissatisfaction among his
audiences. In thirty-seven seasons, Stock has performed more
than 300 different works by American composers. And he is
still the friend of the American composer: In 1940-41 (based on
figures compiled by the National Music Council), the Chicago
Symphony Orchestra took first place among American orchestras in the number of performances of American works.

*

Though the Chicago Symphony is the third oldest orchestra

in the country, it has known only two permanent conductors in its fifty-odd years of existence: The other conductor was its founder, Theodore Thomas. He had been brought to Chicago by a group of important business men to organize a major symphony orchestra. These business men were prepared to supply a handsome subsidy. Thomas, who had been conducting his own orchestra in New York and on tours throughout the country, brought with him thirty of his own musicians. He felt that in the Chicago orchestra his lifelong ambitions would be realized. He was given an orchestra which would not be dependent for support on its audiences, and which, therefore, could reach for the highest in symphonic art.

On October 7, 1891, the Chicago Orchestra gave its inaugural concert featuring the Beethoven Fifth Symphony and the Tchaikovsky Piano Concerto (Rafael Joseffy, soloist). That Thomas was determined to sound an incomparably high tone for his new orchestra was proved with subsequent concerts which were held at the now historic Auditorium. At his second performance, the program included major works by Bach, Gluck, Schumann, and Tchaikovsky. The third concert featured two symphonies; the fourth was devoted to Wagner, and to the Schubert C major Symphony. This was an unpleasantly rigorous diet for audiences which up to now had been accustomed only to cream-puffs and desserts. It turned many a stomach. Thomas played to half-empty houses. The first season showed a deficit of $53,000; the second, $50,000. "If it is desirable to educate the 'masses' to a liking for any certain style of music," lamented one Chicago critic (and he was voicing the sentiments of most Chicago symphony patrons) "sound policy dictates that some effective means be adopted for bringing the 'masses' aforesaid within the reach of the educative influences and that the uniform and exclusive offering of what they will not tolerate is hardly to be reckoned among effective means. Mr. Thomas and his advisers seem to think otherwise, and if the Orchestral Association members are willing for their own gratification to pay the cost of what has been given them, nobody else has the right to object."

The backers of the Chicago Orchestra paid the bills without complaint. They had faith in Thomas, and confidence in his ultimate victory. They were determined to have their orchestra one of the greatest in the country. Except, therefore, for minor concessions to the public (such as the occasional substitution of shorter numbers for symphonies), Thomas remained true to his ideals; and his backers remained true to him. In 1901, he directed a Beethoven cycle; in 1902, a historical series tracing the evolution of orchestral music from Gabrieli to Tchaikovsky. The modern composers were consistently featured; even American composers, at that time the *bête noir* of the concert hall.

The antagonism of Chicago audiences to Thomas and his programs was ultimately overcome. Thomas' battle for great orchestral music had not been fought in vain. As they grew accustomed to the music, audiences began to take to it. The Auditorium grew more and more crowded with each season; the deficits decreased sharply. Then, in 1904, came the most convincing proof of the esteem of Chicago citizens for their orchestra. A public subscription was asked for the purpose of building a new auditorium for the Chicago Orchestra. Eight thousand music lovers proved their devotion to their orchestra by contributing $750,000.

"The money began to come in, not only from millionaires and such men of means as had hitherto paid the orchestra's deficit; it came from the public at large, including that great part of the public that is never supposed to know or care a stricken thing about classical music. The rich were asked to give, but it was the common run of humanity to whom we turned and that now spoke out. Working men, merchants, clerks, bookkeepers, schoolteachers, shop girls, scrub women—it is the most amazing thing I know of, but these were the people that responded."*

From this time on, the orchestra was self-sustaining, and was no longer compelled to turn to generous patrons for support.

Theodore Thomas died on January 4, 1905. He lived long enough to have given his orchestra permanency, and to have established for it large audiences of enthusiastic music lovers. It has been recorded that the last words spoken by him before death were: "I have had a beautiful vision, a beautiful vision." He was speaking, no doubt, of his orchestra.

*

Upon Thomas' death, the directors of the orchestra scanned the European horizon with searching eyes, hoping to find a worthy successor. Many famous Europeans expressed their willingness to come to Chicago, among them the world-famous Richard Strauss. Yet when a successor was finally chosen, he was found not in Europe, but at hand, in the orchestra itself.

Young Frederick Stock had, as a matter of fact, the approval of Thomas on his brow. Thomas had brought him to the orchestra from Europe; then (with his keen scent for real musical talent) had elevated him to the post of assistant conductor. This was in 1899; and for the next five years, Thomas had frequent evidence of the sound musicianship of his disciple.

Stock was twenty-three years old when he first came to Chicago to fill the post of first violinist. But already he was an experienced orchestra musician. He had been born on November 11, 1872 in a fortress in the garrison town of Jülich (near

---

* *The American Orchestra and Theodore Thomas,* by Charles E. Russell. Doubleday, Page, 1927.

Cologne) where his father, an army bandmaster, was stationed. Frederick's mother died when he was still an infant. At four, he began to study the violin and at eleven he had his first opportunity to conduct. Young Stock was present at a band rehearsal, and one of the bandsmen good humoredly asked him to substitute for his absent father. The child climbed the bandstand and, having long learned the music by heart, proceeded to beat the time with an accurate hand. The performance, to to amazement of the musicians, went smoothly.

Poverty made it impossible for Stock to get a comprehensive musical training during childhood. What he learned, he had to learn by himself—by reading books, and by experimenting on musical instruments. Yet he acquired so much information, that, in his fourteenth year, he won a scholarship for the Cologne Conservatory where he studied with such masters as Jensen, Humperdinck, Wüllner, and Zöllner.

Upon graduating from the Conservatory in 1887, he was given a violin post with the Cologne Municipal Orchestra. For eight years he played under the batons of world-famous musicians—among them, Brahms, Tchaikovsky, and Richard Strauss.

Thomas came upon Stock in Cologne, was impressed by his sincerity and enthusiasm, and urged him to come to Chicago to his orchestra. When Thomas selected Stock as his assistant conductor, there was no little amazement in the orchestra— for Stock had been one of the more unassuming musicians, and had thus far shown no special conductorial gifts. But Thomas seemed to have a sixth sense for genius, and it told him that Stock was his man. Under Thomas, Stock received the final touches to his musical education particularly during the years when as Thomas' assistant, he worked with the older man, learned his methods, and accepted advice and criticism. Stock helped Thomas rehearse. He accompanied the soloists. He took over some of Thomas' out-of-town engagements. He made valuable orchestral arrangements of old music for Thomas' use. He proved himself Thomas' indispensable right hand. Thomas was satisfied that the intuition which had led him to Stock had once again not failed him.

When, suddenly, Stock was called upon to take the post vacated by Thomas's death, he was already self-assured with the stick. He knew the business of conducting from every possible angle, and could wield the baton with a minimum of fumbling. From the very first, he was able—without the least sign of ostentation—to conduct most works in the repertoire from memory. Even in those days he could learn an entirely new score during a two-hour train ride.

*

A conductor who rises from the ranks of his orchestra is not in the most advantageous position. A few weeks earlier he had been an intimate friend and fellow-worker of the other orchestra players. Suddenly, he was in a position where he had to exert his authority over his friends, where his success demanded that he command and be obeyed. The moment called for tact and wisdom. If he had put on airs of superiority and arrogance, the orchestra would have been permanently antagonized; and an antagonistic orchestra can spell ruin even for a great and experienced conductor. But Stock was never the man for fake attitudes. He maintained his warm and friendly relationship with his men. He kept his rehearsals on a human basis. He even accepted, and gratefully, the advice and opinions of his fellow musicians. But at the same time, he let it be known that his authority was not to be questioned. And his tact won the day for him.

At one other time, and under quite different circumstances, Stock was to profit by his innate tact. It was during our first

139

months of the First World War, shortly after America's official entry into the conflict. War hysteria was in the air. Before long, some of the greatest musicians in America would be persecuted as suspected spies. Stock sensed the situation and rose to it. He asked to be excused from his duties for an entire season, until his American citizenship became official.

Since 1919, he has conducted the Chicago Symphony Orchestra uninterruptedly; with quiet and undramatized competence he has kept his orchestra in the front rank of American symphonic organizations. Always the restrained and well-poised musician, he has kept his performances tightly in check. His performances may not soar on wings, as do those of, say, Koussevitzky or Stokowski. Stock is not the man to excite his audiences with skillfully contrived climaxes, and overwhelming emotional impulses. But dignity he has, and taste. His readings are beautifully proportioned and balanced. They reveal the musical understanding, sensitivity, and discernment of their interpreter. His span is wide; his intelligence, searching.

And always he keeps himself in the background. At his concerts he has conveyed to his audiences that the music is the only important consideration. When, in 1940, the Chicago orchestra celebrated its fiftieth anniversary, the attention was directed on the orchestra itself. Only incidentally were there tributes paid to the conductor who led it for so many years. Like Toscanini, Stock detests applause. He frequently interrupts the welcoming round of handclaps with the opening bars of the first composition. Once the audience adopted the custom of rising to its feet whenever he came on the stage. This tribute so embarrassed him that he was finally driven to make a point-blank demand from the platform that such nonsense cease.

Of European Traditions

1

Bruno Walter

The fact that Bruno Walter was one of the two leading conductors in Germany, and that he had a reputation which circled the globe, did not save him from being the first important musician to be exiled from Germany when the Nazis rose to power. In the spring of 1933, he was ordered to leave the country without further delay, and never to return. The concert he was scheduled to conduct with the Leipzig Gewandhaus Orchestra on March 16, 1933 was hurriedly assumed (without so much as a blush of shame) by Richard Strauss—because, so ran the official explanation, Walter's appearance "threatened public order and security." Another concert, scheduled with the Berlin Philharmonic a few days later, was cancelled altogether; this time, without mincing words or seeking escape in subterfuge, the Nazis stated that it was found undesirable to have a Jew direct a great German symphonic ensemble.

Thus Walter's fifteen years of artistic endeavor for German music was brushed aside contemptuously because he was a Jew. That he was one of the great artists of our generation was forgotten overnight. No stronger indication could have been given by the Nazis at the time that they meant business in their policy of *Säuberung*—the cleansing of Germany of non-Aryan influences. For not even his world fame had saved Walter.

Strange paradox! Walter, who had always felt that art was in a world removed from politics, and that the artist had no place at the side of statesmen, was henceforth to feel the shattering impact of political forces more than any other musician. Having lost his native country, Walter transferred his home to Vienna, the city where he had achieved his first triumphs, and where his name was hallowed. Vienna itself was torn by anti-Semitic hatreds; but it received him warmly, for Vienna, though it hated Jews, was too musical to disown a great artist because of his Jewish blood. His first Viennese concert following his exile from Germany saw an overwhelming public demonstration for him—a spontaneous and heart-warming manifestation of affection and admiration. Walter conducted symphonies and operas in Vienna, and for a year was artistic adviser to the Vienna Opera. During the summers, he continued his work at the Salzburg festival which, more than any other single person, he had helped to make world-famous. Austria was now his adopted fatherland; in Austria he felt at home, at peace with his art. The banishment from Germany had been less of a searing wound only because Austria meant so much to him.

But the political cataclysm which had devastated Germany in 1933 was soon to have its profound repercussions in Austria. It was at a Bruno Walter concert of the Vienna Philharmonic that, during the intermission, Chancellor Kurt von Schuschnigg was formally introduced to the new ambassador from Germany, Franz von Papen. They exchanged polite salutations. Franz von Papen told the Chancellor that he had come for the express purpose of cementing the then strained relations between the two countries. They shook hands; and with that handshake the fate of Austria was sealed.

It was also at a Bruno Walter concert that von Schuschnigg made his last public appearance in Vienna. Soon after this, he went on an ill-fated journey to Berchtesgaden. Bruno Walter also left Vienna (fortuitously) for some performances in Paris. A few weeks after this, Austria fell to Germany; and Bruno Walter had lost his second home.

He now became a French citizen, devoting himself principally to performances in France and England, and to festival concerts in Italy and Lucerne. But he lost Italy when that country, showing greater Axis solidarity, launched its own anti-Semitic program. And he lost Lucerne when, in 1939, Europe plunged into a new world war. In the spring of 1940 his French citizenship was abrogated when France capitulated to Nazi Germany.

*

He came to the United States not only for concert performances, but also to seek American citizenship and to settle his roots permanently in this country. He appeared in guest performances with most of our leading orchestras. For the first time, he conducted opera in America, projecting magnificent performances at the Metropolitan Opera House. The honors which this country accorded him must at least partially have compensated him for his sad adventures in Europe. Here— where an artist does not have to apologize for his race or creed —Bruno Walter continued to occupy the position which had been his throughout the world for more than thirty years.

Whatever may be the fate of Europe, whatever may be its musical destiny, it is certain that henceforth Bruno Walter will play a major role in our musical life. He has said that now, more than anything else, he wishes to be a part of us; that he realizes what a privilege it is for him to practice his art in this arsenal of freedom. In view of the part he is destined to play here, it might be of moment to review his career in this country.

It was not always paved with triumphs. He came here for the first time in 1923 to be guest conductor of the New York

Symphony Society. Behind him already lay a formidable career in Germany and Austria, including major successes in Vienna, Munich, and Salzburg. Yet, to the New York audiences of the 1920's—more concerned with spectacular personalities than with spectacular music-making—Walter was no sensation at first. I recall his first concerts vividly. His programs were soundly constructed (there were, if memory serves, two major symphonies at his introductory concert) and presented with dignity, and often with majesty. There were no fireworks either in Walter's stage personality or in his interpretations. No breath-taking eccentricities. Only profound musicianship; only the cultured speech of a scholar. Some discriminating music-lovers in New York sang his praises from the first; but the public in general remained apathetic to him.

He returned to conduct the New York Symphony in 1924 and 1925, with hardly greater success. A few discerning music lovers, of course, appreciated him for his true worth; but the public in general remained comparatively disinterested. Then, possibly discouraged by his failure to earn here the fame that was his due, he did not return to America again until 1932, when he was invited to conduct the New York Philharmonic. During his absence, a subtle transformation had taken place in American musical taste: it had become refined and sensitized. Americans were growing less concerned with personalities, and more with good music itself. And in this new scheme of things, Bruno Walter could now take his deserving place of honor. He remained two seasons with the Philharmonic, his beautifully fashioned performances, rich with poetic fervor and feeling, finding large and appreciative audiences. He was again with the Philharmonic during its centenary celebration season. He conducted most of the leading American orchestras from New York to Los Angeles as well. Then, in

1940, he earned his crowning triumphs in America, when he joined the Metropolitan Opera House and gave incandescent performances of operas by Beethoven, Mozart, and Smetana.

Without minimizing Bruno Walter's gifts as symphonic conductor, it can be said with full justification that the true Bruno Walter was not known to America until he came to the Metropolitan Opera House in 1940. He is always a sensitive and poetic interpreter, whether he conducts symphonies or operas, and there are always qualities in his readings which delight the discriminating. But there has been little question to those of us who have heard him in Paris, Salzburg, Vienna, or Florence, that he is greatest in the realm of opera.

In the symphonic repertoire he yields too often to the urge to overinterpretation. He is so carried away by the music he is playing that he cannot resist the temptation of caressing a lyric line affectionately, or permitting the full tide of his feelings to overflow. He indulges in some of the indiscretions of the von Bülow school of conductors: sometimes inserting uncalled for pauses *(Luftpausen)* to heighten suspense; utilizing rubatos with too lavish a hand; touching lyric pages with saccharine. He has the taste of a fine artist, and such indiscretions are often not objectionable except to the purist. But one often prefers less interpretation, and a more meticulous accounting of the composer's own intentions when listening to Walter.

In the opera house we hear a quite different Bruno Walter, a more restrained and disciplined artist. It may be that, subconsciously, he is held in constraint by the artists on the stage; or that his personality is better adapted for the theatre than the symphony hall. In any case, he is one of the great operatic conductors of our time. In Mozart, in Weber, in Gluck, in most of the Italian repertory he has Toscanini's intensity, scrupulous attention to details, spaciousness of design. His hand integrates all the various elements of operatic performance into a unity. His adjustments between orchestra and singers are sensitively achieved; he is one of the few opera conductors who can pluck out of the texture of an orchestral accompaniment, a phrase, or a rhythmic pattern (formerly unnoticed by us) which gives new meaning to the action of the stage. He has, when the music calls for it, passion and strength; his is an extraordinary range of dynamics and nuances. He can play a melody with a soaring line, and can provide accompaniments pronounced with clarity and unpretentiousness. He bends elastically with every changing mood, carrying orchestra and singers with him.

He is essentially the aesthete, the worshipper of beauty in every form. He is passionately fond of painting, lyric poetry, the theatre, books; with whatever art he comes into contact he searches hungrily for beauty of design. It is for this reason that the composer he adores above all others is Mozart, the composer in whom he also finds his happiest vein as an interpreter. Mozart is the quintessence of beauty in form and substance, and in the presence of Mozart Bruno Walter melts.

To see him conduct Mozart is to realize how deeply this music moves him. His eyelids become heavy and droop over his dreamy eyes; a beatific smile creeps across his lips; his face has an other-worldly look. As his body moves ecstatically with the rhythm of the music, he seems to be floating, buoyed by the wings of the music. He is so completely under the spell of the music that it is some moments after the end of the performance before he recovers. He leaves the platform somewhat dazed, high-strung, his eyes dreamy, his face pale.

*

His training and background have particularly adapted him for the opera house. He was born in Berlin on September 15,

1876 (his original name was Bruno Schlesinger), and he was educated at the Stern Conservatory. Long before his graduation from the Conservatory he knew that he wanted, above everything else, to be a conductor; not even early successes as a prodigy pianist in Germany could deflect him from his ultimate goal. As a boy, he frequently visited the State Library, begging his way in, for it was against the rules to admit one so young. There he would study the scores of great operas. At an interesting musical passage—a striking melodic phrase, or an unusual progression, or chord—he would make a notation on a piece of paper. Then, when he was able to hear an actual performance of these operas, he would take his notes out of his pocket and wait to hear the passages he had singled out.

After he graduated from the Conservatory, he accepted a few minor posts as conductor in small German opera houses. Then he was engaged as coach, chorus master, and general assistant for the Hamburg Opera.

The Hamburg post was a turning point in Walter's life. It brought him into contact with the artist who was to exert the greatest single influence over his life: Gustav Mahler, principal conductor in Hamburg. To work with Mahler, to assist him in his fastidiously prepared performances, was a university education for a young conductor. The two years in Hamburg taught Walter many things about the art and technique of conducting. But more than this, Walter learned from Mahler the idealism, self-effacement, and consecration to the highest standards of art with which every true artist must concern himself.

Conducting in theatres in Breslau, Pressburg, and Riga, and filling an engagement at the Royal Opera in Berlin, brought Walter the necessary experience and self-assurance for his first major assignment. In 1897, Mahler had been appointed director of the Vienna Royal Opera. He freshened and enriched the opera house with transfusions of new blood. He brought young singers to Vienna (many of them to rise to world fame there). And he called upon young conductors to assist him. Mahler had not forgotten his energetic and idealistic young co-worker of Hamburg. In 1901 he called Walter to Vienna.

No greater or more soul-satisfying experience could a young artist ask for than to assist Mahler during one of the great epochs in the history of Viennese music-making. Mahler was at the zenith of his powers as a conductor. Gustav Mahler's herculean energy, brilliantly analytical intellect, maniacal pursuit after perfection, unsparing zeal and industry, and high artistic devotion created a revolution at the Vienna Opera. The repertoire was reshaped and freshened as one novelty after another was introduced, and as the old operas were subjected to the most painstaking re-study. Mahler drove those who worked under him; and he drove himself. And through hard work—and the revitalization of Mahler's interpretative genius—the Vienna Opera was transformed into the leading musical institution of the world. To work at the side of Mahler, and to be subjected to his will and artistic purpose, was to be given a dazzling vision of the interpretative art at its noblest. In Vienna, under Mahler's vigilant, exacting eye Bruno Walter emerged from a talented conductor into a great one.

Mahler left the Vienna Opera in 1907. "A great epoch had come to an end," wrote Walter, "the achievement of one man and his inspired co-workers. Everyone had learned from him, everyone had been led to the utmost of his capacity."

Walter never forgot his debt to Mahler. He has paid the debt—and paid it handsomely—by passionately espousing the cause of Mahler's music, and directing it with all the skill, devotion, and reverence of which he was capable in every music center in the world. It was Walter who directed the première of *Das Lied von der Erde* in Munich, and that of the Ninth Symphony in Vienna. It was Walter who, twenty-five years after Mahler's death, directed a monumental Mahler festival in Vienna. It was Walter who persistently furthered the cause of Mahler's music in America in spite of the general apathy of the public. And (with eloquent appropriateness!) it was with a Mahler Symphony that Bruno Walter made one of his last appearances in Vienna in 1938.

Walter remained in Vienna until 1913, and it was he who was largely responsible for some of the brilliant moments which persisted, recollections as it were, of the Mahler epoch. Then, already considered among the most brilliant conductors of the period, he was engaged as Felix Mottl's successor as general music director of Munich. In Munich, Walter's fame became international, enhanced by his remarkable contributions to the Salzburg festival beginning with 1922.

Anti-Semitism and envy, finally, drove him out of Munich. But his stature grew. Subsequent to his first appearances in America, Walter's star kept rising in Europe. In 1924, he gave his first performances in Covent Garden and was so successful (particularly in Wagner) that his annual visits henceforth became musical events of striking importance in the London season. In 1925, Walter was appointed principal conductor of the Charlottenburg Opera in Berlin which, largely through his efforts, became one of the great opera houses in Germany. In 1930, Walter became conductor of the historic Leipzig Gewandhaus Orchestra.

Ejected from Germany in 1933, Walter continued his performances in France, in England, at the Florence May Music Festival, in Salzburg, Vienna, and the United States.

Particularly noteworthy was his work in Vienna. During this period, the Vienna State Opera had fallen upon sorry days, especially under the regime of Felix Weingartner, once one of the truly great conductors of the world, but now a tired, old man, set in his ways, and deaf to all advice and criticism. His best days as conductor were long past; yet he was determined to conduct the most important performances. He had many blind spots, and was responsible for a stodgy repertoire. Hating Jews, he ruthlessly dismissed some of them from the company. Besides, he was inefficient, reactionary in his musical tastes and stubborn. Weingartner's promise to conduct in Japan in 1936 offered the Vienna Opera a welcome excuse to ask for his resignation. To lift the Opera out of its degeneracy, the directors called on Bruno Walter to assume direction. Bruno Walter worked against impossible odds; but, in spite of petty intrigues, the rising ocean of anti-Semitism, and the lack of fresh musical material, he succeeded in restoring some measure of dignity and self-respect to the Vienna Opera.

But his reign, unfortunately, was brief; in 1938 the Nazi entered Vienna.

*

"Nur Mut, und Kopf oben"—only courage, and head high —Mahler had often said to Bruno Walter.

No phrase could more aptly sum up Bruno Walter's career. He has had courage—of that there can be no doubt. One has merely to recall how valiantly he has fought his musical battles—the battle for Mahler and Bruckner, for example— to realize that he is of heroic stature. One has only to speak to Walter today—a man who has lost his world and his setting —to recognize that he has moral and physical courage to face disaster and to emerge from it with unvanquished spirit.

And his head has been high: few artists of our time have remained so true to their art and to their principles as Walter.

Nothing is quite so illustrative of the nobility of the artist

152

as his attitude toward Richard Strauss. Walter was recently asked why he persisted in directing the music of a man like Strauss, who had done him such personal injury; and why he sponsored the music of a composer who was the leading musical figure of the detestable Nazi regime. "I dislike Strauss as a person," Walter answered simply, "and I abhor everything for which he has stood in recent years. But Strauss is a genius, and some of his works are masterpieces. I cannot in all honesty boycott masterpieces because I detest their composer."

2

Fritz Busch

Fritz Busch was another early victim of the Nazi purge. He was not, like Bruno Walter, a Jew, but a political suspect. It was known that he had no great enthusiasm for the Nazi party, and no intentions to curry favor with it now that it had acquired power. Besides, he was a liberal whose political philosophy was sharply opposed to that of a dictatorial regime.

As in the case of Bruno Walter, not his world fame, nor his monumental contributions to the Dresden Opera, nor the admiration and respect with which he was regarded by his fellow Germans could save Busch once the Nazis designated him as their enemy. During a rehearsal at the Dresden Opera, on March 7, 1933, Nazi storm-troopers noisily entered the auditorium and demanded that Busch resign his post in favor of a proved Nazi. That same evening, at a performance of *Rigoletto,* the front rows of the opera house were occupied by brown shirts. As Busch made his way to the conductor's stand they chanted in unison: "Out with Busch!" Quietly, Busch withdrew, announced his resignation, and left the country.

Handsome compensation and gratitude for his historic artistic achievements and for his unsparing devotion to German music!

Fritz Busch, older brother of the famous violinist, Adolf, was born on March 13, 1890, in Siegen, Westphalia. His father, who had abandoned a musical career for carpentry in order to support his family, was determined to realize his own artistic ambitions through his children. All of them were given comprehensive musical training from early childhood. They grew up in a musical setting, and became saturated with a musical atmosphere. A small orchestra, conducted by their father, met regularly at their home, filling the days and evenings with music; besides this, the children often joined their father in chamber music performances.

Fritz began to study the piano in his fifth year, and two years later began concert work with success. Concerts (and, later, hack work in music halls and ballrooms to earn a sadly needed mark) did not interfere with the systematic study of music. By the time he was twelve years old, he had a working knowledge of every instrument in the orchestra.

In 1906, he was enrolled at the Cologne Conservatory. One year after this came his debut with the baton—at the State Theatre at Riga. Other engagements, in Gotha, Aachen, and Bad Pyrmont, brought experience and self-assurance to the young conductor.

In June, 1918, he was invited to conduct the Berlin Philharmonic in a festival devoted to the music of Max Reger held at Jena. It was his first taste of triumph, and brought him his first major post; the direction of the Stuttgart Opera in succession to Max von Schillings. Three years at Stuttgart made Busch famous throughout Germany. His next post, as director of the Dresden Opera, extended his fame beyond Germany throughout the rest of Europe and even to America. Under his guidance, the Dresden Opera became one of the great opera houses of the world. Besides its admirable performances of the standard repertory—the operas of Mozart and Wagner particularly, for which Busch proved himself especially adapted —there was the progressive and fearless promotion of new music to bring it its deserving fame. Modern opera owes a debt to Fritz Busch and the Dresden Opera, for it found in them stout-hearted champions. At Dresden, many of Hindemith's operas were first performed, including the controversial *Cardillac*. There, too, took place the world première of Kurt Weill's *Der Protagonist*. Many of Richard Strauss' later operas were officially introduced in Dresden, for example, *The Egyptian Helen* and *Joseph's Legend*. And whether the opera was of the classic repertory or the modern, it received at the hands of Fritz Busch a studiously prepared performance which was the delight and admiration of German music lovers.

*

Fritz Busch's first contact with the United States came in 1927 when he was invited to serve as guest of the New York Symphony Society. He did not make a forceful impression. His appearance, suggesting a department store manager rather than an artist, and his unexciting stage manner were not likely to fire the interest of New York concertgoers to a boiling point. His performances—intelligently prepared but without any suggestion of the dramatic—were also unspectacular. New York found his concerts unimpressive. A hero in Dresden, Busch remained unsung in New York.

It cannot be said that America has given Busch any greater homage since 1927. After his exile from Germany, Busch conducted a season of opera in South America. Then he was engaged as musical director of the Danish Broadcasting Company. At the same time, he filled engagements as guest of opera and symphony performances throughout Europe. Wherever he came he was honored as a major figure of the baton—particularly at the annual summer Glyndebourne Festival in England where his performances of the Mozart operas were accepted as models of classic perfection.

In 1936, when Toscanini resigned as principal conductor of

the New York Philharmonic, he suggested Fritz Busch for the post. He personally sent Busch a cable urging him to return to America in order to take over the direction of the Philharmonic. Busch (no doubt recalling the frigid reception he had received in this country) politely turned down the offer. He was happy at his various posts in Europe, and he had no desire to court the favour of the American music public. But the outbreak of the Second World War forced him to revise his plans. With Europe in conflagration—reducing its musical activity to ashes—Busch came to the United States. He conducted opera with the recently organized New Opera Company in New York (a not altogether successful attempt to transplant the Glyndebourne Festival to America). He also appeared as a guest of several major symphony orchestras, including the New York Philharmonic during its centenary season.

If Busch has failed to conquer America as decisively as he has stormed other music centers, it is not altogether the fault of our audiences. The standard of conducting is incomparably high in this country. Well executed performances are not enough to excite widespread enthusiasm. The truth is that Busch is an example that sound musicianship, scholarship, taste, and artistic discrimination are not sufficient to create great performances. To speak to Busch personally is to realize that he is a musician to his very fingertips: few conductors have his phenomenal command of the symphonic and operatic repertory. Intellectually he need feel inferior to none. But intellect, too, unfortunately, does not suffice. Busch lacks the personal fire, the voltaic electricity to create sparks and cause conflagrations. He does not excite his men or inspire them with the dynamism of personality. He has not the despotic will to dominate, nor the capacity to be obeyed implicitly.

The result, too often, is a rather stodgy performance in which things are usually correctly said, but not with eloquence, passion, nor moving spirit. I have heard some performances (but they have been very rare) in which he has been superb: the music of Max Reger, for example, offers an idiom in which his heavy Germanic accent can express itself happily. I have heard performances by Busch which have been artistically prepared in every detail, in which the workmanship is expert, and the taste unimpeachable—his Mozart performances in Glyndebourne for example. I have heard performances of Beethoven and Brahms which betrayed the intelligence and understanding of their interpreter. But, personally, I have never been stirred by Busch in the way that I am affected by Toscanini or Koussevitzky or Bruno Walter. My own reaction seems to be the reaction of most American music lovers. They will applaud him politely for his musicianship and integrity; but I have yet to see them demonstrate enthusiasm.

3

Sir Thomas Beecham

Sir Thomas Beecham has more titles than any other English musician, including those of knighthood and baronetcy. But those who know him well have always felt that a formal title is not quite appropriate for a man of such simplicity, lovable humor, and unpretentiousness. In appearance he may suggest a member of Parliament: he has the dignity of height and carriage; his bullet-shaped head converges into an aristocratic pointed beard; an impressive nose separates a high forehead and finely shaped lips. In reputation he may rank with the immortal musicians of England. In background, he may suggest the highborn. Yet to his friends (and to the many musicians who have worked with him) he is simply "Tommy," a genial fellow, a gentleman in the finest meaning of the term, a devoted and lovable friend.

There is more than his genius with the baton to make him a famous personality. There is, for example, his fabulous memory. Like Toscanini, he seems to know intimately about the entire symphonic and operatic repertoire. Whenever a question arises in London about a debatable point in some obscure work, it is "Tommy" who is consulted; and invariably he has the correct answer at the tip of his tongue. His fellow musicians have long stood in awe of his encyclopedic knowledge of musical scores. An amusing story describes his command of the repertory. He was a guest conductor at an opera performance in Birmingham. A few moments before the per-

159

formance he coolly smoked a cigarette. When curtain time arrived, he snuffed out his cigarette, and on his way out to the pit, quietly asked the manager: "By the way, what opera are we playing tonight?"

His courage is almost as formidable as his memory. Perhaps the most illustrative example is a performance of Mozart's *The Marriage of Figaro* which he directed at Drury Lane during the First World War. An air-raid took place, during which a bomb destroyed a wing of the theatre. But "Tommy" realized that panic was a greater danger than the descending bombs. Without seeming to notice the explosion, he continued his conducting. The audience, inspired by his courage, remained in its seats. The air raid passed without any casualties in the theatre; and the performance went on without interruption.

He has always had the courage to speak his mind without mincing words. He has violently excoriated English music schools and their system of music education (even though, at the same time, he was wounding the sensibilities of some of his personal friends). He has attacked English music critics with devastating verbal attacks, without giving a thought that he might be wounding his own position at the same time. In America, in 1941, he bitterly denounced Hollywood music, pricking many open sores in the movie colony. Not that he is neither tactful nor diplomatic; he would not be so much the Englishman if he weren't. But where he sees abuses in music he cannot remain silent. Expediency cannot restrain him from shouting his criticisms.

Then there is his fleet, pointed sense of humor. When he was first invited to conduct the London Philharmonic he remarked (remembering that his father had become world-famous by virtue of a medicinal preparation): "I suppose now they will call the orchestra the London Pillharmonic." While conducting a performance of *Aïda* in a small town in England, he was disconcerted to notice the shabby presentation. During the course of the performance, the horse on the stage yielded to physical necessity. "Tommy" put his hands on his hips and alertly applying the famous *mot* of David Garrick, whispered to his men: "Upon my word, gentlemen, he's a critic!" Once, in commenting on English music, he remarked sadly: "British composition is in a state of perpetual promise. It might be said to be one long promissory note."

Most important of all, however, is his idealism. He has consecrated his life to great music—sparing neither his health nor his fortune—thereby carving musical history in England. Few people of our time have made such fabulous personal sacrifices for the development of music culture in their countries as Beecham. Over a period of several decades he brought England the greatest operas in the world (many of them heard there for the first time) in brilliant performances, frequently paying the necessary expenses out of his own pocket. The Diaghilev Ballet, Russian operas with Chaliapin, opera in English, people's opera, world famous premières and revivals, new operas by living composers, neglected modern English composers, all were sponsored by Beecham to the greater good of English music. It is said that his operatic ventures entailed him the loss of several million dollars, enough certainly to have thrown him at one time into bankruptcy. No wonder, then, that one critic was able to say of him: "I think that unbiased British musicians would agree with me that Beecham has done more to stimulate and enrich the musical life of England than any other musician of his time."

*

His first adventure was the organization of a symphony orchestra in London in 1905. The New Symphony Orchestra paid tribute to old music, neglected by other English composers. In doing this, it brought a deepening and an enrichment of musical experiences to London's musical life. The New Symphony Orchestra soon passed into other hands (eventually it was transformed into the famous Royal Albert Hall Orchestra). In 1908, Beecham created another orchestra, the Beecham Symphony—this time to do heroic propaganda work for the modern composer. What a debt contemporary English composers owe to Beecham for his labors at this time cannot easily be calculated. Many of them—Delius especially—stepped out of the total darkness of obscurity to the limelight of public attention only because Beecham had worked for them.

Then Beecham turned to opera, first creating his own company in 1910 (when he gave the world première of Delius's *A Village Romeo and Juliet*), then, in 1911, taking over the management of Covent Garden. During his regime, one of the greatest in Covent Garden's history, every major opera in the repertory was given performance; with that, more than sixty novelties were presented. Opera performance in England acquired a healthy stimulus from its contact with Beecham, and it thrived. There was a season of Russian opera with Chaliapin ("my Russian season," once remarked Beecham, "was eminently successful; no one understood a word"), and another with the Diaghilev Ballet; there was a season of *opéra comique* in English, and another of grand opera in the same language; there were magnificent cycles of the Wagner music-dramas, and first performances of all the major Richard Strauss operas. Beyond this, there was a seemingly inexhaustible parade of new operas and fascinating revivals by Richard Strauss, Dame Ethel Smyth, Debussy, Eugen d'Albert, Rimsky-Korsakow, Sir Arthur Sullivan *(Ivanhoe)*, Stanford, Holbrooke, and Delius.

For his services to English music, Beecham was knighted in

SIR THOMAS BEECHAM

FRITZ BUSCH   BRUNO WALTER   PIERRE MONTEUX

1914, and in 1916 succeeded to the title of baronetcy. But titles and honors, unfortunately, do not pay the expensive bills for opera-making such as Beecham offered. In 1919, Sir Thomas announced that his personal funds had been exhausted by his experiments and musical ventures, and that he was forced to go into bankruptcy.

His retirement was temporary. In 1923, he conducted a symphony concert at the Royal Albert Hall, and with this concert his return to London musical activity became official. Henceforth he was to be feverishly active, with no necessity of financing his own ventures. He directed all the major English orchestras, and was one of the principal conductors at Covent Garden. His guest appearances brought him to the head of the leading orchestras and opera houses in Europe. In 1928, he made his debut in the United States with the New York Philharmonic, marking the beginning of a long and successful association with this country. In the same year, he evolved a monumental plan for a people's opera in England, in which he promised to present the greatest operas for the masses at popular prices if 150,000 music lovers throughout England would contribute two-pence weekly for five years; this scheme, unfortunately, was never realized. In 1929, he directed a monumental Delius festival in London, the successful culmination of his lifelong effort to bring recognition to this great composer; Delius, now an invalid, was brought to these concerts in a wheelchair to witness, at last, the tribute so long due him. In 1932, with the aid of society backing, he founded the London Symphony Orchestra, and became the artistic director of Covent Garden. Illness brought about another temporary retirement shortly before the outbreak of the Second World War. But once again the retirement was only temporary. During the first year of the war, Sir Thomas played a major part in creating music as a force for morale. And, in 1941, he came again to this country—England's ambassador of good will—associating himself with our leading orchestras, and making unforgettable guest appearances at the Metropolitan Opera House.

*

Sir Thomas was born in St. Helens, Lancashire, on April 29, 1879. His father, the famous manufacturer of Beecham's Pills, at one time must have questioned himself—as did the King in the *Pirates of Penzance*—"For what, we ask, is life, without a touch of poetry in it?": He advertised his product throughout Europe with the following poetic flourish

> "Hark, the Herald Angels Sing
> Beecham's Pills are just the thing."

Beecham's Pills, carried to success on wings of poetry, was also to become a silent partner of music; for it was its earnings which were later to pay the bills for Sir Thomas' many musical adventures.

His early musical education was haphazard: some piano and theory instruction at the Rossall School in Lancashire, and some additional theory lessons at Wadham College. But his infatuation for music was obvious. From earliest childhood—when he would listen breathlessly to the sounds emerging from an "orchestrion" which his father purchased him as a toy—he responded to every form of musical expression. At the age of ten, he founded a children's orchestra, which he directed with no small delight.

After leaving Oxford (without a degree) he began to participate in musical performances by organizing an amateur orchestra in Huyton. At one time, the famous Hallé Orchestra of Manchester, directed by Hans Richter, came to Huyton for a concert. The orchestra preceded its conductor who was so long delayed that he was unable to direct the concert. At the last moment, young Beecham substituted for him and gave an admirable account of himself in symphonies by Beethoven and Tchaikovsky.

He found it hard to discover a niche for himself, though he knew it would have to be in music. For a period, he wandered throughout Europe, enjoying a vagabond's existence. He listened to concerts and opera everywhere, absorbed hungrily all the musical experiences that could be acquired, and spent his idle hours in memorizing musical scores.

In 1902, he was engaged as one of the conductors of the Kelson Truman Opera Company, which toured the European provinces. Three years after this, he made his baton debut in London, directing a concert of the Queen's Hall Orchestra. This last experience, and the success that was his, told him that he was artistically prepared to undertake an important assignment. Digging into the Beecham fortune, he founded the New Symphony Orchestra.

*

Though a part of the Beecham fortune went into Sir Thomas' numerous musical undertakings, it would be a sorry mistake to say that he has bought his career. He has long ago proved himself to be one of the great conductors of our time, a remarkable interpreter of many different schools and styles. His solid musical scholarship (despite his inadequate schooling), discerning intellect, extraordinary musical instinct and feeling, and his capacity to make an orchestra a pliant instrument in his hands would have always insured him a glorious career.

His feeling for classic style—his capacity to play Mozart and Handel with purity and detachment—is matched only by his ardor in his performance of music by Berlioz or Tchaikovsky. He has brilliance and grandeur of expression—a capacity to set the orchestra aflame with color when the music calls for it. Yet his simplicity is one of his most ingratiating qualities when he treats the music of the distant past.

His conductorial manner is not one which can be imitated to advantage. At rehearsals he is likely to be fussy, unsystematic, given to making windy speeches, wasting time with pleasantries. His baton technique is the most complex among modern conductors. His mad gyrations of the body and head, and the throwing of his arms in all directions, have tempted one English critic to describe him as a "ballet dancer." The wonder of it is that his gesturing is not confusing to his orchestra.

But whatever his method, he gets results—and that is the only important consideration. His performances, when they are projected, are beautiful in their artistic finish, sense of proportion, lucidity. His orchestra is an eloquent instrument in his hands (and this is true whether he is conducting the New York Philharmonic or a WPA group like the New York City Symphony Orchestra). He is not equally great in all music: some of the modern scores, not of English origin, lack conviction in his hands; some of the classics, like those of Brahms and Schubert, do not soar to heights. But in numerous other works he is magnificent: in Rossini and in Wagner; in Mozart and in Handel; in Beethoven and in Delius. Speaking this music, he is with the great interpretative spirits of our time.

Pierre Monteux

Pierre Monteux has never received in this country that full measure of appreciation which has been his due. The critics have always been appreciative; and in recent years he has found devoted audiences in San Francisco. But an artist of Monteux's rank should have earned for himself the nationwide recognition that belongs to Stokowski and Koussevitzky—for, over a period of more than three decades, he has been among the elect of the baton.

He is not a spectacular figure on the stage. Short, stocky, he appears more like a French *Maître d'Hôtel* than an artist. His performances do not discharge fireworks. In place of dramatics, or excessive emotionalism, there is beautiful proportion, restraint, simplicity, profound musicianship. In some of the French literature for orchestra he is a master: to hear him perform the César Franck Symphony (for example) is to hear a masterpiece with the majesty of a Sophocles drama without the bluster and fake heroics so many other conductors bring to it. In modern music, his range is flexible, his judgment astute, and his appreciation sensitive. It should not be forgotten that he helped to create the musical history of our times by performing the world premières of such masterpieces as Stravinsky's *Petrushka* and *Le Sacre du Printemps,* and Ravel's *Daphnis et Chloé.* But even when he is not at his very best (and, to repeat, his very best can stand comparison with the great orchestral performances of our time) he is a musical interpreter who combines intelligence, discrimination, and scholarship. That he has not won for himself the adulation that attends so many other (and, in some cases, less gifted) conductors, is not easily understandable.

His latest achievement, in a lifetime cluttered with achievements, has been his reorganization of the San Francisco Symphony Orchestra.

This organization had come upon evil days when Monteux came to California: artistic and economic disaster had hit it simultaneously. Founded in 1911 under the sponsorship of the Musical Foundation of San Francisco, it was conducted respectably (but not inspiredly) by Alfred Hertz until 1929. By 1934, the orchestra—the permanence of which was not questioned during the Hertz regime—was shaken to its very foundations. The depression had cancelled some valuable sponsorship and contributions, making the existence of the orchestra precarious from one season to the next. And a series of guest conductors hardly succeeded in revitalizing it from its now lackadaisical state. During the 1934-35 season, the orchestra gave only four concerts; and these were made possible only because the municipality offered to pay all the bills. Evidently, a revolution was in order, if the orchestra was to survive.

Not one revolution, but several, took place. The first was the reorganization of the Musical Association of San Francisco to include several new, far sighted officers. The second was the acquisition of public support for the orchestra. The new Association began a vigorous and highly publicized campaign which resulted in a vote by the citizens of San Francisco for an amendment to the city charter whereby the orchestra would henceforth be supported by public funds. Its existence assured, a third revolution now overhauled its artistic policies. A conductor had to be chosen, whose experience and technical equipment was such that he could rebuild the orchestra in a short period. More than this, a world-famous conductor was needed, a conductor with a historic career behind him, to bring with him to the orchestra the lustre of his own fame.

*

Hardly a wiser choice could have been made than Pierre Monteux. Monteux's long activity with the baton had been of historical significance. He first achieved world fame as the conductor of the sensational Diaghilev Ballet Russe, which inaugurated such new directions not only for the dance but for music as well. He joined the group in 1911, and at once was assigned to prepare the world première of Stravinsky's *Petrushka*. He was well prepared for so exacting a task, having had many years of experience as a professional musician, besides possessing unusual conductorial qualities. Born in Paris on April 4, 1875 and a graduate of the Paris Conservatory where he had been a pupil of Lavignac and Berthelier (winning first prize in violin playing in 1894), Monteux acquired his first musical experiences as a member of a string quartet, then as violinist in the Colonne and Opéra Comique orchestras, then as chorus master of the Colonne Orchestra. A short season as assistant conductor of the Colonne Orchestra gave him the equipment with which to organize and direct his own orchestra, the Concerts Berlioz in Paris in 1911. It was his work with this organization which attracted the attention of Serge Diaghilev who, with his keen capacity for recognizing genius, saw at once that Monteux had the ideal temperament and technique with which to direct the forces of his adventurous ballet corps.

It was no sinecure—that conductorial post with the Diaghilev Ballet. The music of Stravinsky, which then burst on the world of music like a bolt of lightning, demanded an exacting technique. With its enormous rhythmic and harmonic complexity it called for all the resources of a conductor's science. That Monteux handled his task with complete competence and distinction has been attested to by no one less than Stravinsky himself: "He knew his job thoroughly, and was so familiar with the surroundings from which he had risen that he knew how to get on with his musicians—a great asset for a conductor. Thus he has been able to achieve a very clean and finished execution of my score." *

In 1912, Monteux conducted the première of Maurice Ravel's complete *Daphnis et Chloé* with the Diaghilev forces. One year later, he was again in the vanguard of modern musical history when he conducted the première of Stravinsky's *Le Sacre du Printemps*.

That, surely, was one of the most sensational evenings ever experienced by a conductor—the première of *The Rites of Spring*. The audience expressed its indignation at the music so hotly and volubly during the performance that it was frequently impossible to hear the orchestra. Saint-Saëns and the critic André Capu loudly denounced the work as a fake; Maurice Ravel, Florent Schmitt, and Debussy just as vehemently proclaimed it the production of true creative genius. The Austrian ambassador laughed loudly; a lady stood in her box and slapped the face of a man near her who was hissing; the Princesse de Pourtalès left her seat in indignation, exclaiming that this was the first time that anyone dared to make a fool of her. In the wings, Stravinsky was holding Nijinsky's collar to prevent the dancer from rushing on the stage and excoriating the audience for its stupidity. Claude Debussy frequently stood up in his seat and begged the audience to listen patiently and tolerantly. "Monteux threw desperate glances towards Diaghilev, who sat

---

* *Stravinsky: An Autobiography,* Simon and Schuster, 1936.

in Astruc's box and made signs to him to keep on playing. . . .
As soon as the first tableau was finished the fight was resumed.
. . . The second tableau began, but it was still impossible to
hear the music. . . . Everybody at the end of the performance
was exhausted."*

No doubt the extensive publicity gathered by the scandal of
Stravinsky's *Rites of Spring* was instrumental in throwing a
great deal of attention on its conductor. For the next year or
so, Monteux's fame grew, and he became busily engaged on
various conductorial fronts: He conducted at the Paris Opéra;
he founded and directed the Société des Concerts Populaires
at the Casino de Paris; and he became a frequent guest conductor in London, Berlin, Budapest, and Vienna.

When the first World War broke out, Monteux joined the
35th Territorial Infantry, and saw action at Rheims, Verdun,
Soissons, and the Argonne. After two years of heavy fighting,
he was officially released from his uniform to tour America
with the Russian Diaghilev Ballet and, through his music, to
spread propaganda in America for the French cause in the war.

*

From the very first, Monteux's career in America has not been
particularly happy. No sooner had he arrived than he became the center of controversy and the object of criticism
because of his provocative statement that he would under no
circumstance perform the music of Richard Strauss or that of
any other living composer from an enemy country. America
had not yet entered the war; and there were those music lovers
who were offended at Monteux's stand: Art, they said, had no
place in political or international controversies.

After a year at the Metropolitan Opera House, where he conducted the French repertory, Monteux went to Boston to be-

* Nijinsky, Romola: *Nijinsky*, Simon and Schuster, 1936.

come the permanent conductor of the Boston Symphony Orchestra. Ordinarily, this would have been a coveted assignment to reveal Monteux's conductorial talent to best advantage. But Monteux—traveling in this country under some unlucky star—had to work against imponderable odds. A general strike among the orchestra men to establish a union had proved unsuccessful, and twenty of the leading musicians resigned. The orchestra Monteux conducted was, therefore, not the great Boston Symphony of the Karl Muck era but a sad approximation of the same. Despite the difficulties facing him, Monteux did well: his concerts were admirable both for the vitality of his programs and the musicianship with which they were presented.

In 1924, Monteux—who never achieved the popularity commensurate with his gifts—was succeeded in Boston by Serge Koussevitzky. Returning to Europe, he once again dominated the orchestral scene abroad by founding and conducting the Paris Symphony Orchestra, and by giving admirable guest performances with most of the great European orchestras. In 1928, he returned to America for a guest period with the Philadelphia Orchestra. Once again, the untoward fate which seemed to dog his footsteps in America, impeded him. The audiences—perhaps too dazzled by their own Stokowski to have eyes and ears for any other conductor at that time—were apathetic, though the critics spoke most eloquently about his talents. The indifference to his performances inspired Monteux to remark acidly that American symphony orchestras were interested only in "slim, well-tailored conductors."

At that time, he said he was through with America, which had no place for true talent minus sensationalism. He returned to his many engagements in Europe determined never again to seek his fortune across the ocean. But in 1935, the San Francisco Symphony Orchestra called him, and he was tempted into making one more effort in breaking down American indifference to his art. To a certain extent he has succeeded: Not only in San Francisco, but with the NBC Orchestra which he launched by conducting its first concerts, he received greater appreciation and understanding. But the acclaim that he deserves is not yet his, though it is reasonable to believe that a musician of Monteux's outstanding capacities and gifts cannot permanently be underestimated.

New Batons for Old

1

John Barbirolli

When John Barbirolli first came to conduct the New York Philharmonic, in 1936, the skeptics told him that he would not last in New York longer than one season. He was assuming a job too big for him, they said. It was impossible to succeed in Toscanini's post without inviting comparisons. Such comparisons had proved death blows to the New York careers of conductors more experienced and of greater international repute than Barbirolli. Besides, the New York music public was said to be the most spoiled audience in the world. It had had ten years of Toscanini, whom it had apotheosized. It was unthinkable that it would now accept as substitute a young Englishman of comparatively little experience with orchestras, whose very name had, for the most part, been unknown in America one year earlier.

And yet, Barbirolli stepped into Toscanini's shoes with comparative grace, and he proved successful enough with his audiences to earn a three-year contract as principal conductor. And when that three-year contract was terminated, at the close of the 1939-40 season, still another awaited his signature.

For from the very first, the Philharmonic directors, the orchestra men, and the subscribers all took to Barbirolli. They seemed to make no attempt to compare him with an incomparable predecessor. They estimated him on his own merits alone, and found him acceptable. They liked his personal charm, his obvious sincerity, his youthful enthusiasm, his simplicity, his musical gifts. If he was no Toscanini—well, they argued (with a tolerance which was never expected in New York) where *could* you find another Toscanini, anyway?

You can ascribe Barbirolli's unexpected success in New York, however, much more to his own tact and astuteness than to New York tolerance. Other conductors, coming to the Philharmonic, immediately tried to set themselves as a counter-attraction to the idolized Arturo. They conducted from memory; they flaunted their idiosyncrasies; they tried to magnetize the audiences with their personal fire; they attempted to impress them with unusually spectacular platform mannerisms. And in competition with Toscanini, they always emerged second best in the eyes of Philharmonic audiences. But Barbirolli made no effort to pit himself as a rival against the greatest conductor of our generation. If he had been selected to step into Toscanini's shoes, he would not spend too much disconcerting thought on the immensity of such an assignment. He would, rather, only think of the task he had in hand, namely, to present symphony concerts which would please and interest a discriminating audience; and he would perform that task to the best of his abilities. "I forced myself to forget that I was supposed to succeed Toscanini," he confided at the time. "I said to myself: 'Look here, Tito. You've been hired to do a job. Do it as well as you can, and let the devil take the hindmost'."

With such an attitude he won the admiration of the orchestra men with his very first rehearsal. After he had been introduced by the manager, he made a short and modest speech. I do not recall the exact words, but the theme was as follows: "I have been appointed to succeed Mr. Toscanini, who is the greatest conductor of our time. No one knows better than I do, my own shortcomings and deficiencies in assuming such an assignment. I would be a fool if I were to try to be another Toscanini. I've got a job here to conduct concerts, and I'm going to try like the very devil to do the best I can with that job. I hope you will help me, for, God knows, I shall need your help." After that, the musicians were all for him—and half his battle was over.

Though Barbirolli made no such introductory speech to his audience, it sensed at once his honesty and self-effacement, and liked him for it. Here was a conductor who made no attempt to conduct from memory, or without a baton; who did not try to flaunt his eccentricities in the face of his public. Music, and not self-aggrandizement, seemed the first consideration with the newcomer. He addressed himself to his music with apparent sincerity and artistic devotion. And for all this, Barbirolli earned the respect and admiration of his audiences.

*

That the audiences of the Philharmonic have always kept a warm spot in their hearts for Barbirolli became particularly evident during the centenary season when, returning to his post after a brief hiatus, he was given a regal welcome. But not even his most devoted admirers will say that he is not without disturbing blemishes as an artist. He has many positive qualities which are admirable: warmth of feeling, enthusiasm, energy, a love for his work, an excellent taste. His baton technique is efficient. He knows his orchestra well. But there are, unfortunately, notations to be made on the other side of the ledger. If he has energy, it is not controlled and disciplined—in the way, say, that Koussevitzky controls his. Barbirolli permits sonorities to get out of hand to a point of distortion; his climaxes are his master, and not vice-versa. He is too impetuous, too hot-blooded, too ardent for much of the

179

music he directs; a little more English reserve and ice would serve him handsomely.

But there is a far greater fault to be found with Barbirolli. He is too often superficial in his readings. He glides over the surfaces of a work like an adroit skater. There may be smoothness and dispatch, but it is only surface work. A deeper, richer note of profound understanding rarely manifests itself. What he gives us, too often, is a fluent enough "reading" of a work, not a penetrating and dissectingly analyzed interpretation.

Not that Barbirolli is without marked talents. He has a native flair for conducting; his musical gifts are many and pronounced. When he first came to the Philharmonic, I felt confident that here was a conductor who would surely develop into greatness, given the necessary time in which to grow and mature. But Barbirolli has not yet developed into a great conductor, though several years have already passed; and there have not been perceptible growth and maturity.

The explanation for this lies with his Philharmonic job which, from the first, was too much for his capacities. Had Barbirolli been permitted to work with an orchestra less pretentious than the Philharmonic, he would have had ample opportunity to give his talents full scope, and to evolve and develop with the experiences he received. But the Philharmonic is most certainly not an orchestra with which a conductor can grow. The extensive repertoire demanded by a full season of concerts—four concerts a week—demands the services of a conductor who has already arrived at the zenith of his powers. The necessity to conduct so much music that was new to him, including so many world premières (the truth was that even some of the classical symphonies Barbirolli had to conduct with the Philharmonic were new to him!), week in, week out has encouraged in Barbirolli a greater and greater superficiality.

He simply did not have the necessary time to subject all this new music to the intensive study that was required, and he did not have the required background and lifelong experience to help him in this task. When he rehearsed many works, therefore, he merely touched upon spasmodic pages; and when he performed them he betrayed more than once that he had only a slight understanding of the music at hand.

Some music he has played beautifully—the Elgar *Enigma Variations*, for example, has given a fair indication of his genuine ability. Barbirolli is one of the best accompanists in the business. But, regrettably, he is still more promise than fulfillment. When he is at the head of the Philharmonic, this great orchestra is no longer one of the great symphonic organizations of the world. It goes through the paces of musicmaking; but the drive, dynamic urge, electrifying vitality, and gorgeous tone textures are simply not there.

*

Those qualities which have been found so meritorious in Barbirolli's conducting—his warmth, exuberance, vitality, simplicity of approach, are also the personal qualities which have endeared him to his friends. Though Barbirolli is English by birth, he is more Latin than English by temperament. It is largely for this reason that his most intimate friends have nicknamed him "Tito." His fullness of heart, lack of reticence, abundance of feelings remind one of the Latin countries. When he greets his intimate friends, it is not with an aloof Nordic handshake, but more often with an effusive embrace, sometimes coupled with kisses on the cheek. He is capable of extraordinary attachments; he always carries with him snapshots of his nephews and nieces which he proudly exhibits. Towards his close friends he has a vein of tenderness which is touching. I recall that at one of his Sunday afternoon concerts there was a delay of several minutes because, at the last moment, a thought occurred to him. He rushed a messenger to his box to bring down to him one of his more personal young friends. When the friend reached him breathless, Barbirolli took his hand, and said warmly: "I want you to know that I am playing this symphony for you. I am speaking to you through this music." Then, with this message delivered, he waited until his friend had returned to the box before he stepped out on the stage for his performance.

Even his palate is more Italian than English. His favorite haunt in New York is a small and intimate Italian restaurant near 60th Street and Central Park West. He eats sparingly, because his health compels him to follow a diet. But he likes good food, particularly well-spiced Italian dishes washed down with a glass of Chianti wine. He is extraordinarily fond of spaghetti, though he does not permit himself frequent indulgence. He says he finds consolation in his abstinence from this favorite food by occasionally cooking some for his friends and watching their delight in tasting his Milanese sauce, one of his culinary specialties.

But "Tito" is also very much the Englishman, very much the young man from Bloomsbury, where for many years he had his London apartment. He has the Englishman's characteristic suave manners and poise, his ready wit, his flair for the neatly turned phrase. He has the Englishman's passion for cricket matches. His English tailor sees to it that he is always dressed with English reserve: The cut of his clothing is conservative, the colors discreet; his favorite get-up is a dinner jacket and striped trousers which he wears even for informal affairs, and which fit him despite his short and stocky build. Above all else, he has the Englishman's allegiance to his country. In the last war. he unhesitatingly enlisted in the army to serve his country. He would have done so again in this war, but for the fact that high government officials convinced him that he could serve England better with the baton than with a gun. At any rate, he patriotically returned to England in the spring of 1942 to conduct its principal orchestras in many concerts, refusing to accept even traveling expenses.

His home is literally cluttered with musical scores, books, and *objets d'art,* of which he is a devoted collector. He is a demon for work. During the music season, his activities occupy his time from early morning until late at night. He rises early, partakes of a meager breakfast (his only meal until evening), then at once leaves for his morning rehearsal. When there are no rehearsals, there is no relaxation in his activities. Manuscripts and musical scores must be studied; there are people to see, letters to write, and a thousand and one other details that absorb the time and energies of an important conductor.

Some of his best work is done late at night. A poor sleeper, he long ago abandoned fighting insomnia by having it serve him. He can study two manuscripts in the middle of the night in the time it takes him to read one during the day. Sometimes he likes to spend his sleepless hours orchestrating a piece of music of which he may be particularly fond: His excellent orchestral transcription of Bach's *The Sheep May Safely Graze* was written at one sitting late one night.

He is a veritable whirlwind of energy. It is an endless source of wonder to those who meet him, and momentarily try to keep pace with him, how he can maintain such a furious activity from early morning until late at night without much relaxation. The truth is that, when he does snatch an hour of relaxation, he has the capacity to divorce himself completely from his problems. At such moments, he likes to read medical books (one of his curious hobbies) or light fiction. Sometimes he will participate with members of the Philharmonic in informal performances of chamber music. Most often, he will take a brisk walk in the park, holding the hand of his wife as he walks.

His wife is Evelyn Rothwell, a well-known English musician in her own right, formerly an oboist of the Scottish Orchestra. This is his second marriage; concerning the first—an unhappy affair almost from the beginning—he prefers to remain uncommunicative. He met Miss Rothwell while conducting one of the English orchestras. Impatient with the performance of the oboist, he demanded a substitute. Somewhat apologetically he was told that the only available substitute was a woman. Barbirolli exclaimed that he did not care if it was a giraffe, just as long as the oboe part would be played satisfactorily. The woman was called for, and she played for Barbirolli. It was a case of love at first hearing. She played with such beauty of tone and grace of phrasing that Barbirolli was enchanted. "After that, I knew I would fall in love with her." Later on, Barbirolli became principal conductor of the Scottish Orchestra and was thrown into daily contact with its oboist. His friends first suspected that Barbirolli had fallen in love with Evelyn Rothwell, when they learned he was composing a concerto for oboe and orchestra; when a cellist composes a concerto for oboe, there is more in it than meets the eye. Because of the complicated legal technicalities in Great Britain involving divorce, Barbirolli could not marry Miss Rothwell until recently. Since then, they have been as happy together as two schoolchildren, and are practically inseparable.

*

Like Toscanini, Barbirolli came to the conductor's stand by way of the cello section of an orchestra. He still loves the cello above any other instrument, though he rarely finds the time in which to play it. Whenever an eminent cellist appears as soloist at a Philharmonic concert, Barbirolli furtively steals away the virtuoso's instrument and, disappearing into his own rest room, proceeds to play on it for several precious minutes. Gaspar Cassado, the Spanish cellist, once complained to a friend: "It's always that way when I have to appear under him. *I* have to play a difficult concerto on the stage, but *he* spends ten minutes before the concert limbering up *his* fingers!"

Both his grandfather and father were professional musicians. His grandfather had been a violinist in an opera orchestra which had included among its members a young cellist named Arturo Toscanini. His father was also an orchestra violinist. They were both employed in the Empire Theatre Orchestra in London when John was a child. Often he was brought to rehearsals and, seated on the floor near his father's foot, he would listen to the music without making a sound. Somewhat later, he asked for a musical instrument of his own, and was given a violin. He was changed by his father from a violin to a cello because he had acquired the habit of pacing the room nervously while practising, which his father felt would be detrimental to his health; and a cello would keep him rooted to one spot, and seated into the bargain.

As a child, he was fascinated by music: His childhood hero was a bandmaster who performed in a local public park. When he was ten years old, he won a scholarship for the Royal Academy of Music in London. He was an excellent pupil. One year after entering the school, he was able to make his official concert debut by performing the Saint-Saëns Concerto at Queen's Hall.

The World War was instrumental in transforming him from a cellist to a conductor. Shortly before the war broke out, he was engaged as cellist in many different orchestras, accepting any and every assignment that came his way. "It wasn't long before I had played everywhere except in the street. Theatres, music halls, cinemas, in opera, orchestra, and chamber music— I went right through the mill."

Then, for the years of the war, he served in the English army. When the war ended, he found that the posts he had vacated were filled. There seemed no room for him in London's musical life (though, for a while, he did serve as cellist in a well-known string quartet which toured Europe). Many other musicians were in a similar plight. Then an idea occurred to him. He would gather some of these unemployed musicians about him into a chamber orchestra and would direct them in concerts of unusual and rarely heard music. Thus the Barbirolli Chamber Orchestra came into being. Its public concerts were so successful from the first that, within a year's time, its conductor was known well enough to be called upon at a last moment to substitute for Sir Thomas Beecham at a concert of the London Symphony Orchestra. At this concert, young Barbirolli gave such a good account of himself (in a particularly exacting program that included the Elgar Second Symphony) that he was given engagements for guest performances with several leading English orchestras. These, in turn, brought him an important affiliation with the two leading London orchestras (the Royal Philharmonic and the London Symphony), and also with Covent Garden where he conducted an extensive repertory of French and Italian operas. In 1933, he received his first important permanent post as conductor of two major symphony orchestras, the Scottish Orchestra and the Leeds Symphony.

Such was his history before he came to New York. It was not a particularly fabulous history, and hardly one which might be expected to culminate with the acquisition of the most coveted conductorial post in the world. Truth to tell, Barbirolli was practically unknown in this country when the announcement of his appointment as Toscanini's successor in the spring of 1936 struck New York music circles like a thunderbolt. It was a well known fact that any one of a half-dozen world famous conductors would have given their right eye for the job; yet it fell into the lap of a comparatively obscure and inexperienced musician.

There were no dark and mysterious forces at play in bringing Barbirolli to New York, as was so often hinted at first; only sound common sense. The directors were eager to have a progressive young musician at the head of the Philharmonic, one whose career still stretched in front of him, so that he might grow with the orchestra and become an inextricable part of it. In short, they wanted to develop a conductor expressly for the Philharmonic, whose allegiance and devotion would belong exclusively to it. Toscanini suggested Barbirolli's name, and several other famous musicians (who had played under him in England) spoke well of his talents and promise.

This is the entire story. And its epilogue, already told in an earlier paragraph, is equally succinct: Where other and far more celebrated musicians had failed, this young Englishman had succeeded. With all his faults, he won his audiences decisively enough to remain principal conductor of the Philharmonic for six years. And—despite the rain of critical denunciation which descended upon him in recent seasons—he was invited to remain a Philharmonic conductor for the 1942-43 season.

*

A long and regal dynasty of conductors marks the history of the New York Philharmonic from its founding fathers to John Barbirolli. In its first years—the Philharmonic was born a hundred years ago—the orchestra was directed by several different conductors at *each* concert. Not until 1865 was the full authority of leadership to be invested in one man: Carl Bergmann, who for ten years previously had shared his baton with Theodor Eisfeld. As I have written elsewhere,* Bergmann's "long tenure of the post might suggest that he was popular—which, to be truthful, was not the case. He was too scrupulous and honest a musician to resort to cheap devices for pleasing an audience. He was too vigorous and uncompromising a champion of the music of Wagner and Liszt—two composers who were generously disliked. The New York music public never quite took to him. Even the press annihilated him for his experiments. . . . The audiences, and the box-office receipts, remained small during the twenty years of Bergmann's office as conductor. More than once it seemed certain that the orchestra, which had staggered through one season, would not survive the next. In 1876 Bergmann was displaced."

Things did not go too smoothly for the Philharmonic during the first decades of its existence. If one of the musicians of the orchestra had a profitable engagement on the evening of a rehearsal, he would send a substitute, or, more often, would simply stay away without further rehearsal. When the absentee was a violinist or a cellist, the rehearsals could proceed without interruption. But if a reed or a wind player stayed away, the conductor was at a loss to proceed with his rehearsal in the face of a gaping hole in the orchestral texture. When coming to a rehearsal, the conductor always scanned the faces of his men eagerly to be sure that all the essential members were there. If all the reeds and winds were present, he would go out of his way to thank them for their kindness in coming.

Musicians did not even have qualms about staying away from

---

* *Music Comes to America,* by David Ewen, Thos. Y. Crowell Co., 1942.

an actual concert if they had assignments elsewhere. More than once the conductor was compelled to make a last minute change in the orchestra—assigning a solo clarinet part to the violin, or a solo bassoon to the cello—because these performers were earning more money that evening at a wedding or a dance.

Often, to fill out his ranks, the conductor hired special musicians only for the public concerts. These musicians performed in the orchestra without the benefit of a single rehearsal, since it was simply impossible to find the necessary funds with which to pay rehearsal fees. A conductor might rehearse a symphony with painstaking care only to have his performance disintegrate at the concert because the flutist or horn player had his own definite conception of the tempo or phrasing which he did not take the trouble to impart to the conductor beforehand. As late as 1900, Walter Damrosch lamented the unhealthy condition of the Philharmonic. "I found to my amazement that of the hundred players at the concert less than fifty were actual members of the organization, the rest being engaged from outside, often changed from one concert to the next. Some of the members were old men who should no longer have played with the orchestra. Most of the wind instruments were outsiders and therefore could not be properly controlled regarding attendance or rehearsals." *

The orchestra struggled for sheer existence; and its musicians with it. The income the musicians drew from public concerts was hardly compensatory for the work they put into it: the high mark of the first fifteen seasons, for example, saw the distribution of $143 to each musician for the entire year (the orchestra was operated cooperatively). Musicians fell from the ranks because they could not afford to remain; many of those who remained were too old to procure lucrative posts else-

* *My Musical Life,* by Walter Damrosch, Charles Scribner's Sons, 1923.

where. And the response of the audience was none too cordial, even after the Bergmann regime. One season, directed by Leopold Damrosch (which saw the American première of the third act of *Siegfried*), the total income of the orchestra for its entire season of concerts was $841!

Yet the orchestra persisted season by season, held together for the most part by a few faithful musicians, growing slowly but perceptibly. After the first season, four public concerts were decided upon for the next season. After the sixteenth season, the number of concerts was increased to five; in 1869, to six.

Dr. Leopold Damrosch's season in 1876 marked the lowest ebb in the history of the Philharmonic. It was doubtful then whether the Philharmonic would not completely disintegrate after that year. The income of $841 meant that there were no profits to distribute to the musicians; they had worked an entire year without remuneration. Many musicians began to speak of abandoning the adventure once and for all. Some of them, as a matter of fact, had offers to join the profitable Theodore Thomas Orchestra which was touring the country. In 1877, Theodore Thomas was called upon to become conductor of the orchestra—a last effort to save the orchestra from extinction. Thomas remained with the orchestra until 1891. His popular appeal and reputation brought about an increased income for the orchestra from the $1,641 average of the Bergmann regime, to the annual average of $15,000.

And yet, the Philharmonic stood on uncertain feet. By 1900, the six season concerts once again began to show a deficit; once again there was talk of disbanding. Early in 1903, Walter Damrosch proposed a plan to acquire financial backing in order to establish the Philharmonic on a permanent basis; but this backing was predicated on a thorough reorganization in which the older men would be replaced by new blood. His offer was politely turned down, because the older men refused to vote themselves out of a job.

In place of reorganization, the Philharmonic offered an expansion of program. It featured a great European conductor at each of its concerts. For the next three years, eight major conductors of Europe were invited to direct the eight different concerts of the Philharmonic season. The greatest personalities of musical Europe came to the head of the Philharmonic, including Felix Weingartner, Richard Strauss, Max Fiedler, Eduard Colonne, Ernst Kunwald, and Vassily Safonov.

But it was soon recognized that permanency for the Philharmonic—and artistic distinction—could not be realized until the orchestra was thoroughly overhauled. The standards of the orchestra were as lax as its personnel was uneven. In 1907, the first attempt at rehabilitating the Philharmonic took place. A sixteen-concert season was entrusted to the permanent direction of Safonov. Two years after this, a group of energetic women procured a large guaranty fund with which to establish the orchestra once and for all on a firm basis. Gustav Mahler was invited to take over the direction. He exerted his authority ruthlessly, replacing older men with younger ones, enriching the repertoire, and raising the artistic standards of each concert immeasurably. The orchestra, for so many years insecure and uncertain of its very existence, had at last acquired stability. Henceforth, it was to play host to some of the greatest conductors of the world, and under their direction was to become one of the world's great symphonic organizations.

2

Eugene Ormandy

The same period which saw young Barbirolli replace Toscanini witnessed the succession of another young and comparatively inexperienced conductor to one of the greatest orchestral
posts in America.

Eugene Ormandy's career offers at least one forcible proof
that American orchestra audiences have grown up during the
past decade. A career such as this, beginning with a post in a
motion-picture theatre and culminating with the directorship of
the Philadelphia Orchestra, would have been impossible twenty
years ago. In those days of hero worship in the symphony hall,
a new conductor who did not have a brilliant career behind
him (preferably a brilliant European career) had little hope of
attracting attention. His gifts were of little consequence if he
sprang from humble musical origins.

But gradually the tastes of symphony audiences in this country became cultured. With it came a deflection of interest from
the performer to the music itself. What the audiences now
clamored for was a concert of great music performed with dignity; they had acquired a sufficiently fine sense of musical
values to be capable of making their own judgments. Any
conductor capable of providing beautiful music-making was
given honor regardless of his background; while not even a
well-recommended European personality could now hope to
catch the passing fancy of the American public if his reputation
were not accompanied by a talent of high order.

When Leopold Stokowski announced his resignation from the Philadelphia Orchestra in 1936, there were those sombre skeptics who felt that the organization was now doomed. Stokowski, idol of Philadelphia, had identified himself so intimately with the orchestra that it seemed impossible for Philadelphia's prime musical and artistic venture to survive without him. Or, if it were to survive, another conductor would have to be found with Stokowski glamour and genius—say, a Toscanini, or a Koussevitzky.

It is known that several world-famous conductors (Wilhelm Furtwängler among them) made a strong bid for the post which, from the points of view of remuneration and prestige, was a coveted one. Yet the appointment fell to a young man of comparatively insignificant background and training: Eugene Ormandy, a graduate from the movies and the radio. Ormandy had no European triumphs to dramatize him to his audiences. His experience, measured by the yardstick of a career like Furtwängler's, was of no great moment. Yet, strange to say, Philadelphia audiences were not alienated from their orchestra by the appointment. The crowded houses that had heard Stokowski remained to listen to Ormandy. And passing favorable judgment, they remained for his concerts week by week.

Ormandy's success in Philadelphia is, of course, a great tribute to his capacity to make his concerts attractive even in comparison with those of his adulated predecessor. There was nothing anticlimactic about Ormandy's performances. His programs were always fresh and inviting; his interpretations revealed authority and imagination. But Ormandy's success is even a greater tribute to the audiences of Philadelphia, who did not permit his comparative obscurity—or their former devotion to Stokowski—to prejudice them against the pronounced conductorial gifts of the younger man.

It was a temptation, not easily resisted, for the new conductor of the Philadelphia Orchestra to expropriate some of the tried methods which made his predecessor such a sensational figure; particularly if the new conductor admired his predecessor as much as Ormandy did Stokowski. Yet much to Ormandy's credit, he made no attempt at becoming a carbon-copy Stokowski. Certain similarities between Stokowski and Ormandy have frequently been pointed out. They both have taken flattering notice of the modern composer; they both have featured extensively orchestral transcriptions of music by Bach; they both conducted from memory. But these are slight links with which to handcuff the two artists. Essentially they are opposites.

By temperament modest and retiring, by training a student (he finished university courses in Budapest for a doctorate in psychology) sensationalism is alien to Ormandy. If he was to win his audiences, he would have to win them in his own manner.

At rehearsals, his musicians saw a quiet, soft-spoken drill-master who worked efficiently and methodically, and who was never given to antics, pranks or eccentricities. After all those years of working under the unpredictable Stokowski, the Ormandy rehearsals appeared to the men placid and restful. What impressed the men particularly was the sureness with which Ormandy attacked his work. His knowledge of the orchestral repertoire seemed all-embracing.

At the concerts, audiences saw a rather reserved and unostentatious musician, dedicating himself exclusively to his music. No speeches—prepared or spontaneous; no playing up to the spotlight; no stirring of a hornet's nest with the branch of some sensational dictum. The Stokowski concerts might have offered greater adventure, but with Ormandy music once

EUGENE ORMANDY

ERICH LEINSDORF

again assumed the only starring role. It was obvious that he had no intention of purchasing his success with counterfeit coin, but only with the legal tender of great music.

His personal life has been as unsensational as his artistic; nothing there to feed the front pages. He lives, together with his wife Steffi Goldner (a professional harpist, formerly a member of the New York Philharmonic) in a spacious and comfortable home in a suburb of Philadelphia. They were married in 1921, a few months after Ormandy's arrival in America, and many years before his success.

He likes to play ping-pong and tennis (as a matter of fact, some years ago he won an amateur championship in tennis in Europe). He devotes himself to photography, his favorite hobby; then, when the urge for excitement comes, he will go motoring in his car at breakneck speed. Beyond these interests, his world is the world of music. He confesses that of all his pastimes, his greatest pleasure comes from poring over the pages of a new, interesting score.

When he works on a new score, he likes to sprawl on the floor on his stomach, and commit the music to memory. He memorizes easily—it is for this reason (and not for display) that he has always conducted his concerts from memory. His is a peculiarly tricky memory which photographs the unimportant with the essentials. He rarely forgets anything, however insignificant. Once in Minneapolis he reminded an offending piccolo player that three years earlier—in a different city, in different music, and under a different conductor—he made the same peculiar, but not particularly noteworthy, mistake in phrasing. Ormandy at the time was in the audience, but he never forgot the mistake. In the same way, the smallest details of a score—markings that so many others might consider as insignificant—are vividly clear in his mind; and this familiarity

195

with details enables him to be painstakingly meticulous about every element of a musical work.

Once when Rachmaninoff was soloist under Ormandy, he asked for an hour and a half rehearsal with the orchestra. However, the rehearsal went so smoothly that not once did Rachmaninoff ask Ormandy to review a passage; instead of an hour and a half, only thirty minutes had been required. "You know," Rachmaninoff told Ormandy, "I have played my concerto under most of the great conductors of our time. This is the first time in my life I ever could play a rehearsal without any stops whatsoever."

No incident could better illustrate Ormandy's diligence in preparing a musical work for performance: He had rehearsed the orchestral accompaniment for Rachmaninoff's concerto so comprehensively that when the time came for Rachmaninoff to join the orchestra no further corrections or changes were necessary. This same thoroughness has always characterized his performances, and has been one of his impressive virtues as a conductor. One has always been conscious of the careful study and preparation that went into his performances. Even when his readings failed to move the listener, it was not because of careless projection, but because he was yet too young to sound a deeper and profounder note.

Besides his careful preparation there were other qualities highlighting his talent, even early in his career. In 1932, Olin Downes already spoke of Ormandy's "healthy musical sense . . . temperament, and a conductor's flair for effect." But even more important than these qualities has been Ormandy's capacity to grow and develop as an artist. As he acquired experience his talent has grown richer and deeper. His performances today have a greater intensity of feeling, deeper musical penetration, greater command of style, subtler moods, and a more elastic span than when he first took over the Philadelphia Orchestra. And he continues to disclose new facets to his interpretative art with each passing season.

It is a different Philadelphia Orchestra we hear today under Ormandy than the one we knew with Stokowski. The ravishing Stokowski tone is Stokowski's secret, and not to be emulated by any other conductor. With Ormandy, the Philadelphia Orchestra has greater sobriety, less lustrousness of color, greater mellowness. But it remains a great ensemble. It has not experienced any essential deterioration with Ormandy. This, perhaps, has been Ormandy's greatest achievement. To replace a conductor like Stokowski, who brought the orchestra to a position of regal magnificence, and to maintain the standards established by his predecessor, called for a talent of the highest order.

*

In the face of what Ormandy has accomplished, and in the face of his extraordinary conductorial gifts, it becomes difficult to remember that his experience was first acquired in the Capitol Theatre, a motion-picture house in New York. He tells us that the schooling he received there was rigorous and comprehensive, such as he could have acquired nowhere else— and, in view of his phenomenal technique and self-assurance, we are inclined to believe him. "We played good music— movements from the great symphonies, and even such modern classics as Strauss' *Till Eulenspiegel*. And, mind you, since each week we performed every work about twenty times, we had an almost incomparable opportunity to learn the music with intensive minuteness. After all, a conductor of a symphony orchestra does not play, say, *Till Eulenspiegel* twenty times in as many years! And so, by conducting each masterpiece twenty times or so in succession over a period of seven days—and doing this for years—I acquired a repertoire, and acquired it by learning each note in the score by heart."

Ormandy had first come to the Capitol Theatre as an orchestra violinist by chance; and it was chance, too, which gave him his first opportunity to conduct its orchestra. Born in Budapest on November 18, 1899, he was a child prodigy who gave great promise of a brilliant future as violinist. At the age of one and a half he could identify any one of about fifty musical works by listening to a few bars. A few years later, he gave unmistakable indications of possessing an ear for perfect pitch: He attended a violin recital which he suddenly disturbed with a childish cry to the performer that "you played F-sharp instead of F-natural!" At four, he began to study the violin—an eighth size instrument of fine quality being built especially for him. He took to it as naturally as if he had been born with the instrument in his hands. One year after this, he became the youngest pupil ever to enter the Budapest Academy. He became a student of Jenö Hubay, after whom, incidentally, he had been named (Jenö is Hungarian for Eugene). "My lessons with the great Hubay filled my days with work and with dreams. My fingers were numb from the exercises of Kreutzer and Cramer, and (later) the showpieces of Vieuxtemps and Sarasate." He learned with such rapidity that, when he was seven, he was encouraged by his teacher to make his concert debut, which he did with considerable success. When Ormandy was fourteen, he graduated from the Academy with the Master's degree, six years younger than any other recipient of a similar degree. It had required a special decree of the Ministry of Education to get him the diploma because of his age.

Though, for a period, he was professor of the violin at the Academy, he aspired not for a teacher's career but for that of a virtuoso. Several tours in Central Europe convinced him that he had pronounced gifts which could appeal to audiences. He dreamed of extending the sphere of his concert successes. It was at such a moment that an enterprising impresario came to him with a contract to tour America. Fabulous America, which paid such idolatrous homage (and such lavish fees) to the Mischas, Saschas, Toschas, and Jaschas of the violin, seemed to offer a happy hunting ground for a young musician with swollen ambitions. Ormandy eagerly signed the contract. With high hopes, he sold his last possession to pay for the ocean voyage, and arrived in America—penniless.

In America, Ormandy discovered that his impresario had overstressed his managerial capacities. The proposed extensive American tour had evidently been only the wandering fancy of a too vivid imagination. Ormandy learned that his contract had no validity whatsoever, that, as a matter of fact, the impresario had discreetly disappeared. Ormandy now found himself in a new, strange country, without funds or friends.

One day he was standing on the corner of 50th Street and Broadway with only five cents in his pocket. He was hungry. He did not know whether to invest his last coin in some food or in carfare back to his room. He chose to satisfy his stomach. He was about to prepare himself for a long hike home when an acquaintance from Budapest stumbled across him. He gave Ormandy a loan, and with it some valuable advice. Erno Rapee, also a native of Budapest, was holding an important music post at the Capitol Theatre in New York—then the leading motion-picture house in New York. Why did not Ormandy apply to him for a job? Playing in a theatre orchestra was not precisely the fulfillment of Ormandy's artistic dreams. Yet it meant a salary and an end to want. Ormandy approached Rapee, and was accepted for the violin section. In a week's time, Ormandy graduated into the concertmaster's chair. He acquired a certain measure of fame as a member of the famous Roxy "gang" over the radio (under his original name of Eugene Ormandy Blau), playing favorite virtuoso numbers on his violin as a regular feature of the popular weekly program. Eventually, he was assigned to some conductorial duties as fourth assistant to the principal conductor, David Mendoza (both Rapee and Roxy had, meanwhile, left the Capitol Theatre for the new cinema palace nearby, the Roxy Theatre). One day, Mendoza was taken ill, and Ormandy, on a fifteen-minute notice, took over the baton, conducting a movement from the Tchaikovsky Fourth Symphony from memory. His performance made such a deep impression that at once he was promoted to first conductor. For the next seven and a half years, Ormandy was principal conductor at the Capitol Theatre. During this period, he acquired an extensive repertoire, not only through actual performance of a wide range of classics, but also through the indefatigable study of innumerable scores which had become his favorite pastime for leisure hours.

*

If you have real talent, it is not always necessary to go out to conquer the world. The world will seek you out, wherever you may conceal yourself. Ormandy's friends had told him that he was virtually committing artistic suicide by devoting himself to motion-picture theatre music. Once a motion-picture theatre conductor, they said, always a motion-picture theatre conductor. Yet good work does not ever pass permanently unnoticed. Before long the word was shuttled that excellent musical performances could be heard at the Capitol Theatre. W. J. Henderson, the music critic of the New

York *Sun,* singled out Ormandy for special praise in one of his columns. Then the famous concert manager, Arthur Judson, went to the Capitol Theatre, heard Ormandy, and decided to take the young conductor under his wing. He first gave Ormandy a contract to conduct the accompanying music for the Duncan Dancers, following the successful consummation of which he offered him some radio work. By 1929, Ormandy felt that he was well on his way toward achieving a certain measure of recognition in music—with the baton, if not with the violin. He resigned from the Capitol Theatre, and put himself in Judson's hands.

From this moment on, his rise was rapid. A brief engagement with the Philharmonic Symphony at the Lewisohn Stadium during the summer of 1929 was followed, in the summers of 1930 and 1931, by summer concerts with the Philadelphia Orchestra at Robin Hood Dell. At the same time, Ormandy conducted regular orchestra concerts over the air through the Columbia Broadcasting System network.

Then came the opportunity which established his reputation. Toscanini had been engaged to conduct a few guest performances with the Philadelphia Orchestra in the fall of 1931. An attack of neuritis compelled the maestro to cancel these performances at the last moment. Desperately, the directors of the Philadelphia Orchestra sought a substitute for these concerts. One conductor after another refused to accept the assignment, feeling that to substitute for Toscanini would invite unwelcome and damaging comparisons. The offer was made to Ormandy, and, in spite of well-intentioned advice, he accepted it. His friends expected that his performances would be subjected to violent criticisms by audiences and critics who had been led to expect Toscanini but instead were forced to play host to a radio and motion picture theatre conductor.

201

They counted, however, without Ormandy's natural gifts, his capacity to give a musicianly exposition of the music he conducted, his powers to dramatize without reaching for vulgarity, his ability to electrify his audiences. From that moment on, Philadelphia was for him.

It was this success in Philadelphia which brought Ormandy a contract from the Minneapolis Symphony Orchestra to become its permanent conductor.

*

The Minneapolis Symphony Orchestra originated as an auxiliary group to a choral society. The orchestra, conducted by Emil Oberhoffer, was at the time pretty much of a haphazard affair: Often, one group of musicians would attend the rehearsal, while another would come for the actual concert. Such a state of affairs was not long to be tolerated by Oberhoffer. In 1903—with the aid of Elbert L. Carpenter—a subsidy of $30,000 was raised to support a permanent orchestra of fifty musicians as an independent musical body in Minneapolis. The first concert, on November 5, 1903, featured a varied assortment of musical bon-bons (the most substantial item of which was the Schubert *Unfinished Symphony*). Oberhoffer, who conducted the orchestra until 1921, was a good musician who achieved a considerable following; it was largely through his effort that the orchestra was established on a permanent basis. In 1905, a new concert auditorium (modeled after Symphony Hall in Boston) was built for the orchestra—its permanent home for the next twenty-five years. Finally, in 1930 the orchestra transferred its habitat to the Northrop Memorial Auditorium on the University of Minnesota campus (which could accommodate 4,000) and, under a special arrangement, the orchestra became a part of university life.

Oberhoffer was neither an inspiring nor a profound conductor. Like his successor, Henri Verbrugghen (conductor in Minneapolis from 1923 to 1931) he was conscientious, sincere, hard-working—with all the qualities of a fine conductor except that of genius. The Minneapolis Symphony, therefore, achieved respectability and a certain degree of artistic prestige in the West; but it was by no means one of the country's great orchestras when Ormandy, then only thirty-two years old, took it over.

But Ormandy possessed at least one gift which had been foreign to both Oberhoffer and Verbrugghen—the gift of transforming an orchestra. His five years in Minneapolis remoulded the orchestra into an ensemble commanding respect. He reshaped it, drilled it with inexhaustible patience, and created a wonderfully balanced organization. The extensive repertoire he instituted—freshened by the introduction of many new works—called for virtuosity and flexibility on the part of the orchestra, and a great technique on the part of the conductor. Both orchestra and conductor rose to meet all the demands of the music: and, thus, a great symphonic ensemble was evolved. It now operated on an annual budget of a quarter of a million dollars—the expense involved not only by its many local concerts, but also by its extensive tours throughout the mid-West. Half of this budget was defrayed from the income; the other half came from contributions from private sources.

Ormandy's achievements in Minneapolis placed him in the front rank of American conductors. When, therefore, Stokowski decided to call it a day in Philadelphia, the directors of the orchestra (encouraged by Stokowski's advice) shrewdly decided to place the fate of the orchestra in the young, energetic hands of a conductor whose career still stretched before

203

him. Ormandy's contract in Minneapolis still had one year to run; but the directors of the Minneapolis Orchestra—recognizing the fact that a great post was awaiting Ormandy—generously decided to release him. Ormandy had won his first successes in Philadelphia some years earlier. These successes, and those which now attended him as permanent conductor, were no temporary and evanescent flashes. In 1938, Ormandy's permanency in Philadelphia was assured once and for all when he was given the Stokowski post of "music director" together with that of conductor. From now on, Ormandy's word—like that of Stokowski before him—was law: his decisions, judgments, and musical plans could no longer be vetoed by any higher officer.

Having established himself irrefutably as the major young conductor in America, Ormandy proceeded to make a name for himself in Europe. He came to Vienna as guest of the celebrated Philharmonic, and then—preferring to have the odds against him—he featured the music of Mahler. Vienna had heard Mahler's music under Mahler himself, then under the batons of the greatest Mahler interpreters such as Bruno Walter and Richard Strauss. It was not likely to listen too tolerantly to a young American conductor discoursing Mahler's music. But Ormandy performed with such dignity that Vienna acclaimed him; he had won his triumph in Vienna the hard way. Then, in Linz—at the Bruckner festival—he substituted for the ailing Bruno Walter at the last moment, and conducted his concert from memory. Other European performances further confirmed his talents and powers. To have swept away the prejudice of European audiences to American-trained musicians—and to have swept it away so decisively—was by no means the least striking of Ormandy's achievements.

3

Erich Leinsdorf

When, early in 1940, the newspapers throughout the country publicized the hostility which had arisen at the Metropolitan Opera House between Wagnerian soprano Kirsten Flagstad and the brilliant, young conductor, Erich Leinsdorf, there were many who apprehensively feared that the brief and sensational career of Leinsdorf at the Metropolitan was coming to an untimely end. Flagstad threatened to resign unless Leinsdorf was replaced; and she underlined her threat by a temporary boycott of all Metropolitan performances. "Mr. Leinsdorf," she exclaimed, "is inexperienced in playing Wagner. He watches the music. I see his arms moving. But I can't tell where the music is." Lauritz Melchior joined with Flagstad in a raucous duet of condemnation. "Leinsdorf," he shouted, "is not yet ready to be senior conductor of the finest department of the greatest opera house in the world."

Leinsdorf had already proved himself—to the audiences of the Metropolitan at any rate—to be a conductor of unusual talent. Only musical gifts of the highest order could have brought him to the most important conductor's post at the Metropolitan at an age when other conductors are neophytes. But Flagstad was the greatest drawing card the Metropolitan has had since the days of Enrico Caruso, and Melchior was likewise a box-office attraction of no mean significance. It was generally felt, therefore, that Edward Johnson, director of the Metropolitan, had no choice but to yield to the gods.

That the 1940-41 season of the Metropolitan found Erich Leinsdorf still at his post as leading conductor of German opera, spoke eloquently for the courage of Edward Johnson in sticking by him. He came to Leinsdorf's defense by deprecating "some old boats in the company who would like to be dictators of the Metropolitan." "The operatic art and this institution are greater than they," he announced contemptuously, "and these will be here, along with Mr. Leinsdorf, long after the old boats have gone. . . . Mr. Leinsdorf will be so acclaimed in a few years that they won't want to remember that they opposed him."

The following week, anger was still at such white heat that Melchior, appearing under Leinsdorf in *Götterdämmerung,* wore his eagle-winged Norse warrior's helmet backwards. Incidentally, at that performance, it was Leinsdorf, and not Melchior, who received an ovation from the audience after the second act. Eventually the storm blew over; Flagstad and Melchior must have realized that they were on the losing side of the war, what with Johnson, the public, and the critics fighting for Leinsdorf. The gods of the Metropolitan's Valhalla resigned themselves to their fate. At the conclusion of a performance of *Die Walküre,* Melchior and Leinsdorf shook hands publicly on the stage. A few weeks later, Flagstad returned from her self-imposed exile. The entire episode would have been forgotten by now—but for one significant fact: It proved that Leinsdorf's position at the Metropolitan is secure. And it is secure because he has proved himself to be one of the greatest baton discoveries in some three decades of opera-making in New York.

*

Such a storm was inevitable—even if it had not been created by Flagstad's desire to bring a conductor of her own choosing to the Metropolitan. Destiny, in the shape of Artur Bodanzky's sudden death, placed in Erich Leinsdorf's hand the entire Wagnerian repertory when he was less than twenty-eight years old; some of these music-dramas he had never before conducted. It was not the happiest or most idyllic of assignments. A conductor must, above everything else, exert his authority —and this was not easy for a very young, and comparatively untrained conductor, if the singers under him had become world-famous as Wagnerian interpreters. If a young conductor permits himself to be influenced by the artists under him, not much can be said for his artistic convictions, nor can he expect much respect. If, however, he has definite ideas about the music he directs, from which he can not be shaken by the weight of the reputations of those working under him, but only by the truth of their interpretations, it is not a simple task for him to impose those ideas on seasoned artists—not if he himself is young and raw.

This was the problem facing Leinsdorf. To exert his will, on singers like Flagstad and Melchior, carried with it almost a suggestion of impertinence. Yet he had too much honesty, too strong a feeling of his own concerning the music, too keen an analytical mind to cater to his artists by subjecting his own ideas to revision only because these artists wished him to do so. Temperaments and artistic tastes rubbed against each other —and there were sparks.

How much justification was there to Flagstad's severe criticism of Leinsdorf? True, Leinsdorf was young and inexperienced, but these were not particularly important disadvantages in the face of his obvious talent and his capacity to grow and develop with every performance. Flagstad said that Leinsdorf's eyes were in the music in front of him, and not on the artists. Actually, in some of the Wagner music-dramas, Leins-

dorf rarely consults the music, so well is he acquainted with
the score. In other dramas, which he was called upon to direct
for the first time (he conducted *Parsifal* for the first time in
his life on twelve-hour notice!) it was to be expected that his
memory should lean heavily for support on the score, at least
for his first few essays. The wonder of it was, rather, that he
did show such familiarity and command of the music as he
did, a familiarity and command which became increasingly
apparent with each presentation.

At times, also, his tempi were erratic, sometimes to a point
of disturbing the singers (was this not, on occasions, equally
true of Bodanzky?). He was sometimes stubborn in his conceptions, overruling the ripened judgment of long-experienced
artists. But these are not formidable faults by any means, not
when there also came to play his insight, his high artistic purpose, his enthusiasm, his natural gifts for conducting. If
Flagstad did not have a definite axe to grind on the stone of
this controversy, it is doubtful if Leinsdorf would have caused
her more than mild irritation to which she would have been
tolerant.

For the most part, it can be said that Leinsdorf handled a
vexing situation diplomatically. Those who saw him rehearse
realized that he was not at all above listening to advice and
criticism; when he was at fault, and it was called to his attention, he displayed humility. He treated the great singers
under him with respect which was evident even when he insisted on exerting his authority over them. What he refused
to do was to revise his own judgments of the way the music
should be played, when he was convinced that his judgments
were the correct ones. Most of the artists who worked with
him were won over by his charm, youthful zest, sincerity, and
remarkable intelligence. In his battle against Flagstad and

Melchior they were all for him—just as director Edward Johnson, the audiences, and the critics were for him.

*

Leinsdorf's history up to the present time is climactic with strange victories, of which the one over Flagstad was only a single example. If, as his most enthusiastic supporters insist, Leinsdorf gives indication of developing into another Toscanini, you are likely to hear recitals of his achievements more frequently as the years pass. He was only twenty-six years old when the Metropolitan Opera House engaged him as a conductor to assist Artur Bodanzky in the performance of the German repertory. At an age when other conductors are cutting their first artistic teeth, he was assigned to conduct the most exacting music in the operatic repertory—the music-dramas of Wagner—at the most celebrated opera house in the world.

His background was well-known to American music audiences when he first came to New York. Born in Vienna on February 4, 1912, he showed unmistakable musical gifts at an early age. His father's death, when Erich was still very young, brought the family face to face with pressing financial problems. But his mother would not hear of his abandoning his study of music, even though his attendance at the Vienna Academy meant great deprivation for herself and the rest of the family. Young Leinsdorf justified his mother's faith in him by proving himself—under a variety of teachers, including Paul Emmerich, Hedwig Kammer-Rosenthal, and Professor Kortschak—a piano pupil of brilliance.

Determined on a career as conductor rather than pianist, he decided to contact and interest Bruno Walter. In the summer of 1934, he walked the 155-mile distance from Vienna to

Salzburg, and while still dusty and tired he entered the Festspielhaus to listen to a rehearsal of *Fidelio* by Bruno Walter. At one point, Walter left the piano to consult with an artist. Leinsdorf suddenly was inspired to strike boldly and vigorously. He slipped onto the stage, went to the piano, and continued playing the music of *Fidelio* (from memory) from the point where it had been interrupted. This exhibition made such a deep impression on Walter that young Leinsdorf was at once engaged by him to assist in preparing his Salzburg performances.

That same winter, Toscanini came to Vienna to conduct a series of symphony concerts. A pianist was needed for Kodály's *Psalmus Hungaricus*. None seemed available (possibly because so many Viennese pianists were terrified at the thought of playing for Toscanini). Leinsdorf came to the rehearsal, asked for a hearing, and played the music with such competence and distinction that Toscanini smiled broadly, and whispered: "Good—very good." Not only was Leinsdorf engaged for the piano part for that concert, but the following summer he worked with Toscanini, as well as with Bruno Walter, in preparing some of the festival performances at Salzburg.

To rehearse the Toscanini and Walter productions was a prodigious task. Often young Leinsdorf had to be in four different places in one afternoon—practicing with the orchestra, directing the chorus, working with soloists, and consulting with the stage director. But the job did not overwhelm him. He would travel from one place to the next, sometimes by bicycle, other times by foot (he did not have the money for taxi fares) and in each new place he would throw himself into his work with as much vim and enthusiasm as though he were just beginning the day. Toscanini told his friends that summer that Leinsdorf's preparations were so painstaking and exhaustive that, when he himself took over, there was little more to do than to apply the final artistic touches.

Leinsdorf hoped to become a conductor at the famous Vienna Opera. Both Toscanini and Walter recommended him for the post. Unfortunately, because anti-Semitic forces were at play, he was rejected by the Ministry of Fine Arts. Although the Opera of his native city turned him down, the rest of the music world stood ready to accept him. Besides collaborating with Walter and Toscanini at the Salzburg festivals, he assisted at several performances during the May Music Festival in Florence, in May, 1935. I recall being in Florence at that time, where one of the most striking performances was that of Gluck's *Alceste* in the Boboli Gardens. One afternoon I was with one of the leading Italian conductors, and told him how much I admired the *Alceste* performance. It was then that he told me about a young man named Leinsdorf who had assisted in its preparation. It was the first time I heard the name, and it impressed itself on my memory because the Italian maestro spoke of the young man as a "born conductor." "Remember the name," the Italian told me. "He reminds us all here of Toscanini, when Toscanini was first conducting in Italy."

The fall and winter of 1936 Leinsdorf spent in Bologna, Trieste, and San Remo directing symphony concerts as well as opera. And, early in 1937, he set out for New York.

It was, therefore, a creditable, though not necessarily epic, background which Leinsdorf brought with him to the Metropolitan. Those who came to his New York debut, therefore, hardly expected to hear much more than a promising, talented, but possibly still immature conductor, who had come with Toscanini's blessings and praises. Very promising, talented, but immature conductors were not particular novelties there. . . .

It was something of a shock to operagoers that January eve-

211

ning in 1938 to see a mere boy on the conductor's platform about to direct a magnificent cast in the complicated music of Wagner's *Die Walküre*. As he took his place, about to give his opening beat, he appeared as self-conscious and diffident as a boy wearing his first long trousers at a party. It was an even greater shock to discover that this youngster had the music, so to speak, in the palm of his hand. As the musical drama unfolded, it became increasingly evident that there was much more than a good memory at work on the conductor's platform. There was a forceful personality, which, despite youth, could command and be obeyed. There were taste and feeling, and a coherent conception of the work at hand.

The Leinsdorf saga was developed at the Metropolitan. During the first season he directed thirty-six performances and acquitted himself nobly. He had been at the Metropolitan a season and a half when Bodanzky fell ill and left him the task of rehearsing the entire German repertory for 1939-40. Leinsdorf disclosed such a masterful command of the music, and, single-handed, fulfilled his duties at the rehearsals with such quiet self-assurance that, when Bodanzky died six days before the opening night of the new season, Leinsdorf was chosen to succeed him as principal Wagnerian conductor—one of the most demanding assignments in the entire field of conducting.

His first year in this important capacity at the Metropolitan —when he officiated at fifty-five performances—was as impressive an achievement as you are likely to find in the entire history of conducting. It will be recalled that during that year there was no perceptible decline of artistic standards in the Wagnerian performances at the Metropolitan. That alone could speak volumes for a young director who overnight inherited such a formidable conductorial position. But one can say much more than this of Leinsdorf's first year as principal

212

conductor. Though there were occasional minor technical lapses in his conducting (and these were to be expected) there were also vitality, charm, musicianship; in certain respects, his performances at times had greater freshness and vitality than those of Bodanzky.

No wonder, then, that there were some now to speak of Leinsdorf as "young Toscanini," just as the Italian conductor had described Leinsdorf to me in Florence. The parallel between the two conductors is striking even after one has pierced beyond superficials. Leinsdorf and Toscanini both made their debuts at a tender age: Toscanini at nineteen, Leinsdorf at twenty-two. Both were still very young when they were given major assignments. Toscanini became principal conductor of a world-famous opera house (La Scala in Milan) in his thirty-first year; Leinsdorf assumed a similar post with another great institution (the Metropolitan) when he was twenty-seven. Both Toscanini and Leinsdorf proved their true worth in the Wagnerian repertory, and both refused to be constricted by any one style or school by conducting works in the French and Italian repertoire as well (one of Leinsdorf's outstanding achievements, for example, has been his performance of *Pelléas et Mélisande*). Toscanini combined his work as conductor of opera with remarkable performances of symphonic music; Leinsdorf, too, has coupled his operatic conducting with excellent guest appearances with major symphony orchestras.

In one respect the parallel grows even more striking; for history has a curious faculty of repeating itself. Toscanini was principal conductor at the Metropolitan a full year when the security of his position was momentarily shaken by the threatened retirement of soprano Emma Eames, who felt that her temperament clashed so violently with that of the young Italian maestro that she could not work with him. Emma Eames was,

213

at the time, at the height of her fame. It was felt by some
that it might even be necessary to dismiss Toscanini in order
to keep the glamorous soprano at the Metropolitan. Gatti-
Casazza, however, stuck by Toscanini, and early in 1909 Emma
Eames made her last Metropolitan appearance. It should not
be difficult to find in this historic feud a similarity, even in
details, with the Flagstad-Leinsdorf feud, even though Flagstad's resignation was not a direct outcome of the quarrel.

*

It is Leinsdorf's consuming love for music that most reminds
me of Toscanini. Like Toscanini, Leinsdorf—whether at work
or not—lives music, breathes it, perspires it. In the presence
of great music he melts. There are passages in Wagner and
Richard Strauss which bring tears to his eyes, even while he
is in the heat and strain of directing them. At other times,
he sings—as with stick he draws a lyric line from the strings
of the orchestra—because he simply cannot control himself.
You must see him at his piano at home, going through an
opera score, to realize how music absorbs his every fibre. As
he plays the piano part, and sings every major role, you become
aware of his extraordinary enthusiasm, zest, and love for what
he is doing. Perspiration bathes his face and body. His shirt
begins to cling to his armpits and shoulders. His eyeglasses
slip from the ridge of his nose and become clouded with mois-
ture. But he is altogether oblivious to his discomfort. He
forgets that there is anyone at his side. He is immersed in his
one-man projection of a mighty music drama. He plays the
piano part musically, which is to say that for the realization
of the composer's intentions he is often willing to sacrifice
digital accuracy. He sings the different parts with a wonderful
instinct both for histrionics and the flow of the lyric line. And
yet, when he is through with a scene or an act, what remains

most memorable is not the musical quality of the performance, which is outstanding, but the bubbling, oozing, geyser-eruption of the performer's enthusiasm.

It is this all-absorbing love for music that gives him his phenomenal capacity for work. Hard work does not exhaust, but stimulates him; the greater the assignment placed in his hands, the more is he energized. His first year as principal Wagnerian conductor at the Metropolitan placed a colossal burden on his shoulders, which would have brought collapse to many more experienced conductors. Not only did he have on his hands all the rehearsals and performances of the Wagnerian repertory (which, because of Flagstad's popularity, dominated the Metropolitan season) but he even had to study several scores which he had never before directed. During that first year, he had to add to his repertoire *Die Meistersinger, Tristan und Isolde, Götterdämmerung,* Richard Strauss' *Der Rosenkavalier,* Debussy's *Pelléas et Mélisande,* and Gluck's *Orfeo!* He was kept at work from early morning until late at night, Sundays included. Yet that was one of the happiest years of his life. His spirits were keyed high, and physically he was in the pink of condition. At the end of that strenuous year, he laughed at the suggestion that he might need a vacation—and plunged into the study of some new scores. "You know," he once said, "a two-hour cocktail party exhausts me more than studying an entire new operatic score."

His integrity, too, has the Toscanini trademark. He has stuck to his principles, and has never been tempted to make compromises with his conscience. I need recall only one example of his integrity; there have been others. He was engaged to conduct the New York Philharmonic for one week at the Lewisohn Stadium during the summer of 1938. There is no young conductor who would not give his right eye for a Stadium assignment which, often, proved to be a convenient springboard from which to dive into a comfortable post. Eugene Ormandy practically began his career with these summer concerts, and so did Iturbi. The young Italian, Massimo Freccia, graduated from the Lewisohn Stadium to the Havana Symphony Orchestra. A success at the Stadium might have meant much for Leinsdorf at the time, since his post at the Metropolitan had not yet been made secure by the occasion of Bodanzky's death. And yet, because he could not at the time get the number of rehearsals necessary for a comprehensive preparation of his programs, Leinsdorf quietly and unostentatiously declined to conduct. He had no sympathy with half measures. If he could not give the best of himself at his performances, he preferred not to conduct at all.

The Dynamic Conductor

1

Fritz Reiner

Our feverish times are more likely to produce the intense, passionate conductor given to nervous and agitated performances rather than one of calm detachment and serenity. These dynamic conductors are vivid personalities who brand the music they interpret with the flame of their individualities. As Virgil Thomson pointed out so admirably, for these conductors "every piece is a different piece, every author and epoch another case for stylistic differentiation and for special understanding. When they miss, they miss; but when they pull it off, they evoke for us a series of new worlds, each of these verifiable by our whole knowledge of the past, as well as by our instinctive sense of musical meaning. Theirs is the humane cultural tradition. And if their interpretations have sometimes been accompanied by no small amount of personal idiosyncrasy and a febrile display of nerves, that, too, is a traditional concomitant of the sort of the trance-like intensity that is necessary for the projection of any concept that is a product equally of learning and inspiration." (Quoted from the New York *Herald Tribune.*)

Fritz Reiner, conductor of the Pittsburgh Symphony Orchestra, belongs unmistakably to these "Dionysian" spirits of the baton. He has the red blood of vitality; all his performances glow with healthy and athletic energy. His is a natural bent for theatrical music calling for brilliant orchestrations and exciting climaxes. Here his wonderful technique, and his exhaustive knowledge of the orchestra, as well as his temperament, are exploited fully. Thus he is excellent in Wagner, in Richard Strauss, in Berlioz, and in the music of most modern composers. Thus, too, he is one of the most gifted opera conductors in America today, and it is to be greatly regretted that he has not been given greater opportunities to reveal his gifts in this direction. In the theatre, even more than in the symphony hall, he reveals himself a master over all the forces under him. In the theatre, his personality finds its fullest scope for self-expression.

His interpretations, whether in symphony or opera, are generally spacious and robust; Reiner thinks along large lines and in expansive designs. Certain of his qualities are most admirable. He can be galvanic without sacrificing tonal balances; he can build dramatic effects with astuteness, and not yield to unpleasant exaggerations. What he does lack as an artist is some ice to contrast the fires; some contemplation to mellow the excitement.

He was born in Budapest on December 10, 1888, and his education took place in local schools (culminating with the study of law at the University) and at the National Academy of Music where he was a pupil of Thoman and Koessler. As was required of students at the Academy, he played in the school orchestra, his instrument being the tympani. One day the conductor was delayed, and Reiner was called upon to substitute for him. That moment Reiner knew that he would be dissatisfied with any future other than that of conductor.

The celebrated teacher and violinist, Jenö Hubay, took Reiner under his wing after the latter had graduated from the Academy and gave him personal instruction in conducting. Equipped with this preparation, Reiner accepted the post of chorusmaster at the Budapest Opera in 1909. One year later, he was the conductor at the Laibach National Opera, and a year after that at the People's Opera in Budapest. He developed rapidly; and as he developed, his reputation grew. In 1914, he was given one of the most desirable posts in Europe when he became first conductor at the Dresden Royal Opera. Here he revealed for the first time the full scope of his interpretative gifts. The Dresden Opera was one of the most progressive musical institutions in Europe, and it paid flattering attention to the modern reportory; in this reportory, Reiner attracted praise for the extraordinary energy and freshness of his readings.

The war made the cultivation of music difficult in Germany. Reiner went to Italy to conduct at the Teatro Reale in Rome and at the Augusteo. Guest performances during this period brought him to different parts of Europe. He was conducting the Wagner music dramas in Barcelona in 1922 when a wire reached him from his wife, then vacationing in the United States. The telegraph agents had obviously garbled the message and it was impossible for Reiner to guess the meaning. In desperation, he wired his wife that he could not unravel the meaning of her telegram, but that, if there was a decision to be made, he stood ready to abide by her judgment.

Thus Reiner came to the United States: for his wife had cabled him that the Cincinnati Orchestra offered him a post as permanent conductor; and she had accepted it.

Fritz Reiner remained eight years in Cincinnati* and proved himself to be a conductor of imperious authority, and (in some works) an interpreter of power and insight. His talent was highly thought of in Cincinnati, as well as in other American cities to which he frequently came for guest concerts.

After the 1930-31 season, Reiner passed his baton on to Eugene Goossens. Settling temporarily in Philadelphia, he became head of the orchestral department of the Curtis Insti-

---

* For the history of the Cincinnati Orchestra see chapter on Eugene Goossens.

tute of Music, and a frequent visitor to most of the leading American orchestras. He now proved his exceptional talent for operatic music by directing Wagner performances with the San Francisco Opera Company, a variety of opera from Gluck to Richard Strauss with the Philadelphia Opera, and several Wagner operas with the Chicago Opera. He also toured Europe frequently and extensively both in symphonic and operatic music: During the Coronation Festivities in London in 1936, he scored a particular success in a cycle of the Wagnerian music-dramas at Covent Garden.

In 1938, the Pittsburgh Symphony Orchestra was reorganized a second time, after a precarious existence of more than forty years. It had been founded in 1895, and from 1898 to 1904 was conducted by Victor Herbert who, though never a great conductor, helped to raise the program standards from what formerly were rather plebeian levels. Distinguished guests, including Richard Strauss, Sir Edward Elgar, and Emil Paur conducted the orchestra during the next few seasons. It was not, at best, a very good orchestra, as Richard Aldrich of the *New York Times* remarked when he heard it in 1907. "Its tone ... has neither fulness nor nobility. The violins sounded especially poor and thin; the wind choirs are reasonably good in most respects. But the ensemble was a little frayed at the edges, and there was not much of distinction or power in the playing."* Failing to fill any indispensable role in Pittsburgh, the orchestra expired in 1910 for lack of support.

In 1926, a few local musicians decided to reestablish the Pittsburgh Symphony. To test public reaction, a free concert was given under Richard Hageman's direction; the reaction was sufficiently favorable to encourage the sponsors of the orchestra to proceed with their plans. From 1927 to 1930, the new

---

* *Concert Life in New York,* by Richard Aldrich, Charles Scribner's, 1941.

organization was conducted by Elias Breeskin, and from 1930 to 1937 by Antonio Modarelli.

It was decided, in 1937, to reorganize the orchestra radically. Otto Klemperer was called from Los Angeles to reshape the orchestra and to direct the first few concerts. This done, one other move was necessary to give the orchestra high ranking. That move was made with the appointment of Fritz Reiner.

Reiner enjoys an enthusiastic following in Pittsburgh; the audiences admire him and are responsive to his electrifying personality. It cannot be said that the musicians who play under him are as affectionate as his audiences. High-handed, dictatorial, given to acidulous criticisms, Reiner (like Stokowski) treats his men severely without permitting a personal relationship to develop between conductor and orchestra. Yet, however much they dislike him personally, his men are never sparing in their praise of his gifts. Under him, they function like a smoothly oiled machine not only because of his extensive knowledge of orchestral literature and his comprehensive grasp of the orchestra, but also because he is one of the most fabulous baton manipulators of our time. "He leads an orchestra through the most complex technique with the ease and sureness of a tightrope walker who performs a backward somersault blindfolded," remarked Oscar Levant. His baton technique is so skilful and its demands are so clearly enunciated that (as one of his musicians is reported to have said) "you have to be an awful dope if you can't follow him."

In his orchestral classes at the Curtis Institute, Reiner places emphasis on gesturing. He himself has said that, after his pupils have worked with him and leave his classes, any one of them "can stand up before an orchestra they have never seen before and conduct correctly a new piece at first sight without verbal explanation and by means only of manual technique."

2

Artur Rodzinski

When the NBC Orchestra was organized for Toscanini in 1937, there was need for a conductor to whip it into shape. A great orchestra is not born overnight. Its virtuosity, the marriage of its choirs, its flexibility and resilience come only after a long period of practice and experience. But a conductor who is also a technician can often bring about these qualities to a marked degree even in a young orchestra. A technician was sought for the NBC Orchestra to do the preparatory work for Toscanini.

Toscanini suggested Rodzinski for the task, because Toscanini knew that Rodzinski had extraordinary organizational gifts, and one of the ablest orchestral techniques among American conductors. Rodzinski knows the orchestra, its strength and weakness. He knows how to blend and balance skilfully the different sections into a rich tone-texture. He knows how to give it permanent solidity. He knows how to adapt its technique pliantly to every requirement of orchestral performance. He can recognize weaknesses which might escape a less observant ear, and knows how to remedy them. Beyond this, he has unquestioned authority: the vibrancy of his personality can subject the men under him to his every wish.

The numerous rehearsal sessions during which the orchestra was trained by Rodzinski were a severe test for any conductor. Here were a hundred men, fine artists all, it was true, but men nevertheless who were playing together for the first time. To make a unified body of these different elements—one mind, one heart, one will, one purpose—and to do this in a brief period, called for the full resources of a conductor's science. Rodzinski met the test squarely. When Toscanini came to conduct the orchestra he gave expression to his delight. He had expected to confront many of the shortcomings of a new organization—a sharp-edged tone (not yet mellowed by time), an imperfectly integrated organism, a technique lacking exactness. But Rodzinski's spadework had been done so thoroughly that, instead, there was a developed orchestra, without any perceptible gaps, ready to serve the master, to respond to his most exacting demands. The NBC Orchestra—molded into a great orchestral ensemble within a few weeks—was a tribute to Rodzinski's orchestral mastery; there were few conductors who could have duplicated this feat.

Once before Rodzinski had proved his mastery: This was in Cleveland, when he was appointed permanent conductor of that orchestra. The Cleveland Orchestra was not an old orchestra, nor was it a great one. It had been organized by a few public spirited music lovers in 1918 (headed by Adella Prentiss Hughes), with Nikolai Sokoloff as its first conductor. Sokoloff was a good musician. To his credit belongs the fact that an increasingly fine standard was achieved at his concerts; also, that they appealed to an ever-growing audience. But Sokoloff worked, for the most part, with inadequate material, nor did he possess that very organizational capacity which could cope with such material successfully. His orchestra was not a good ensemble; it was definitely of provincial stature, with marked defections in various departments. And it did not become a great orchestra until Artur Rodzinski came to Cleveland.

About a year and a half after the Cleveland Orchestra entered its new home—beautiful Severance Hall, the gift of Mrs. J. L. Severance in memory of her husband—Sokoloff retired as its principal conductor. Artur Rodzinski was named his successor.

*

When Rodzinski came to Cleveland—it was in 1933—he was ripe for the major appointment of his career; for he had profited by many years of intensive apprenticeship with the baton.

His debut had taken place in Lemberg where, shortly after the end of the First World War, he had been engaged to conduct first choral music, then opera. "Sad to relate," Rodzinski recalls his first adventure with the baton, "during the rehearsal the musicians laughed at me. Came the intermission and the very kind concertmaster showed me the rudiments of beating three-quarter and four-quarter time. While I was holding on to this job, I took another playing the piano in a vaudeville house. I recall with merriment now (though it was no joke then) that once a dancer gave me a sound berating for spoiling her act. She called me a rotten pianist, and a worse musician."

Truth to tell, his musical education up to that time had not been comprehensive. He was born on the Dalmatian coast of the Adriatic Sea, in Spalato, on January 2, 1894, where his father, an army officer, was stationed upon a military mission. Law was chosen as the career for Artur. He was, therefore, sent to Austria for his schooling, completing it at the University of Vienna. He supported himself by tutoring backward students in mathematics and languages. Such hours as he could steal from his legal studies and tutoring he devoted to music. Music had attracted him magnetically since his childhood. But he had been compelled to follow it as an amateur. In Vienna he studied some theory by himself, took some music courses at the University, and spent most of his leisure evenings at the

226

FRITZ REINER   VLADMIR GOLSCHMANN

FABIEN SEVITZKY

ARTUR RODZINSKI   ALEXANDER SMALLENS

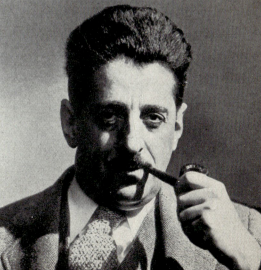

opera house and concert hall: this was the entire extent of his early musical education up to that time.

During the First World War, he joined the Polish army, fought on the Russian front, and was wounded in action. Demobilized, he returned to Vienna. The war had given him an entirely new perspective on his future. He knew now that it was music, and not law, which appealed to him most. He studied the piano with Sauer, and conducting with Franz Schalk. At the same time, he took courses in music at the University which brought him a doctorate.

He went to Lemberg for his first musical assignment. Then the progressive Lemberg Opera engaged him for a few performances. Evidently he had the capacity to learn quickly. The young and inexperienced conductor who had caused such merriment at his first rehearsal because of his ineptitude, gave such authoritative performances of *Carmen, Ernani,* and *Eros and Psyche* (a Polish opera) that the directors came to him with a contract as first conductor of the opera house. They asked him which operas he was prepared to conduct, and he answered with quiet assurance that he knew the entire Italian and German repertory. Actually, he had never even seen many of these scores. When he signed his contract for the following season, he devoted his time to a rigorous study of the classical operas. The following season he undertook an extensive repertory, frequently having to step briskly in his studies to keep one step ahead of his rehearsals. But he had an alert and receptive mind, a sound musical instinct, and an irrepressible enthusiasm for his work. He mastered the routine of the conductorial profession and acquired a sound technique.

He was invited for some guest engagements in various European cities, which he despatched with impressive self-assurance. He was then called to Warsaw to direct the famous Philhar-

monic, and to give an occasional performance at the opera
house.

He was conducting a performance of *Die Meistersinger* at
the Warsaw Opera one evening when Leopold Stokowski was
present in the audience. Stokowski recognized Rodzinski's
talent and urged him to come to the United States. Rodzinski
accepted Stokowski's invitation, arrived in 1926, and for three
years served as Stokowski's assistant in Philadelphia. During
these years, Rodzinski acquired the finishing touches to his conductorial training. Stokowski was a ruthless master; Rodzinski,
an alert pupil. By helping Stokowski prepare the Philadelphia
concerts, by directing the orchestral and operatic departments
at the Curtis Institute, and by assisting the performances of the
Philadelphia Grand Opera Company, he acquired a mastery of
conducting, and a command of baton technique.

During this period he was invited to serve as guest conductor
of several major American orchestras. At one of these appearances—in Los Angeles in 1929—he gave such an impressive
account of himself that he was asked to become permanent
conductor of that organization.

At that time the Los Angeles Philharmonic was ten years old.
Founded by William Andrews Clark, Jr., in 1919, it had been
conducted by Walter Henry Rothwell—a conductor of rich
experience—from its initial season until 1927. Under Rothwell the Los Angeles Philharmonic was not one of America's
great orchestras; but it gave respectable concerts of good music
which, if they never clutched at greatness, never on the other
hand offended sensitive musical tastes. Georg Schneevoigt
took over the orchestra from 1927 until 1929. After this, the
need for young blood was felt. Rodzinski came for some guest
appearances and made a profound impression. The direction
of the orchestra was offered to him, and he accepted.

Rodzinski was principal conductor of the Los Angeles Philharmonic until 1933. With each passing season, there was perceptible the growth and development of a fine artist; at the same time, a truly admirable symphonic organization was being evolved. In 1933, the Musical Arts Association of Cleveland engaged him as the permanent conductor of the Cleveland Orchestra. Rodzinski's contract in Los Angeles still had one year to run, but the directors generously freed him, and at the same time showed him their gratitude for his remarkable services to the Los Angeles orchestra by tendering him a banquet and a scroll. The post in Los Angeles was inherited by that admirable German conductor, Otto Klemperer.

Rodzinski's association with the Cleveland Orchestra had historic significance for that city. He developed one of the great orchestras in America out of a comparatively unimpressive ensemble. He enriched the repertoire with particularly flattering attention to the new works of modern composers. Recently he launched a notable experiment in the selection of new works for performance by the orchestra: New music is given an anonymous audition before a carefully selected committee; those compositions that receive the highest rating are selected for exhibition at the Cleveland Orchestra concerts. In this way, Rodzinski feels, his own personal prejudices and idiosyncrasies play no part in the selection of new works for his repertoire.

He has also introduced opera into Severance Hall, directing searching performances of *Tristan und Isolde, Parsifal, Der Rosenkavalier, Lady Macbeth of Mtsensk* (Shostakovitch), *Die Meistersinger, Elektra,* and *Tannhäuser* as part of the symphonic season. When he first introduced opera to his programs—it was in 1937 with *Parsifal*—the event immediately assumed such artistic importance that it attracted visitors from forty different cities! For these opera performances, Rodzinski recruited his principal singers from the Metropolitan Opera House. But it is interesting to note that he depended exclusively on local talent for the minor roles, feeling that it offered an enviable opportunity to encourage undiscovered singers in Cleveland.

That he had become one of the great conductors of our time was proved by the flattering assignments that now came his way. In 1936, he was invited to perform at the Salzburg Festival. When Toscanini heard his concert he exclaimed: "You do not need me any longer here. You now have him." The following summer he was a guest conductor in Salzburg, London, Vienna, Warsaw, and Prague. In the spring of 1937 he conducted an eight-week session with the New York Philharmonic, scoring triumphs with his performances of the last act of *Parsifal* and the complete *Elektra,* in concert versions. In the fall of the same year, he was called to New York to condition the newly organized NBC Orchestra. In 1938, he directed a Polish program at the Paris Exposition, and was awarded the *Diplôme d'Honneur.* In 1939, he directed another Polish program, this time in conjunction with the New York World's Fair. In June, 1941, he conducted the opening concert at the Lewisohn Stadium before the largest attendance in the history of these concerts.

*

One ideal is ever before him: that of democratizing music in America. "Music," he argues, "belongs to the people who hear it. Opera houses and orchestras should belong to the people." He hopes to see, some day, the elimination of patrons from all music-making in this country. At one time he suggested that each radio owner be taxed one dollar a year for the support of all musical organizations in the country—the fund to be administered by a special bureau in Washington.

For he is essentially a man of the people; he likes people; he likes to feel that he is one of them. There is no aristocratic aloofness about him. On his twenty-seven acre farm in Stockbridge, Massachusetts—where he leads the simple life of a farmer, dressed in overalls, and tending to his goats—he has a sign which reads: "Visitors Welcome." He does not mind the summer tourists wandering all over his place, casting an inspecting eye as he tends to his farming activities, poking around and literally stumbling over him.

His daily habits are of an almost ascetic simplicity. There is his farming in the summer. In the winters he reads a great deal, studies, and pursues the hobby of photography. He likes some sports, swimming and skiing particularly. Except for an infrequent brandy, he never drinks. His only real indulgence is smoking cigarettes, which he rolls himself from specially imported Egyptian tobacco.

On days of concerts, he usually spends hours in quiet seclusion, as if to fill in the reservoir of his physical and nervous strength, which is greatly sapped by every performance. He eats almost nothing—some toast and milk is about the extent of a full day's diet. After a performance he is usually so exhausted that he cannot find the energy to eat. Some time in the middle of the night, he will suddenly awake, and shout that he is starved. His dining table, covered with cold meats and pastries, awaits him. He gorges himself, and then returns to bed.

His wife, Halina, is the niece of the famous Polish violinist, Wieniawski. They have one son, Witold, who works at the NBC studios in New York City. Once Rodzinski stopped an elevator boy and spoke to him in Polish. He was later praised for his democratic spirit in stopping to speak with a mere elevator operator. "Why shouldn't I talk to him," asked Rodzinski, "if he is my son?" Rodzinski insisted that his son accept the humble position of elevator operator, so that he might learn the radio business from the ground up; whether he intended a pun in this, it is difficult to say.

The simplicity of the man is evident the moment he steps on the stage. He gives a passing gesture of recognition to the applause of the audience. Then, without further ceremony, he proceeds to direct the music of the day. His baton technique is the last word in unostentation. His beat is firm and clear; his movements are sparing; his directions to his men explicit. There are no extravagant rotations of the body or head. Rodzinski is an almost austere and unspectacular figure on the platform.

His command of the orchestra and his knowledge of all its resources make him particularly effective in music that is complex in design. Where a work is brilliantly orchestrated, where it has intricate rhythmic or harmonic constructions, where it demands expansive dynamics, in such music he is in his element. If he has versatility (and he can play many different styles well) it is not the versatility of, say, a Toscanini or a Bruno Walter. He is not the ideal interpreter of Haydn or Mozart, for example; his touch is too heavy for such fragile items. He is not completely at his ease in lyric pages that call for contemplation, introspection, or serenity. His Beethoven, therefore—particularly the Beethoven of the slow movements —frequently leaves much to be desired. But where the call is for vigor, dynamic drive, virtuosity of a high order, brilliant coloring, there Rodzinski stands with the great musical interpreters of our time. In Sibelius, Richard Strauss, Shostakovitch —in most of the modern composers for that matter—he brings vitality and power, wonderful blendings of sonorities, irridescent tonal colors. One recalls his electrifying and cogent recreations of such works as the Shostakovitch First Symphony or Richard Strauss' *Elektra,* in which works one is almost tempted to say that he is incomparable.

He is equally impressive in Scriabin and Wagner, in Berlioz and Rimsky-Korsakow, in Debussy and Tchaikovsky. In fact, his catholic musical tastes—he himself has no leaning towards any one style or school of music—give him a wide and plastic range to his interpretative gifts. "I like all good music," he has said. "The year it was written and the number of times it has been played mean absolutely nothing to me." In listening to his concerts, one recognizes the sincerity behind such a statement. He presents all music, whether it is in his happiest interpretative vein or not, as if he loved it. Even where he fails artistically, the failure is not the result of careless preparation or a lack of musical penetration; it is only because the music is not an expression of his temperament, and does not lend itself to his many talents as an interpreter.

3

Vladimir Golschmann

Others, besides Rodzinski, have created excellent orchestras out of unimpressive materials. Vladimir Golschmann, for example. Before he came to St. Louis, its orchestra was just another musical organization, undistinguished but serviceable; there were many such orchestras throughout the country.

It had had a long career. Its origin dates not from 1881 when, strictly speaking, it was founded, but more accurately from 1894 when it was reorganized along professional lines. Its principal conductors after 1894 were Max Zach (1907 until 1921), and Rudolph Ganz (1921 to 1927). It would be exaggerated enthusiasm to speak of the reign of either conductor as particularly fruitful, when comparison is made with other orchestras of the East. From 1921 until 1931, the St. Louis Symphony continued its existence with guest conductors. One of these, Vladimir Golschmann, made sufficiently striking an impression to be retained as a permanent fixture. Golschmann —young, spirited, adventurous, and experienced—was the tonic needed by a tired and dispirited orchestra; and under him the orchestra became rejuvenated.

Golschmann is the son of a noted writer, mathematician, and translator. He was born in Paris on December 16, 1893, and received his academic education at the Buffon College, and his musical training at the Schola Cantorum. He began music study by concentrating on the piano, then abandoned the piano for the violin because "there were too many pianists in the world." Then he preferred to concentrate on composition and theory. Actually, all the while he knew only one compelling ambition in music: to become a conductor. Like Koussevitzky he used to direct imaginary orchestras in play when he was a boy.

His schooling ended, Golschmann served as violinist in three major orchestras of Paris. He realized only too well that playing in orchestras was essential preparation for the career he had set for himself. When he was barely twenty-three, he joined a small orchestra of seventeen musicians, which included among its members José Iturbi, Lucien Capet, and Jacques Thibaud. The conductor of this ensemble was at one time unable to attend the performance and Golschmann was asked to substitute. This was his first experience with the baton; and it went well.

A wealthy music patron of Paris, Albert Verley, became acquainted with Golschmann and, on one occasion, begged him to try out for him on the piano some pieces which he (Verley) had lately composed. Golschmann, always a fluent sightreader, went through the music smoothly. "When you play these things of mine," Verley remarked, "it seems to me I can hear a full orchestra playing. Why don't you become a conductor?"

Golschmann confessed that that was the ambition of his life.

"In that case," answered Verley, putting a blank check on the table, "you can have your orchestra."

In 1919, therefore, Golschmann founded the Concerts Golschmann in Paris which soon proved among the most eventful concerts of the season. He placed emphasis on modern music (though the classics were not neglected), featuring particularly the work of the "French Six,"* and other modern spirits

---

* The *"Groupe de Six"* were MM. Darius Milhaud, Arthur Honegger, Francis Poulenc, Georges Auric, Louis Durey and Mlle. Germaine Tailleferre.

of French music. Frequently his concerts became the scene for scandals; hissing, verbal and fist fights, cheers, guffaws, reflected the varied reactions of the audiences. But these concerts were vital, pulsatingly alive. Because of Golschmann new music found a hearing; and through its dynamic performances, young Golschmann acquired fame.

He was invited to direct guest performances with many leading French orchestras; and—sign of his growing reputation—was singled out by the French government to become director of the *Cercle musical* at the Sorbonne University. Besides this, he arranged electrifying festivals of Ravel and Stravinsky music in Paris, took over the direction of the Diaghilev and the Swedish ballets, and toured all of Europe in guest appearances with the foremost orchestras. In 1928, he was appointed permanent conductor of the Scottish Orchestra in Glasgow and Edinburgh.

Meanwhile he made his reputation in America, first coming here in 1924 as the conductor of the visiting Swedish Ballet. He was invited by Walter Damrosch to conduct several concerts with the New York Symphony Society. He made an appealing figure on the stage; his music had (as Lawrence Gilman remarked) "vitality . . . power and intensity." Golschmann returned to the head of the New York Symphony in 1925. In 1931, after successful visits to St. Louis, Golschmann was given the post which kept him permanently in this country. Through this post, he has provided young composers everywhere a haven for their new works.

4

Fabien Sevitzky

Of the major American symphonic orchestras, the Indianapolis is one of the youngest. That it is by no means a provincial orchestra is proved by the facts that during the last five seasons it has broadcast about seventy-five times over the three major networks, it has made recordings for Victor, it has toured seasonally in about thirty cities in nine states, and it ranks with the Boston and Chicago orchestras in the percentage of first performances of American works.

It was founded in 1930 on a cooperative basis by Ferdinand Schaeffer, its conductor until 1936. But it did not become an orchestra of importance until 1937 when Fabien Sevitzky became its permanent conductor, and its support was transferred to a special organization founded for that purpose, the Indiana State Symphony Society. It is an orchestra of comparative youngsters: almost all the players are under thirty-five, and a good many of them are still in their early twenties. Seventy-two of the eighty-five musicians are American born; all others, except one, are citizens. This, then, is a young, enthusiastic, energetic American orchestra. And it is led by an enthusiastic and energetic conductor. It was inevitable for the orchestra to rise to national prominence.

Fabien Sevitzky has always felt that the first duty of every conductor in America is towards American music. Not even Koussevitzky, Stokowski, or Stock have sponsored the music of our composers more passionately than he. When he first took up a baton (in 1925) he inaugurated a policy for himself to which he has since adhered faithfully: that of including as least one American work on every program he conducted. He continued this policy when, in 1937, he came to Indianapolis. Of course, there are times when an all-Beethoven or an all-Tchaikovsky program made the inclusion of an American work artistically undesirable. But, in restitution, Sevitzky always directs at least one all-American program during the season.

He plays American music so indefatigably because he believes in it. "There is unlimited vitality, unlimited power and beauty in American music. . . . In modern American music there is much that is worthwhile, and some that is great. American composers have a right to a fair hearing by their compatriots, and I am doing my best to see that they get it."

About two hundred American manuscripts reach Sevitzky each season. He is scrupulously diligent about looking through every piece of music that is sent in to him. He is compelled to discard about half of the works as unsuitable for public performance. The other half he gives a reading at rehearsals. Those which stand the test of performance successfully are eventually selected for his programs. During the 1940-41 season he played thirty-two different works by twenty-five American composers; the season after that the average was equally high. In May, 1940, he inaugurated and conducted Indiana's first festival of American music which promises to be an annual affair.

In recognition of his efforts for American music, Sevitzky was honored in 1938 by the National Association of Composers and Conductors which designated him as having done a greater service for the American composer than any other single conductor. Also because of his contributions to American music, he has been given an honorary doctorate by DePauw University, the third such degree given by the University since its founding in 1837.

*

Fabien Sevitzky, a nephew of Serge Koussevitzky, was born in Vishni-Volotch, near Tver, Russia, on September 29, 1893. While he was still a boy he moved with his family to St. Petersburg. There he applied for the César Cui scholarship for the double bass at the Conservatory (because, as in the case of his uncle, no scholarship was open for any other instrument). He won the scholarship, studied under such masters as Glazunov, Liadov, and Rimsky-Korsakow, and was graduated in 1911 *magna cum laude* with the gold medal for double bass (the first time this coveted medal had ever been awarded for that instrument).

After his graduation he played in the orchestra of the Moscow Imperial Theatre. Then he toured Russia as a virtuoso, giving more than 150 concerts in six months. He acquired a reputation on his instrument second only to that formerly known by his uncle. In 1915, Sevitzky abandoned music temporarily to enlist in the army. He joined the infantry and during the war served at the front as a despatcher, a particularly perilous assignment. After the Revolution he went to Moscow, which now remained his home until 1922, playing in the orchestra of the state theatres and studying acting. For a while he actually fulfilled a few important roles as an actor in the movies and acquired a considerable reputation as an interpreter of character parts.

He escaped from the Soviet Union in 1922. After a harrowing experience (which he does not like to describe) he came to Poland. There, for eight months a year, he worked as double-bass performer in the orchestra of the State Opera and in the Warsaw Philharmonic. During the other four months he knew the privations of cold and hunger.

In 1923, shortly after his marriage, he sailed for America. That summer he toured Mexico and South America in joint concerts with his wife, a well-known singer (Maria Koussevitzky). In the autumn of 1923, Sevitzky joined the Philadelphia Orchestra as a double bass player.

His first venture at conducting was with a string orchestra— the first permanent string orchestra in the world, incidentally— which he founded in Philadelphia. The Philadelphia Chamber String Simfonietta toured the country giving excellent concerts of rarely heard old and new music. Besides his work with this group, Sevitzky gave guest performances with the Philadelphia Grand Opera Company, and the Pennsylvania Opera. The demand for his baton services grew so great that, in 1929, he retired from the Philadelphia Orchestra to devote himself exclusively to conducting. He settled in Boston where, from 1930 to 1935, he directed numerous organizations, some of which he himself had organized among young people. After 1930, he undertook several tours of Europe conducting the great orchestras of Paris, Berlin, Vienna, and Warsaw. He also directed many American orchestras in guest appearances, including the Philadelphia Orchestra, the Los Angeles Philharmonic, and the National Symphony Orchestra of Washington, D. C. In 1936, he was invited to Indianapolis, where he gave such an electrifying concert that he was given a thunderous ovation. One year later, he returned to Indianapolis—this time as the permanent conductor.

His forceful personality recreated the orchestra; it is acknowledged that the history of the Indianapolis Symphony Orchestra as a major musical organization actually dated from the moment Sevitzky took command. He built an orchestra of virtuoso caliber, youthful in spirit and age. He fired it with the flame of his own personality. His performances had verve and passion. His dramatized readings made concertgoing an exciting experience for Indianapolis music lovers.

*

Equable of temperament, Sevitzky is the answer to the orchestra's prayer: a conductor who is a friend to each of the men (he knows them all intimately) without sacrificing his authority. He is likeable, gentle in manner, capable of great affections. He has a ready sense of humor, and a quick, nervous laugh.

He speaks volubly, and usually with the heat of enthusiasm. (He prefers to classify his broad Russian accent as "Hoosier.") His conversations reveal his expansive range of interests which embrace literature, art, politics, and gastronomy.

He is capable of extraordinary passions. His one hobby is shooting: He is an expert skeet and trapshot, and has won many medals for marksmanship. The members of his orchestra recognized his interest in guns when they gave him a gift of a fine holster. In foods, he has an insatiable appetite for carrots. For eighteen years he has eaten carrots in one form or another for every lunch and dinner. In dress, he has an amazing partiality for ties. He has what is believed to be the second largest collection in America (the first largest belongs to Adolphe Menjou). His 980 ties come from every part of the world; and some of them have been woven according to his own designs.

He is interested in clothes, and is always well tailored. When he selects his day's wardrobe, he usually chooses his tie first, and then arranges his other clothing to harmonize with it. For his conductorial assignments, he has evolved a special evening dress which brings him comfort without making any sacrifices on his appearance. The secret for a conductor's attire, according to Sevitzky, is room for movement. His stage clothes are between one and two sizes larger than his street dress, and so cut as to provide him particular freedom in the movement of his hands and body without throwing his clothing out of shape. His stage shoes are high, with special support for arches and ankles. His stiff-bosomed shirt, fastened down in a manner originated by himself, withstands the most violent movements of Sevitzky's conducting.

5

Alexander Smallens

If Alexander Smallens is more the craftsman than the artist of the baton, it can at least be said of him that he is a craftsman of unusual skill. With his adept technique—and his flair for selecting the possible sore spots of an operatic performance and concentrating on them until they are remedied—he can, in short order, create a highly creditable performance. In a great variety of operas, ranging from Gluck to George Gershwin (his repertoire includes more than 150 operas, representing every school and idiom) he is able to produce a smoothly functioning performance in which everything proceeds in well-ordered fashion. It is for this reason that, though officially attached to no single opera house or symphony orchestra, he is probably one of the most active conductors in the country.

If there is an unusual first performance which might elude the experience and capabilities of other conductors, Smallens can always be counted upon to serve well. He has given the world, or American, premières of such diversified modern fare as Prokofieff's *Love of Three Oranges,* Richard Strauss' *Feuersnot,* Stravinsky's *Mavra,* Schönberg's *Pierrot Lunaire,* Virgil Thomson's *Four Saints in Three Acts,* and George Gershwin's *Porgy and Bess;* in at least three of these performances—the works by Prokofieff, Thomson, and Gershwin —the composers themselves designated Smallens for the conductor's post. If an opera performance has to be presented swiftly and efficiently, Smallens is the man most often called upon; he is probably the most active summer-season conductor in the world. Resourceful, intelligent, versatile, a master of all the technical resources of the baton, he may not have the interpretative insight, the personal dynamism, or the capacity to project intensity, passion, or soaring beauty which other conductors possess. But for all these limitations, he is a valuable conductor, with an extraordinary span; and our country is all the richer for his participation.

His extensive experience as conductor began in 1911, when he was appointed an assistant of the newly-organized Boston Opera Company, that admirable institution created by Henry Russell which, during its short career, gave some of the most impressive opera performances in the country. At that time Smallens was only twenty-four years old. Born in St. Petersburg on January 1, 1889, he came to this country as a child and was educated at the New York public schools, and then at the College of the City of New York. His music studies took place at the Institute of Musical Art, and were completed in Paris at the Conservatory.

Once he assumed his chosen career, he was to hurl himself into an almost feverish activity with the baton. He became conductor of the Anna Pavlova troupe, following his apprenticeship with the Boston Opera Company, touring South and Central America and the West Indies over a period of two and a half years. During this time the distinction of being the first North American conductor to direct at the Teatro Colon in Buenos Aires became his. Other major engagements included those with the Century Opera Company, and the National Theatre in Havana. In 1919, he was appointed first conductor of the Chicago Opera Company, a post he held for four years. There he directed an extensive repertoire which comprised some important first performances, including those of Prokofieff's *The Love of Three Oranges* and Reginald de Koven's last opera, *Rip Van Winkle*. At this time he also toured Europe, appearing successfully at the Staatsoper and Volksoper in Berlin and the Royal Opera in Madrid, featuring for the most part the Italian repertory (though in Madrid he also introduced Max von Schilling's *Mona Lisa,* at the express request of the composer). He was the first American ever to conduct opera in Berlin and Madrid.

In 1924, he was appointed music director of the Philadelphia Civic Opera Company, where he gave admirable performances of operas by Mozart, Gluck, and Richard Strauss. Shortly after this he became director of the Philadelphia Society for Contemporary Music, introducing to Philadelphia music audiences such outstanding new works as Stravinsky's *Apollon Musagètes* and *L'Histoire du Soldat,* Hindemith's *Hin und Zurück,* and Malipiero's *Sette Canzone.* In 1934-35, together with Fritz Reiner, he conducted an opera season launched by the Philadelphia Orchestra. After 1934, he conducted every opera performance at the Lewisohn Stadium, as well as opera and symphony concerts in summer stadiums throughout the country. He introduced Gershwin's *Porgy and Bess* during its initial run in 1935, and was again its director during its successful revival in 1942. He has also directed premières of other interesting American operas by Marc Blitzstein *(Triple Sec),* Leo Ornstein (incidental music to *Lysistrata*), and Virgil Thomson *(Four Saints in Three Acts).* And, in 1940, he became the musical director of the newly organized Ballet Theatre in New York, with which organization he has introduced such novel scores as Henry Brant's *The Great American Goof* and Milhaud's *La Création du Monde.*

Other Orchestras — Other Men

1

Hans Kindler

Under the astute guidance of Hans Kindler, the National Symphony Orchestra of Washington, D. C., has become a "people's orchestra"—an integral element of the cultural life of the city. It is today supported by the contributions of seven thousand music lovers who see to it that the orchestra suffers no deficits. As a people's orchestra, the National Symphony has a far more elastic program than merely providing series of subscription concerts. It has organized students' concerts, visiting schools and small public auditoriums and (in 1940-41) playing for some 20,000 children at an admission fee of twenty-five cents. In 1935, it launched free summer concerts on the Potomac River (the orchestra plays on a barge moored off the shore); an average of 20,000 listeners attend each of these concerts. More recently, it has instituted early Fall "Pop" concerts when good music combines with refreshments to create an atmosphere of charming informality.

The orchestra was founded in 1931, year of the economic famine which was laying waste to many fortunes and, simultaneously, to so many different phases of our cultural life. Kindler's friends tried to dissuade him at the time from an undertaking so quixotic as the formation of a symphony orchestra during a period when hardly an American family existed which had not been affected by the financial disaster. They pointed out, besides, that seven different orchestras had previously (and in happier years) been organized in Washington, and all of them had failed: Washington, it appeared, was simply not a city of music lovers. But Kindler insisted that the nation's capital deserved a great orchestra of its own, and should not be dependent for its musical diet on the crumbs which visiting orchestras left behind them. Kindler felt that if a fine orchestra were to function in Washington, there would surely arise audiences to listen to it.

With driving perseverance, Kindler found ninety-seven donors ready to provide the necessary funds. Carefully selecting the personnel of his orchestra, Kindler inaugurated a first season of twenty-four concerts—which, much to the amazement of his friends, and to his own quiet satisfaction, were so well received that at the end of the season the backers were returned 31% of their original investment. The second and third seasons were even more successful. Since then, in line with Kindler's ambitions to make it a people's orchestra, and to expand its artistic program, the original ninety-seven donors grew into seven thousand regular contributors. In 1938, the orchestra increased its schedule of season's concerts to eighty-five. It had also launched numerous series of ambitious tours which brought it as far north as Canada, and as far south as Florida: between 1932 and 1941, the orchestra gave 263 concerts in 94 cities outside of Washington.

The work of the National Symphony Orchestra has become familiar to music lovers throughout the country not only as a result of these extensive tours, but also through its performances on Victor records, and over the air. It is an excellent ensemble, one which must be included among the great orchestras of America. It has spirit and vitality in its performance; a rich tone and a facile technique. Beyond everything else it is Kindler's orchestra: It responds to his every demand with amazing resilience.

The same musicianship and discernment which made him one of the great cellists of our time, has also made him a discriminating interpreter with the baton. Kindler has instituted in Washington one of the most extensive repertoires known by any of our younger orchestras—more than 700 numbers, of which a fair proportion is novelties rarely to be heard elsewhere. And this extensive and varied repertoire—extending from transcriptions of music by the venerable Frescobaldi to a new work by the young American, William Schuman—is played with dignity and an appreciation for style. Kindler may not rise to those empyrean heights to which some other conductors may soar, but at the same time it can also be said that he never descends to the depths of cheapness, superficiality, or sensationalism. He is a self-respecting and respected musician who does justice to the great music he performs, and serves his art with humility.

He was born in Rotterdam, Holland, on January 8, 1893. As a student of the Rotterdam Conservatory he won first prizes for piano and cello. When he was seventeen, he was cello soloist with the Berlin Philharmonic, and at eighteen he became professor of the cello at the Scharwenka Conservatory, as well as first cellist of the Berlin Opera Orchestra. During this period he began his concert career and achieved such fame that within a few months he was invited to give a command performance before the Queen of Holland.

Coming to the United States in 1914, he was so impressed by the country that he extended his stay indefinitely. He became first cellist of the Philadelphia Orchestra, retaining this post under Stokowski until 1920. Then his fame as cello virtuoso had grown to such proportions (and his concert engagements became so numerous) that he was compelled to resign his orchestral post and to devote himself exclusively to the concert stage. He appeared as soloist with the major orchestras, and as recitalist in the leading concert halls. In Europe he was spoken of as the "Kreisler of the violoncello"; in America no one less than James Gibbons Huneker wrote that "I do not expect in my life to hear duplicates of an Elman or a Kreisler, a Casals or a Hans Kindler."

In 1927-28, he was asked to conduct a special series of orchestral concerts in Philadelphia and to appear as a guest in other cities. One of these invitations brought him to Washington, D. C. It was probably at this time that he first conceived the idea of organizing an orchestra for the nation's capital.

His baton successes in America and Europe persuaded Kindler to exchange his cello for a conductor's wand. After completing the record tour of his career as cellist in 1929—he played 110 concerts that season, performing as far west as California, and as far east as Java—he began plans for becoming a conductor permanently. He had numerous offers to appear in guest performances with many great orchestras of America and Europe, which would have kept him busily engaged throughout the season. But such a nomadic existence, journeying from one orchestra to another, did not altogether satisfy him: He wanted an orchestra of his own, one which he could shape according to his own tastes. He decided that the place for such an orchestra was Washington, D. C.

His work in Washington, and his guest appearances with world-famous orchestras, has placed him among the most gifted of our younger conductors: It was in recognition of his place in modern American music that, in 1939, Kindler's name was inscribed on a panel at the World's Fair as one of the Americans of foreign birth who has made vital contributions to our culture. What he lacks in sensational appeal, he more than makes up with sound musicianship and ideals.

Victor Kolar

Although the Detroit Symphony Orchestra has, for the most part, been in the hands of guest conductors since the death of Ossip Gabrilowitsch, a sizable portion of each season's concerts has been allocated to Victor Kolar.

The Detroit Symphony Orchestra was founded in 1914; but not until 1919 did it become an organization of national importance. In 1918, Gabrilowitsch—at that time a novice with the baton, but one of the world's great pianists—was invited to direct a guest performance with the Detroit orchestra. His concert made such a profound impression on the audience that, spontaneously, it rose to its feet to honor him. Gabrilowitsch's success brought him a permanent assignment as principal conductor of the orchestra. He reorganized it completely. "Introspective, extremely sensitive, poetic by nature, soft spoken and gentle, in horror of display of any kind, disinterested in self-exploitation, he appealed to his audiences . . . for qualities far different from those of Stokowski; but his appeal was no less potent," I have written elsewhere about Gabrilowitsch's conductorial career in Detroit.* "The public came to his concerts, and they worshipped him. When he firmly announced that he would resign his post if a new and suitable auditorium were not built for the orchestra in time for the opening of the 1919 season, the funds were easily procured. Detroit would not think of losing its appealing conductor."

* *Music Comes to America,* by David Ewen, Thos. Y. Crowell Co., 1942.

Besides rebuilding his orchestra along new and modern lines, inaugurating a repertoire such as Detroit had never before known, and using his influence to acquire a new concert auditorium, Gabrilowitsch was responsible for another far-sighted move which was to benefit the orchestra immeasurably. He imported Victor Kolar from New York to be his assistant in the preparation of the Detroit concerts. From 1919, therefore, Kolar's history as a conductor has been inextricably associated with that of the Detroit Symphony.

He is Hungarian by birth, having been born in Budapest on February 12, 1888. His musical precociousness was early recognized by his father, a professional musician; his talent was, therefore, nursed and permitted to develop naturally. Before he could read or write, Victor Kolar could play melodies on the violin and the piano. As a child, he became a pupil of Jan Kubelik. Then, after six years with Kubelik, he entered the Prague Conservatory, where one of his masters was Antonin Dvořák.

He graduated with honors. In 1904, he came to the United States and entered the professional ranks by playing the violin as soloist with the Chicago Orchestra, then on tour. For a period, he was a violinist in the Pittsburgh Symphony Orchestra, rising to the position of assistant conductor. In 1907, he was discovered by Walter Damrosch who brought him to New York to become a violinist and assistant conductor of the New York Symphony Society. Kolar remained with Damrosch's orchestra until 1919, when he received a call from Gabrilowitsch to join him in Detroit.

Besides being Gabrilowitsch's valuable right hand man, Kolar was, from time to time, called upon to conduct concerts of his own; and whenever he did so, he revealed his competence. During 1934 he was engaged to direct the Detroit

Symphony Orchestra at the Century of Progress Exposition in Chicago. At this time, he established what must surely be an orchestral record by directing 162 two-hour concerts, including forty-eight national broadcasts, over a period of eighty-six days. More than 800 different compositions were performed. Such an assignment calls for an enormous repertoire, and a facile baton technique; and it can be said that Kolar met his commitments gracefully.

When Gabrilowitsch died in 1936, Kolar became a principal conductor of the Detroit Symphony. He has remained at this post continually since then, sometimes sharing the season with Franco Ghione, at other times dividing the season's schedule between himself and a series of visiting leaders.

3

Eugene Goossens

Eugene Goossens of Cincinnati is not of the dynamic school of conductors. His performances have classic objectivity—high polish, grace, refinement. Perhaps what keeps these performances from achieving greatness, for all the talent and studied care which go into their preparation, is the absence of that very energy and galvanic drive that we find, say, in Koussevitzky or Rodzinski. Goossens is an artist in the finest meaning of the term: Fastidiously he carves each line and phrase with the discernment of a sculptor moulding clay. It is easily understandable why he enjoys conducting the music of Mozart more than that of any other composer; for Mozart's classicism suits Goossens' temperament most happily. Goossens has a talent of high order: His is an infallible instinct for correct accent, for proper nuance, for exact phrasing. If we are not always deeply impressed by his performances, it is not because they have not been musically conceived, and brought to life with artistry—it is because an element is lacking; and that element is the burning fire which is in every immortal conductor, which sets the music aflame, as well as the musicians and audiences.

Eugene Goossens, now occupying the post in which Stokowski served his apprentice years, is not without honor; and it is honor he well deserves. Eugène Ysaÿe and Fritz Reiner held permanent conductorial posts with the Cincinnati Symphony before Goossens received the appointment in 1931. One sound reason for Goossens' instantaneous success in Cincinnati may well have been that the music lovers of the city had known the dynamic type of conductor for so many years, beginning with Stokowski, through Fritz Reiner, that they were now receptive to more placid music-making.

Goossens accepted the post eagerly, for the Cincinnati Symphony Orchestra offered desirable opportunities for a high-minded conductor. There were no financial problems for the orchestra to struggle with—one certainly enviable condition under which a conductor can function to best advantage: In 1929, the Cincinnati Institute of Fine Arts, with a treasury of three and a half million dollars, took over the direction and financial responsibilities of the orchestra. There were no artistic problems either. The Board of Trustees, governing the orchestra, (elected by the Institute of Fine Arts) was quite ready to place the full control of the orchestra in the hands of the conductor.

Under Goossens, the Cincinnati Symphony Orchestra has enjoyed a dignified regime during which its right to be numbered among the great orchestras of America cannot be subject to question. Goossens has established himself solidly in Cincinnati: There are those who say that he has won his audiences so completely that he can have his job as long as he wants it.

Dapper, elegant, well-poised—with the air and manner of a born aristocrat—Eugene Goossens is as neatly trimmed as his performances. Everything about him is in perfect taste, everything is under control. He is a suave figure, dressed in best possible taste by an English tailor and a French shirtmaker (up to 1939 at any rate). A cane is an inevitable part of his everyday attire. His interests traverse a wide range, and reveal the English gentleman: In sports, he indulges in golf and

257

fencing. A solitary evening at home finds him browsing among his books, of which he is a voracious reader. He likes to dabble in architecture, making sketches of every house that interests him. He is particularly fascinated by the sea (a throwback, no doubt, to his boyhood in Liverpool). He finds excitement merely in idling around a busy harbor, absorbing the sights and sounds. He occasionally indulges in sword-fishing because it brings him so much closer to the sea. For the same reason, he once made a hobby of studying the construction of ships, and could actually recognize any transatlantic liner from a distance.

The one plebeian note in his diversions is his passion for locomotives. "Locomotives," he will tell you, "have a definite relation with music; they are all rhythm." Pictures of locomotives line the walls of his office and study (side by side with his valuable illuminated manuscripts of early music). He gets a schoolboyish delight in putting on regulation railroad attire, and sitting on an engineer's stool in the cab of a train. He has frequently done this, in runs between Rochester and New York, and Cincinnati and Dayton; not so long ago, he even made a cross-country run on a Southern Pacific train in the engineer's booth. His one great disappointment is that federal laws prohibit him from handling the throttle, an experience for which he long ago trained himself with professional competence.

Goossens, who was born in London on May 26, 1893, comes from a family of musicians. His grandfather was a well-known opera conductor whose name deserves a place in English music-history books by virtue of the fact that he conducted the first performance of *Tannhäuser* in England. He was the first conductor employed by the Carl Rosa Opera Company, a position which he passed on to his son (Eugene Goossens' father). "Between them," remarks Goossens, "they pro-

HANS KINDLER

VICTOR KOLAR   EUGENE GOOSSENS   KARL KRUEGER

duced probably every well-known opera in the repertoire." Goossens' mother was a well-known contralto. His brother, Leon, is one of the greatest living virtuosos of the oboe. Two sisters are professional harpists; and still another brother distinguished himself musically before he was killed in the First World War.

Music, therefore, was destined as his career almost from his very birth. He was taught it in early childhood. When he was ten he entered the Conservatory in Bruges. Three years after this, he became a pupil at the Liverpool College of Music where he won medals for piano, violin, and composition, as well as a scholarship for the Royal College of Music in London. He moved perpetually in an atmosphere of music. Besides his studies at school and at home, he would spend many of his free hours attending the rehearsals conducted by his father, absorbing, in the dark and empty auditorium, the musical sounds. "When I was ten or eleven years old, I was already familiar with most of the standard operas, having heard them rehearsed again and again by my father.

"One of my first professional engagements as a boy in London was when I was called in an emergency to Covent Garden to substitute for a second violin in the orchestra. Old Hans Richter was conducting *Die Meistersinger,* and that gave me a wonderful experience with one of the greatest of Wagner interpreters. I played in the orchestra also under Nikisch and several other noted conductors." This took place when Goossens was sixteen years old. A year later, he was graduated from the Royal College, entering music professionally by joining the Queen's Hall Orchestra conducted by Henry J. Wood. "I played in the orchestra for several years. My love of the classics was ingrained from that time on. If there is anything to the word 'tradition,' I acquired then my feeling for it that I hope I have not lost. Even taking one season at the Promenade

Concerts at Queen's Hall and playing a different symphony every night—you can imagine that the field of music was well covered—proved a wonderfully comprehensive training in orchestra literature I could get nowhere else. Not having concentrated on any particular school or ism, I was better able to realize the great features of each school of writing."

Sir Thomas Beecham discovered Goossens and urged him to become a conductor. In 1916, through Beecham's influence, Goossens was given his first opportunity to conduct a performance, when he was assigned, at a last moment, to direct an opera by Stanford, *The Critic*. The ease with which he went through this assignment convinced him of the wisdom of Beecham's advice. "I put my fiddle in its case and never took it out again." He became one of the conductors of the Beecham Opera Company, assisting Beecham in all his performances over a period of eight years: Beecham, always generous with advice and criticism, played no small role in Goossens' rapid development as conductor. Then Goossens received an appointment with the British National Opera Company. During these few years he was called upon to direct no less than fifty different operas. Besides these operatic engagements, he was also assigned performances with the Diaghilev Ballet, the Handel and Haydn Society, and with orchestras in England and Scotland.

In 1921, he founded his own symphony orchestra in London which specialized in the performance of modern music. With this orchestra he once and for all established his reputation, and was henceforth frequently invited to give guest performances with the leading European symphonic organizations.

He came to the United States in 1923—already a distinguished conductor—to become the head of the Rochester Philharmonic, an office he held with no little distinction for eight years. During this period, he paralleled his European fame in this country by leading most of the great American orchestras in specially invited performances, beginning with 1925 when he directed three splendid concerts with the Boston Symphony Orchestra. Then, in 1931, following his success in a pair of guest appearances, he was appointed the permanent conductor of the Cincinnati Symphony Orchestra.

Karl Krueger

The Kansas City Symphony Orchestra is the product of its founder-conductor, Karl Krueger. Born in New York on January 19, 1894, the son of a Leipzig University professor, Karl Krueger was brought up in Atchison, Kansas, where he attended the University, graduating in 1916. He studied the cello and organ, then pursued an advanced musical training in Boston and New York. His studies ended, he became an organist in a New York church.

His father urged him to become a lawyer. Acquiescing, Krueger went to Europe where he studied law and philosophy at the universities of Vienna and Heidelberg. At the same time, he continued with his pursuit of music, particularly in Vienna with Robert Fuchs. When he completed his law courses, he knew that he still wished to become a professional musician; and, in music, what interested him most keenly was conducting. He approached Artur Nikisch and asked to be his pupil. Nikisch was impressed by Krueger's talent and accepted him. Krueger not only took lessons from the master, but he also toured with him as his protegé and assistant.

Nikisch sent Krueger to Vienna with an effusive letter of recommendation to Franz Schalk, the conductor of the Vienna Opera. Schalk appointed Krueger an assistant conductor of the Vienna Philharmonic and the Vienna Opera; it was here that Krueger acquired his extensive experience in a great and varied repertoire.

In 1926, Krueger received from the United States an offer to assume the principal conductor's post of the Seattle Symphony. "I have no doubt," Franz Schalk wrote at the time, "that he will play an important role among the leading orchestral conductors of his time." In Seattle, at any rate, Krueger played a role of importance, for it is generally credited that his vital performances succeeded in raising the orchestra to a position of note; there were many who felt that, with Krueger, the Seattle Symphony had joined the twelve or fifteen leading orchestras in America.

In 1933, a symphony orchestra was founded in Kansas City, sponsored by the Chamber of Commerce. It called on Karl Krueger to assume artistic direction and he accepted. He has since remained the principal conductor of the orchestra, and through his sincerity and gifts has brought prestige both to himself and to his orchestra. In May, 1937, Krueger returned to Vienna for the first time since his apprentice years under Schalk, and was asked to give several guest performances with the Vienna Philharmonic. The fact that he had been preceded by Toscanini—who had scored a sensation in Vienna—did not dissuade Krueger from accepting the invitation. "To conduct the Philharmonic immediately after Toscanini," commented the Viennese critic, Ernst Decsey, "and right after his concert to make an impression, yes, even to win laurels—that is something!"

Men Over the Radio

1

Howard Barlow

When Howard Barlow became a conductor at the Columbia Broadcasting System, he shocked its directors by performing an entire symphony (Haydn's *Military*) at one of his radio concerts. "The public doesn't want symphonies," they told him. "Give them short, light numbers." But Barlow insisted that radio audiences had a higher intelligence quotient than a six-year-old, and he played his symphony. He was deluged by letters of gratitude from every part of the country. Shortly after this, inspired by the success of his first bold thrust, he inaugurated a symphony series in which a famous symphony was played in installments, one movement at a time.

With radio music today on an artistic plane with our concert halls, it becomes difficult to remember that only a few years ago it required the adventurous spirit of a pioneer to play a complete symphony on the air. Today, not only the symphony but even the esoteric music of modern composers, is an everyday radio event. In this phenomenal growth of radio music from childhood to full maturity, only Walter Damrosch played a role of greater significance than Howard Barlow. Barlow first came to the radio on the afternoon of September 18, 1927, when he officially helped to inaugurate the Columbia network by conducting twenty-two musicians in Luigini's *Ballet Egyptiènne*. Since then, his work with the Columbia network, where he has risen to the post of music director, has been decisive in revolutionizing the standards of musical programs over the air. His orchestra has grown from twenty-two to sixty-five men; from Luigini, his programs have developed until they included the greatest works of the symphonic repertory. This evolution must inevitably form an epochal chapter in the history of music-making in this country.

Howard Barlow was born in Plain City, Ohio, on May 1, 1892. As a child he was unusually responsive to music. He sang in church choirs, in one of which he made his official debut as soloist at the age of six. He also studied the cello, and was so devoted to his instrument that he wore out one pair of trousers after another at the knees until his mother sewed a pair of kneepads to his garment. He was eight when he heard excerpts from *Il Trovatore* on a player piano; from that moment on, he was convinced that his life's ambition was to become a professional musician.

"Music was my greatest source of enjoyment," he recalls, "and as our town boasted neither music teachers nor music stores (except the place where dance records were sold) I was hard put to it to find the enjoyment I wanted. My only pieces were a book of Czerny exercises, Schumann's *Album for the Young,* and a volume of baritone solos. I learned all of these on the piano, and then began all over again studying them on the violin and cello. After that I came to a stop."

His father, who was in the furniture business, had hoped to see his son succeed him. But once he recognized Howard's extraordinary aptitude for music, he would not stand in his way. Perhaps he realized the futility of interference. In those days he used to say, "Howard is as stubborn as a mule. If he wants something, he'll get it, even if it takes him ten years." At any rate, when the Barlow family moved to Denver, Howard became a music pupil of Wilberforce J. Whiteman (the father of the famous jazz-orchestra leader). He had a taste of conducting, as well, by directing glee clubs and his school orchestra. At the same time, he continued with his academic studies, attending the University of Colorado and Reed College.

A scholarship for Columbia University brought Barlow to New York. New York, musical Mecca, excited the young music lover. He began to study music more seriously than ever before. He haunted the concert halls. With the hope of finding for himself some opening in the professional music world (for, as he has said, the only letter of introduction he brought with him to New York was to a cheese merchant!) he registered at the Columbus Circle Employment Agency as an "American singer."

He did not get any engagements as singer, but he found plenty of other work for his talents. He earned his living by directing choral groups in Bronx, Brooklyn, New Jersey, and Long Island; by assisting small instrumental groups; by coaching singers. When the First World War broke out, he served first in the Fosdick Commission, then as a private.

It was immediately after the war that Barlow received his first major assignment as conductor. In 1919, he was invited to direct the festival of the National Federation of Music Clubs at Peterboro, New Hampshire. Four years later, he organized an orchestra of his own, the American National Orchestra, in which every member was American born and American trained. The orchestra was not destined for a long life (it continued functioning for two seasons); but it was important in bringing Barlow some experience in the performance of symphonic music. At about this time, too, he was called upon to conduct the world première of Charles Wakefield Cadman's opera, *The Garden of Mystery*, at a special Carnegie Hall performance.

For a period, he worked at the Neighborhood Playhouse, in downtown New York, where he arranged the music, wrote ballet numbers, conducted the orchestra—and on one occasion even appeared as singer under an assumed name. One of his notable achievements was his performance of the accompanying score to the Neighborhood Playhouse successful production of *The Dybbuk*.

In 1927, he was offered the job of conductor at the newly organized Columbia Broadcasting System. At that time, the post did not promise a great deal of artistic satisfaction for a young musician with ideals. Good music over the air meant Victor Herbert, and more Victor Herbert. It meant Godfrey Ludlow in his fifteen minute violin recitals. It meant Slumber Music. The great classics (so the radio executives insisted) were not for mass consumption; and by the same token, the radio was not appealing to exotic tastes.

But Barlow did not see radio in the same light. He saw it as a heaven-sent educational force which could educate the masses into the beauties of great music. He had faith in the innate intelligence of the people. If they did not like good music it was only because they had never before come into direct contact with it. Bring music to them, in full diets— not with spoon feedings—and they would learn to appreciate it. Of this Barlow was convinced; and to that end Barlow was determined to devote his efforts over the air. Barlow also knew that a musical post is as important as the man who holds it. He accepted the radio job, determined to make it a weapon in his battle for good music.

For such an assignment he was particularly adapted. He was a man of rather unpretentious musical background. He had always loved music, and learned about it more as a devoted amateur than as a professional. His own background had taught him what the public would take to, and through what steps. Besides, he had patience and persistence. Howard Barlow did not expect to change the musical tastes of the country overnight: He would feel his ground, move cautiously, then, when he felt that the moment was ripe, would plunge ahead to his goal.

"I was certainly nervous before my debut radio performance. I pictured the 'mike' as a central spot from which countless wires, endless in length, stretched all over the country. I felt like a tiny fly caught in the center of a spider's web. But when the music started, and I felt the baton in my hand, I forgot everything but the music."

He took naturally to the radio. And he set about raising the standards of radio music, deaf to advice and discouragement. After introducing a full symphony, and a series of symphonies a movement at a time, he started a cycle of great piano concertos with Ernest Hutcheson as soloist. He conducted special educational programs called "Understanding Music" and "Understanding Opera." He inaugurated afternoon symphony concerts, the programs of which gradually approached symphony hall standards. The fact that his increasingly ambitious gestures did not alienate his radio audiences but rather brought into his office an avalanche of congratulatory letters and telegrams gave him the encouragement he needed; that, and the weapon with which to break down the resistance of the radio executives.

Having elevated the standards of radio music (assisted in this effort by other far-sighted musicians) Barlow launched in 1937 a missionary program for radio on behalf of American composers. He commissioned the foremost American composers to write music expressly for radio use. He featured these works extensively on his programs. Such famous American composers as Roy Harris, Aaron Copland, Howard Hanson, Robert Russell Bennett, and Quincy Porter wrote new

271

symphonic works for use by Barlow's orchestra. Other composers, like Louis Gruenberg and Randall Thompson, wrote radio operas. In this way, Barlow has been a force of incalculable importance in the development and encouragement of modern American musical expression.

Short, slight of build (he weighs only one hundred and twenty-three pounds), soft-spoken, unassuming, Barlow does not make a forceful impression at first glance. He has two outstanding likes: His Boston bull pup, and orange shortcake. His one violent prejudice is against cheap music of all kinds. Though he likes good music, whether it is old or new, classical, romantic, or ultramodern, he confesses that one work above all others is his favorite: the prelude to *Tristan und Isolde*.

2

Frank Black

Like Howard Barlow, Frank Black (music director of the National Broadcasting Company) has risen from comparatively humble musical origins. No great and glamorous career paved his way to the radio microphone.

He was born in Philadelphia, on November 28, 1894. His father, founder and head of a prosperous dairy business, had every hope that his son would some day take over his work. But Frank Black had a mind of his own. He studied at Haverford College where he majored in chemistry; he also dabbled with music, concentrating on playing the piano. Soon after graduating from college, he was offered two different posts. One, as chemical engineer, promised a stable economic future. The other, as a pianist in a hotel in Harrisburg (Pennsylvania), guaranteed more personal satisfaction than financial stability. Frank Black went to Harrisburg.

After a season of playing the piano, he returned to Philadelphia to devote himself to further music study. He became a pupil of Rafael Joseffy, commuting regularly to New York for his lessons. Joseffy frequently spoke of Black as his favorite pupil.

Black entered music professionally as a writer of songs for vaudeville. Later he became assistant to Erno Rapee at the Fox Theatre in Philadelphia, then he edited a magazine devoted to popular music, then assumed the direction of a phonograph recording company. During a recording session, he came into contact with a vocal quartet called The Revelers. Black became their piano accompanist and coach; he also made some tasteful four-voice arrangements of musical masterpieces. These arrangements were largely responsible for later bringing this quartet its nationwide fame over the radio.

It was the great success of The Revelers which brought Frank Black to the attention of radio executives. They asked him if he would consider a radio post. Black (thinking of the deplorable lack of good music over the air) said he would; but his ambition in this direction was to organize a string symphony orchestra, and to conduct it as a regular radio feature in the best music of all time. The idea, at the time, appeared fantastic to the executives, convinced as they were that there was no place for good music over the air. However, when there was a need for some orchestral music, Black was frequently called upon to serve as conductor. It was the success of these performances—and the clamor of radio audiences for more of them—that finally tempted radio officials to gamble with Black. They permitted him to organize his own orchestral group, and assigned him a regular radio spot.

From this time on, Black devoted himself assiduously to the cause of good music over the air; and few musicians have served this cause so stubbornly. In 1928, Black was appointed musical director of NBC. With this appointment, good music over the air reached man's estate. As conductor of the Magic Key Hour, the String Symphony, and the NBC Orchestra, Frank Black persistently brought the greatest music of the past and the present to his nationwide audiences. He was not afraid of striking new trails. One of his more recent radio series, for example, was devoted exclusively to the works of young and lesser known American composers who, Black felt, deserved a hearing.

274

ALFRED WALLENSTEIN

HOWARD BARLOW

FRANK BLACK

ERNO RAPEE

The post of music director of NBC—make no mistake about it!—is no sinecure. It has been some years since Black has enjoyed a vacation from his many arduous and taxing assignments. He rises early enough in the morning to be at his desk at Radio City well before eight o'clock. Between eight and nine, he outlines his work for the day, and attends to numerous routine details. At nine o'clock his office becomes a beehive of activity: Letters, telegrams, messages have to be read and answered; the phone rings almost uninterruptedly; manuscripts of musical compositions have to be acknowledged.

A day's work for Frank Black could exhaust the energy and time of a half-dozen different men. New scores have to be read and passed upon; radio auditions of young artists have to be attended; there are consultations with staff conductors and musicians; the purchase of all musical instruments must be personally supervised; orchestral arrangements of various musical masterpieces have to be made for use on his programs (Black has made numerous charming and effective string orchestra arrangements of great piano sonatas of Mozart and Beethoven); there are the rehearsals with the orchestra; and there are conferences with radio executives. A day of work does not end for Black until nine in the evening; but frequently Black is still hard at work at his office till well past midnight.

In this feverish program of activity which consumes six days a week, fifty-two weeks a year, there is no time for diversions. Black enjoys rifle-shooting, and he would consider himself fortunate if he could find the time to putter around aimlessly on a farm. But the pursuit of such hobbies must wait for some distant future. Meanwhile, Black gets his exercise by walking briskly each day from his home in East 57th Street to Radio City; and he finds relaxation by handling his precious collection of first editions and musical manuscripts.

3

Alfred Wallenstein

Alfred Wallenstein of the Mutual Broadcasting System has come to radio work by way of a comprehensive training in several great American orchestras and under world-famous conductors. Like Barlow and Black, he is of American birth. He was born in Chicago on October 7, 1898, of distinguished German lineage: one of his ancestors was Waldenstein von Wallenstein, the national German hero of the seventeenth century. Soon after Alfred's birth, the Wallenstein family moved to Los Angeles. When he was eight years old he was asked which he preferred for a birthday gift: a bicycle or a cello. He chose a cello, and began its study with Mme. von Grofe, mother of the famous jazz arranger and composer, Ferde Grofé.* After a period of additional study in Leipzig with Julius Klengel, Wallenstein made his concert debut in Los Angeles, five years after having taken his first lesson. He achieved a certain measure of fame in Southern California as a prodigy. For a year he toured the vaudeville houses of the country on the Orpheum circuit. Then, returning to California, he assumed a post with the San Francisco Symphony Orchestra. He was so young at the time that before he was given a contract with that orchestra, he had to promise its conductor, Alfred Hertz, that he would henceforth wear long trousers.

In 1917, he was engaged by Anna Pavlova to tour with her in South and Central America.

---

* The real family name was "von Grofe."

After three years with the Los Angeles Philharmonic, which he had joined in 1919, Wallenstein was engaged by Frederick Stock to occupy the first cello chair of the Chicago Symphony Orchestra. For seven years he remained in Chicago, not only performing the orchestral repertoire, but also frequently appearing as soloist. His work attracted the attention of Toscanini who, in 1929, brought Wallenstein to New York for the first cello post with the New York Philharmonic. Toscanini had a high regard for Wallenstein's musicianship. He frequently advised him to abandon his cello and to turn to conducting. Such advice—and coming from such a source—was not to be taken lightly; it touched the strings of Wallenstein's inmost ambitions. He had, as a matter of fact, already acquired some taste for conducting an orchestra. In 1931, he directed a radio concert. After a summer session at the Hollywood Bowl in 1933, he organized his now famous Sinfonietta for WOR. Then his swift rise to popularity brought him the office of musical director of WOR in February, 1935. That he did not abandon his orchestral job impulsively to consider only conductorial work was only because of his devotion to Toscanini. Toscanini had often said that, in conducting the Philharmonic, he counted heavily on such men as Wallenstein. As long as Toscanini needed him, Wallenstein was determined to stay.

Then, in 1936, Toscanini resigned his Philharmonic post. Wallenstein no longer felt bound by his conscience to remain at his desk. By this time he had already made a name for himself in radio. He, therefore, forsook his orchestral duties as cellist and devoted himself exclusively to his radio assignments.

A man of many different tastes, ranging from the indoor sport of poker to the outdoor pastime of deep-sea fishing, from playing tennis and billiards to watching boxing matches,

Wallenstein's one abiding passion remains music. He has betrayed that passion through the catholicity of his tastes; and through his restless bent for musical explorations which have sent him into forgotten lands in search of new musical spices. In his office as music director of the Mutual Broadcasting System, he has brought a veritable horn of plenty to radio; there have been endless riches for every taste and every preference. One series he has devoted to all the church cantatas of Johann Sebastian Bach; another to all the piano concertos of Mozart (with Nadia Reisenberg as soloist); still another, to operas by Mozart, including some never before heard in this country. He has unearthed old music, long forgotten, and restored it to the world—symphonies by Stamitz and Telemann, suites by Rameau, Couperin and Alessandro Scarlatti, overtures by Johann Christian Bach and Sacchini. He has conducted other works, the ink of which was still wet on the manuscript: Not the least distinguished of his many memorable cycles was one dedicated to modern American choral music, and another to modern American operas.

His distinguished work over the radio has not passed unnoticed. For several years successively he won the award of the National Federation of Music Clubs because of his significant contributions to American music. In 1940, a national poll of radio editors placed him third among those who made the most eventful musical contributions to the radio, the other two being Toscanini and Barbirolli. In 1942 he was given the George Peabody Radio Award for distinguished musical services, sometimes referred to as the "Pulitzer Prize of the Radio."

*

That orchestral concerts over the air frequently cannot stand measure with those in symphony halls is not exclusively the fault of their conductors. Unfortunately, radio symphonic performances call for hasty preparation, except in the case of the NBC Orchestra directed by a Toscanini or a Stokowski. It is not possible for a Wallenstein or a Barlow to concentrate on the minutiae of a performance as other conductors are able to do for a public concert. There is, in consequence, some superficiality and there are evidences of hasty preparation. Yet conductors like Howard Barlow, Frank Black, and Alfred Wallenstein have proved their baton gifts even under such unfavorable auspices. Listening to their concerts over an extended period is to be aware of their sound musicianship, their versatility, their fine flexibility in changing with every different idiom. Their performances might lack the breadth, epic scope, sweep, dimension which other conductors can achieve; but they are sensitive interpreters, who fill their posts with dignity.

They have also proved their gifts with excellent guest performances with American orchestras, where they are permitted to work to best advantage. Howard Barlow combines his radio work with the post of principal conductor of the Baltimore Symphony Orchestra, in which he succeeded Werner Janssen in 1939; he has also given guest performances with the New York Philharmonic (at the Lewisohn Stadium), and with the Philadelphia Orchestra (at Robin Hood Dell). Frank Black has conducted the NBC Orchestra. Alfred Wallenstein has directed concerts with the major orchestras of Philadelphia, Cleveland, and Los Angeles. In these performances—even more than in their concerts over the air—the musicians have proved their worth. They may not be in the class of Toscanini, Stokowski, or Koussevitzky; but conducting has room for others besides immortals. Radio need not feel apologetic about the three major conductors it has produced; they can stand with self-respect in the company of America's foremost exponents of the baton.

4

Erno Rapee

Erno Rapee belongs in this group of conductors not because he is a great interpreter, but because he, too, has wielded a noticeable influence. As a conductor of a New York motion-picture house orchestra, it would seem that his musical sphere is a limited one. Yet by enlisting the radio microphone, he has extended that sphere until its periphery borders the entire country. Eloquent words might be spoken of the manner in which he improved the standard of music in the cinema theatre; how, where other conductors satisfied themselves (and their audiences) with a convenient library of musical *charivari*—you know, *Hearts and Flowers* and *Rustle of Spring,* (in a more expansive mood) the *Raymond* and *Poet and Peasant* overtures *ad nauseam*—he leaned more heavily on great music. He introduced a modern and fully equipped symphony orchestra into the movie theatre, instead of employing the haphazard assortment of instruments which satisfied the other conductors. And with this orchestra he proved that the greatest music of all time could be as palatable to movie audiences as the more banal pieces, and much more serviceable for the purposes of good theatre.

All this is very significant in its own way; but it is hardly significant enough to have assigned to Rapee national importance as a conductor. His fame, and his significance, stem rather from his work over the radio. Each Sunday afternoon he has conducted the Radio City Music Hall Symphony Orchestra in programs which did not speak down insultingly to its audiences; on the contrary, it quietly assumed that symphony hall standards applied to the radio as well. Rapee has featured cycles which would do honor even to the greatest of our orchestras: One was devoted to all the Sibelius symphonies; another to the Rachmaninoff piano concertos; still another to modern music—the first time, I believe, that an American orchestra attempted such a panorama and on such a scale; a fourth to the Wagner music-dramas, and a fifth to Italian opera; a sixth to the nine Mahler symphonies, including that gargantua of orchestral music, the Eighth Symphony, last heard in New York in 1912 under Stokowski.

However much one may wish to be generous to Rapee because of these (and other) achievements, it is difficult to ascribe to him any outstanding distinction as a performer. He has played a rich repertoire over a period of many years, touching every style and idiom; he has a long list of first performances to his credit as well. Yet rarely has he satisfied us, and never (to the best of my memory) has he moved us. He plays all the notes—and that is about all. The guiding hand of the artist is never in evidence. It is surface music, more in the nature of a fluent reading than an interpretation of an artistic conception. Granted that his performances are necessarily hastily prepared—yet, if he were a compelling personality of the baton, guided by sound musical instincts and strong artistic compulsions, there would occasionally emerge, even in superficially rehearsed performances, moments of grandeur, moments when the poetic speech of an artist rings loud and clear. Besides, as a guest of many famous orchestras in the East and the West—including the San Francisco Symphony and the Philadelphia Orchestra—he has had the opportunity to prove himself; and it cannot be said that he has done so.

Yet, we must repeat, if he is not an artist to inspire emulation for his interpretations, he does arouse admiration for his high purpose. When the musical historian of the future traces the evolution of our musical growth, he will no doubt find that in this growth Rapee played his part, and played it well.

*

Erno Rapee was born in Budapest on June 4, 1891. A child prodigy on the piano, he studied at the National Academy of Music in Vienna with Emil Sauer. Graduating, he accepted his first baton assignment, as assistant to Ernst von Schuch with the Dresden Orchestra. Not given enough work to satisfy his restless temperament, he resigned to return to his piano. He toured Europe in recitals and in guest appearances as soloist with the great orchestras.

In 1912 he came to the United States and became a pianist at the Monopole Restaurant on New York's East Side. For the next few years he fulfilled a variety of musical assignments, ranging from an assisting artist with such chamber music ensembles as the Letz Quartet to conductor of Hungarian opera at Webster Hall in downtown New York.

He met S. L. Rothafel (the Roxy of motion-picture fame), then the enterprising manager of the Rivoli Theatre, who offered him the post of conductor at this theatre. From this time on began an association between Rothafel and Rapee which was to continue for many years and exert a decisive influence on music in the motion-picture theatre. Wherever Rothafel went, in his meteoric rise as showman, there Rapee went with him: from the Rivoli to the Capitol, to the Roxy, finally to the grandiose Radio City Music Hall. In these various theatres Rapee has given some 20,000 performances of serious musical works since 1918, when he launched his ambitious plans by directing Mendelssohn's *Fingal's Cave Overture* (the first time, I believe, that so dignified a work was performed in a motion-picture house). As early as 1921 he had advanced sufficiently toward the goal he had set for himself by performing for his movie audiences a work so esoteric as Richard Strauss' *Ein Heldenleben*—and it must be remembered that in 1921 *Ein Heldenleben* was not quite so familiar to music lovers as it is today! "Movie theatre orchestras, I am sure, helped to pave the way for the splendid growth of symphony orchestras in America," Rapee once told an interviewer. There can be no doubt that they played at least a minor role in this development.

There have been several brief periods of interruption in Rapee's long and active career in the motion-picture theatre field. In 1925, Rapee went to Germany to serve as director of a chain of 180 UFA motion-picture theatres, at which time he introduced to Germany American standards of motion-picture entertainment. Shortly after this he worked in Hollywood, and in 1931 he became music director of the National Broadcasting Company. But, feeling that his place was with the baton, Rapee always strayed back to his duties as conductor, frequently sacrificing a more substantial annual income to do so.

Conductors for Tomorrow

1

Izler Solomon

Because so much more than native musical talent is required for conducting—integration of personality, maturity, culture, and experience—the baton has never been kind to child prodigies. From time to time there emerges a youngster whose innate musicianship and intuitive feelings for musical expression bring him (momentarily at any rate) to the head of an orchestra. But these have never been very happy musical events; they always assumed the aspects of a circus performance rather than a respectable and dignified artistic exhibition. Children have been known to perform major concertos of Mozart, Beethoven, or Brahms on the violin or the piano with insight and stylistic distinction—children like Heifetz, Josef Hofmann, and Menuhin. I do not know of any occasion when a symphony of Mozart, Beethoven, or Brahms was conducted with equal understanding by a child conductor, though many have tried. I will go even further: Of the children who have attracted some notice as prodigy conductors not one, to my knowledge, has developed into a fully realized artist. Willy Ferrero, the American born son of an Italian clown, is no exception, though he is today a professional conductor. He made his debut at the age of six at the Teatro Costanzi in Rome, following which he appeared with many leading European orchestras. He inspired admiration because of his intuitive feeling for rhythm and tempo, which made it possible for him to direct works like Wagner's *Meistersinger Overture* and Beethoven's Fifth

Symphony with technical assurance. Ferrero has been conducting in Italy in recent years—but it can hardly be said that he is a formidable artist or that he has in any way lived up to his early promises.

Only recently a child conductor excited admiration and publicity in New York with guest performances with the NBC Orchestra. Lorin Maazel, aged eleven, was the first child ever to direct a major American orchestra, and he directed it in programs which would have taxed the experience and equipment of a much older musician. The story goes that at the age of eight he revealed he could read a full orchestral score; that on his ninth birthday (as his gift) he was given the opportunity to rehearse an orchestra in Tchaikovsky's *Marche Slav*. His career began officially with the National Youth Orchestra which he directed at the New York World's Fair. A guest performance at the Hollywood Bowl (where he shared the baton with Stokowski) prefaced his New York appearances with Toscanini's orchestra.

But young Maazel, for all his apparent talent, has proved himself to be little more than a routined time-beater. He seems to know the music he conducts, and he responds to it emotionally. He has a good ear. But he has no understanding of the artistic forces which give the music its dramatic, emotional, or lyric greatness. He plays bar by bar as if he had been taught to do so by rote; of imagination, sensitive refinement, artistic planning or design there are not the slightest traces.

Consequently, if we are to search for the conductors for tomorrow, we will not find them among child prodigies, but rather among young men who have already reached man's estate and have had an opportunity to prove their talents. Your prodigy conductor is a man having approached maturity.

Erich Leinsdorf, aged thirty, is unquestionably one of tomorrow's conductors; but Leinsdorf already is of our own time as well, holding as he does one of the major conductorial posts in this country—at the Metropolitan Opera House.

One of the younger men who has yet to acquire a permanent post of first importance—but who most certainly will—is Izler Solomon. His work with lesser organizations has been so meritorious that he bears careful watching. Solomon has never had a conducting lesson in his life. But he has such a natural bent in that direction that he has acquired an entire conservatory education from his experiences. There is nothing about his performances today to suggest inadequate preparation. He has mastery of the baton and orchestra and score; he has sound instincts and tastes; he has authority. These qualities—and his extraordinary personal magnetism—have brought him far; and they will carry him much further.

He was born in St. Paul, Minnesota, on January 11, 1910. In 1919 his family moved to Kansas City, where he began to study the violin. His aptitude for music attracted some attention. A Kansas City organization subsidized him. Coming East, he divided his time between New York and Philadelphia, studying music, playing in orchestras, and attending concerts. The concert hall was, as a matter of fact, his principal conservatory. It was there (most frequently at Stokowski's concerts in Philadelphia) that he acquired discrimination and background—these, and his ambition to become a conductor.

In 1928 Solomon was appointed faculty member in the department of music at Michigan State College in East Lansing. He was assistant there to Michael Press, who took him in hand and gave him private lessons in violin playing and in musical interpretation.

Solomon first tried his hand at conducting in East Lansing.

He was responsible for the formation of a city orchestra, of which he was designated to be the concertmaster. The sudden death of its conductor, just before the concert, placed the directorial responsibility in Solomon's hands. He remained the conductor of the orchestra after the first concert.

It was the Music Project of the Federal Works Administration that discovered Solomon. He had convinced the Emergency Relief Administration of the need for a state music-director and was given the post. He worked out an elaborate program for the musical activity of the state which later became a model for all other similar ventures throughout the country. Guy Maier, regional director, was so impressed by Solomon's capabilities that, before long, he transferred him to Chicago and there placed him in charge of the Illinois Symphony Orchestra, a WPA organization.

Solomon led this orchestra for six years, and matriculated as a professional conductor. He compiled an admirable record of first performances of modern works by European and American composers, and gave Chicago its first hearings of symphonies by Shostakovitch, Sibelius, and Khrennikov. Besides this, he developed an admirable symphonic body which made important artistic contributions to the cultural life of the city. Nikolai Sokoloff, national director of the WPA, referred to the Illinois Symphony as the best WPA orchestra in America.

In 1939 Solomon was appointed director of the Women's Symphony Orchestra in Chicago. This orchestra was also developed by him into an excellent ensemble. One year later it was sponsored on a weekly national hook-up radio program which, incidentally, helped to popularize Solomon's name. During the past few seasons he has also made numerous guest appearances with major American orchestras, including the Philadelphia Orchestra, the NBC Orchestra, the Chicago

IZLER SOLOMON

DEAN DIXON

SYLVAN LEVIN

Symphony, and the Buffalo Philharmonic. In these assignments Solomon has again and again given striking evidence of his growing powers as interpreter and his ever increasing command of an extensive and varied repertoire.

There seems every reason to believe that his continued growth and evolution will place him in an imposing position among the leading American conductors of tomorrow. Certainly no other young conductor of recent years has given us so much reason for optimism.

2

Dean Dixon

Another young conductor whose work gives us every reason for faith in his future is Dean Dixon, the only Negro conductor ever to direct a major American orchestra. Dixon's career is the triumph of talent over the greatest obstacle which can be placed in the way of a young musician acquiring conductorial assignments: race prejudice. His appearances with the NBC Orchestra and, at the Lewisohn Stadium, with the New York Philharmonic revealed a definite baton personality with fine interpretative gifts and an ability to lead men. It is not an easy road that has brought a Negro to the conductor's stands of two great American orchestras. That the road has, at last, been traversed speaks well both for Dixon's capabilities and for the capacity of true talent to assert itself.

His mother, who was passionately fond of music, designated him for a musical career. She would carry him in her arms, while he was still a baby, to the gallery of Carnegie Hall, where he would listen attentively for part of the program and then would comfortably fall asleep. Popular music was tabu in the Dixon household. Dean was never permitted to touch the radio. "As soon as he came in the house," his mother confessed, "the radio got out of order. That was a kind of family custom. And when he complained that all of the other children, in other homes, listened to the radio, we told him that somebody had to play the music that came over the air and that if he studied hard he might do that when he grew up."

He showed a native equipment for music. He had perfect pitch, and was able, as a child, to identify any note or combination of notes that were struck on the piano. Beginning the study of the violin at the age of three-and-a-half, he proved he could learn musical lessons easily, though only the firm insistence of his mother could keep him at the merciless grind of daily practice. His music teacher definitely pronounced him a boy of talent when he was thirteen. A few years later, through the offices of Harry Jennison, head of the music department of De Witt Clinton High School (from which Dixon was graduated in 1932), he entered the Institute of Musical Art. At the same time he continued his academic studies at Columbia University, acquiring a Master's Degree, then taking the necessary courses for a doctorate. In 1936 he was passed on to the Juilliard Graduate School with a fellowship in conducting.

He had been conducting as early as 1932 when he organized his own orchestra at a Harlem Branch of the YMCA. At first his orchestra consisted only of one violin and one piano; and his baton was a pencil. But he continued building up and working with his orchestra until it grew into an ensemble of seventy musicians recruited from the neighborhood. He used his own lunch money to finance the venture—for the purchase of the music and musical instruments, and for renting rehearsal rooms—until (in 1937) a group of women became interested in his venture and decided to subsidize it. The Dean Dixon Symphony Orchestra gave annual concerts which eventually attracted such widespread attention that word of its outstanding work reached Mrs. Eleanor Roosevelt. A concert by Dixon's orchestra was arranged at the Heckscher Theatre which succeeded in focusing the limelight upon its brilliant young conductor.

293

Sometime before this Heckscher Theatre concert, Dixon conducted his first concert at Town Hall. Several other minor engagements followed until, in 1940, he was given the baton over the National Youth Administration Orchestra. He conducted a cycle of Beethoven symphonies, and many other ambitious programs (including new music by young American composers). His pronounced baton talents were always in evidence. "Working with a group of inexperienced youngsters whose natural boisterousness was not always under control, he was confronted with a special disciplinary problem," wrote Ella Davis in the New York *Times*. "He solved it with patience. Once when a player persisted in talking while other instruments were rehearsing, Dixon stopped and asked the offender to play his own part, which he did, from beginning to end. When the solo was finished—and the others had remained perfectly still throughout—Dixon said quietly, 'All right. Now you can talk while we play'."

Samuel Chotzinoff, music director of the NBC, attended Dixon's concert at the Heckscher Theatre and was so impressed by the performance that he contracted the young conductor to direct the NBC Symphony Orchestra for two concerts. Young Dixon, who had already proved that he could handle youngsters and amateurs, now displayed professional skill in directing a world-famous ensemble.

Once again quoting Miss Davis: "He literally never raises his voice. When he does get impatient or angry, which isn't often, he resorts to withering sarcasm. . . . His authority stems, not from a sense of personal power, but from his knowledge of the music. Dixon can play, and is familiar with the difficulties and limitations of every instrument in his orchestra— which makes him appear to the lay observer surprisingly tolerant of poor playing in the face of his avowed desire for per-

294

fection. For this very reason, however, he is able to convey without lengthy explanations just what he wants from the various instruments.

"When Dixon appeared for his first rehearsal with the NBC Orchestra . . . Mr. Chotzinoff had some qualms as to how the players, veterans all, would react to this young man whose name was unknown to most of them. The guest conductor stepped to the podium, raised his baton (he conducts without one now)—and the men gave him everything he asked for. He knew exactly what he wanted—and wasted no time talking. From the very beginning he was master of the situation."

3

Sylvan Levin

A major experiment in opera performances successfully operated in Philadelphia has brought the work of its resourceful young conductor, Sylvan Levin, to the attention of the music world. The Philadelphia Opera Company was founded in 1938 by C. David Hocker and Sylvan Levin "to attract a new audience to opera as well as to revitalize the art itself, and at the same time to offer opportunities not available elsewhere for American singers and composers to develop in the lyric art." It has succeeded well in all these aims. It has attracted new audiences to opera by presenting it in the English language, and in freshened and modernized translations. It has, to a measure, revitalized the art by boldly inaugurating experiments in stage direction (at the hands of Dr. Hans Wohlmuth) and in scenic design. It has also undertaken a fresh and inviting repertoire combining old operatic favorites with such less frequently heard masterpieces as Mozart's *The Marriage of Figaro* (performed one year before the Metropolitan Opera House revival), Ravel's *L'Heure Espagnol,* Reznićek's *Spiel oder Ernst,* and the Puccini trilogy of one-act operas, now presented in America in its complete form for the first time. Opportunities have been offered to American singers provided by no other source—by offering them the major roles as well as the minor ones: There is no "star system" in Philadelphia. In the same season one singer may be called on for a minor role in one opera and for a leading role in the next. All the members of the company are required to attend every rehearsal of every opera, so that they might become intimately familiar with every role. Finally, the American composer has been represented by the world première of Deems Taylor's *Ramuntcho* and by the first opera house performance of Gian Carlo-Menotti's radio opera, *The Old Maid and the Thief.*

All this—and Sylvan Levin's intelligent, painstaking and sensitively musical direction—have put the Philadelphia Opera Company prominently on the musical map of our country.

Levin, like Rodzinski and Ormandy, is a Stokowski discovery; the direction of his career was given a powerful impetus by the Philadelphia conductor. Born in Baltimore on March 2, 1903, he studied at the Peabody Conservatory. After his graduation he supported himself by playing the piano in motion-picture theatres, night clubs, and hotels. In 1927 a scholarship enabled him to return to music study—to the Curtis Institute, where he was a piano pupil of Moriz Rosenthal.

He met Stokowski in 1929, and from that moment on his ambition was to become a conductor. Stokowski became interested in him, encouraged him to think of conducting as a career, and gave him all-important advice and criticism. When Stokowski decided to present Moussorgsky's *Boris Godunov* (in its original orchestration) with the Philadelphia Orchestra, he entrusted the task of coaching the singers to Levin.

From now on Levin was intimately associated with Stokowski, and was his right hand man in the preparation of every ambitious concert. Stokowski's performance of Alban Berg's *Wozzeck,* one of the most pretentious undertakings of the Philadelphia Orchestra, was prepared in every detail by Levin.

His official debut as conductor took place in 1930 when he directed a performance of *Gianni Schicchi* with the Philadelphia Grand Opera Company. Levin remained conductor of this organization for three years, conducting ten different operas. He also turned to the direction of symphonic music, appearing as a guest at the Robin Hood Dell in the summer of 1932, and, one year later, collaborating with Leopold Stokowski in a commercial fifteen-minute broadcast of symphonic music over a nationwide network (Levin conducted some sixty of these programs). In 1933 he helped to found the York (Pennsylvania) Symphony Orchestra, which he led until 1936. He also conducted several other orchestras throughout the country.

When C. David Hocker decided to launch a new opera company in Philadelphia—along original and progressive lines—he called upon Sylvan Levin to help him. Levin has remained the principal conductor of this organization since that time and, despite the variety of operas he was called upon to direct, has always performed with dignity and distinction.

Appendix

Major American Orchestras

BOSTON SYMPHONY ORCHESTRA (see Koussevitzky)
CHICAGO SYMPHONY ORCHESTRA (see Stock)
CINCINNATTI SYMPHONY ORCHESTRA (see Goossens)
CLEVELAND ORCHESTRA (see Rodzinski)
COLUMBIA SYMPHONY ORCHESTRA (see Barlow)
DETROIT SYMPHONY ORCHESTRA (see Kolar)
INDIANAPOLIS SYMPHONY ORCHESTRA (see Sevitzky)
KANSAS CITY SYMPHONY ORCHESTRA (see Krueger)
LOS ANGELES PHILHARMONIC (see Rodzinski)
MINNEAPOLIS SYMPHONY ORCHESTRA (see Ormandy)
NBC ORCHESTRA (see Rodzinski)
NATIONAL SYMPHONY ORCHESTRA, WASHINGTON, D. C.
    (see Kindler)
NEW YORK PHILHARMONIC SYMPHONY (see Barbirolli)
PHILADELPHIA ORCHESTRA (see Stokowski)
PITTSBURGH SYMPHONY ORCHESTRA (see Reiner)
RADIO CITY MUSIC HALL SYMPHONY ORCHESTRA (see Rapee)
ROCHESTER PHILHARMONIC (see Iturbi)
ST. LOUIS SYMPHONY ORCHESTRA (see Golschmann)
SAN FRANCISCO SYMPHONY (see Monteux)

1

A Select Bibliography

A. On Conducting

BACHRACH, A. L. (Editor), *The Musical Companion* ("The Conductor's Role," by Julius Harrison). London: V. Gollancz, 1934.

BARBIROLLI, JOHN (with STEPHEN WEST): "The Conductor and his Orchestra." *Etude,* October, 1938.

BERLIOZ, HECTOR, *Art of Conducting.* New York: Carl Fischer, 1936.

BOULT, ADRIAN, *Handbook on Conducting.* London: H. Reeves, 1922.

EARHART, WILL, *The Eloquent Baton.* New York: Witmark & Sons, 1931.

GEHRKENS, K. W., *Essentials in Conducting.* Boston: Oliver Ditson, 1919.

HOWARD, JOHN TASKER: "The Orchestra Conductor," *Harper's Magazine,* November, 1937.

MALKO, NICOLAI (with LUDWIG WIELICH): "Practical Hints for the Conductor," *Etude,* February, 1941.

ORMANDY, EUGENE (with JAY MEDIA): "Be Ready for Your Opportunity," *Etude,* June, 1938.

REINER, FRITZ (with ROSE HEYLBUT): "The Secrets of Conducting," *Etude,* July, 1936.

SAMINSKY, LAZARE, *Music of Our Day.* New York: Thos. Y. Crowell, 1932.

SCHERCHEN, HERMANN, *Treatise on Conducting*. London: Oxford University Press, 1934.

SIMON, ROBERT E., Jr. (editor), *Be Your Own Music Critic* ("Facing the Conductor," by Leon Barzin). New York: Doubleday, Doran & Co., 1941.

WAGNER, RICHARD, *On Conducting*. London: William Reeves, 1897.

WEINGARTNER, FELIX, *On Conducting*. London: B. and H., 1906.

WILSON, ROBERT B., *The Technique of Orchestral Conducting*. London: The Macmillan Co., 1937.

B. ON CONDUCTORS

ARMSBY, LAURA WOOD, *Musicians Talk*. New York: The Dial Press, 1935.

CHOTZINOFF, SAMUEL: "Practical Orpheus: Stokowski," *New Yorker*, March 21, 1931.

DAMROSCH, WALTER, *My Musical Life*. New York: Charles Scribner's Sons, 1926.

DREYFUS, G.: "Notes on Conducting: Conversations with Koussevitzky," *Atlantic Monthly*, December, 1936.

EWEN, DAVID, *Living Musicians*. New York: H. W. Wilson Co., 1941.

EWEN, DAVID, *The Man With the Baton*. New York: Thos. Y. Crowell Co., 1936.

FRANKENSTEIN, ALFRED V.: "Meet Mr. Monteux," *Victor Record Review*, September, 1941.

FRANKENSTEIN, ALFRED V.: "Twenty-five Years a Conductor: Frederick Stock," *Review of Reviews* (U. S.), January, 1930.

GILMAN, LAWRENCE, *Arturo Toscanini and Great Music*. New York: Farrar & Rinehart, 1938.

HEYLBUT, ROSE: "Sir Thomas Beecham Has His Say," *Etude,* April, 1942.

HUSSEY, D.: "Bruno Walter at a Rehearsal," *Saturday Review* (London), January 3, 1925.

LEVANT, OSCAR, *A Smattering of Ignorance.* New York: Doubleday, Doran & Co., 1940.

LOURIE, ARTHUR, *Serge Koussevitzky and His Epoch.* New York: Alfred A. Knopf, Inc., 1931.

LUDWIG, EMIL: "Bruno Walter: Leader and Dreamer," *New York Times Magazine,* October 8, 1933.

MCMAHON, THOS. P. (with KATHARINE HOFFMAN): "Front Page Maestro: Leopold Stokowski," *Today,* April 18, 1936.

NEWMAN, ERNEST: "Serge Koussevitzky," *American Mercury,* January, 1924.

NICOTRA, TOBIAS, *Arturo Toscanini.* New York: Alfred A. Knopf, Inc., 1929.

PIASTRO, MISHEL: "Genius Fortissimo: Arturo Toscanini," *Collier's,* December 25, 1937.

PIERCE, ARTHUR D.: "Stokowski," *American Mercury,* March, 1931.

SHORE, BERNARD, *The Orchestra Speaks.* London: Longmans, Green & Co., 1938.

SINCLAIR, D. W.: "Six Orchestral Conductors" (including Damrosch and Monteux), *American Mercury,* February, 1924.

STEFAN, PAUL, *Toscanini.* New York: Viking Press, 1936.

STEFAN, PAUL: "Toscanini at Seventy-five," *Opera News,* March, 1942.

TAUBMAN, HOWARD: "Rare Musical Bird: Stokowski," *Collier's,* August 19, 1939.

TAUBMAN, HOWARD: "Strenuous Maestro Stokowski," *New York Times Magazine,* November 16, 1941.

WALKER, STANLEY: "He Knew What They Wanted: Alfred Wallenstein," *Woman's Home Companion,* November, 1940.

YEISER, FREDERICK: "My Friend Eugene Goossens," *Victor Record Review,* July, 1941.

The *Chesterian* Magazine (London) published a series of critical essays on modern conductors between 1937 and 1939. This series included the following:

Sir Thomas Beecham, by Robert H. Hull (Vol. 17, No. 124).

Eugene Goossens, by A. Walter Kramer (Vol. 17, No. 126).

Serge Koussevitzky, by Terence White (Vol. 18, No. 133).

Dimitri Mitropoulos, by Frank Choisy (Vol. 18, No. 132).

Leopold Stokowski, by David Ewen (Vol. 16, No. 120).

Arturo Toscanini, by P. O. Ferroud (Vol. 16, No. 118).

Bruno Walter, by Corrado Farigliano (Vol. 20, No. 141).

*

INDEX